'Nigel Barlow's book is simply brilliant! Is there anything left to say about superior customer service? The answer is obviously a resounding "yes". This book proves it! Incidentally, heed Barlow's words: "Legendary" service is a far cry from even "excellent" service!'   Tom Peters

'After ten years studying best practice, what a joy to find a book that exposes customer service as it really should be, with wonderful vignettes from real organisations to help us appreciate what can be done. A "must read" for all SOCAP members'   Tony Mosely, Executive Director, SOCAP (Society of Consumer Affairs Professionals)

'This is one of the most thought-provoking and stimulating books I've read on customer service in a long while. Not only is it an incredibly good read, but it does offer some profound and new insights into that elusive subject – how to create legendary service. I know at least one thousand companies which could benefit from the lessons in this book'   David Freemantle, author of *What Customers Like About You*

'Customer "pull" has replaced supplier "push" as the engine of economic growth, and customers now expect more from you than ever before. Nigel Barlow's inspiring book shows you how to stand out from the crowd by delivering legendary service experiences; the kind of experiences that turn customers into walking "advocates" for your organisation. This is new territory for most organisations: customer service, but not as you know it! Barlow brings fresh thinking and inspiration to a discipline that has long been in need of an overhaul to match its new-found central importance. You need to be customer-centred to survive in the 21st century, the Customer Century as it has been dubbed. Nigel Barlow provides you with your essential route map'   Phil Dourado, Editor, *Customer Service Management*

'As ever, Nigel's thinking is insightful and thought provoking – particularly if you manage a business with "Premier" in the title'   John Church, Managing Director, Premier Banking, Barclays Bank

'*Batteries Included!* made me want to cheer – as a professional responsible for customer contact but, more importantly, as a customer. If you care about customers and want to do something about it, *Batteries Included!* provides the right balance between passion and pragmatism and humanness and profitability. It ought to be required reading for everyone who has customers (before they go near one) from the boardroom (especially the boardroom) to the front-line. In the tradition of story-telling, I hope there's a sequel!' Carol Borghesi, Director, BT Call Centres, Customer Service

'*Batteries Included!* will challenge any business's notion of Customer Service. It dares you to be human, to risk acting on your customers' suggestions and being passionate about it – now that's different. It's not only a great read, but an experience that steps you into a world of heartfelt empathy with your customers that is synonymous with memorable brands and lasting relationships – Legendary indeed'   Graham Ellis, General Manager, Consumer Lubricants, Mobil, Europe

'Nigel Barlow is a master in understanding customer requirements. He truly knows how to get under the skin of the customer to unlock what is key to creating the required service culture in any business. Read this book and ensure that you don't let the "post honeymoon slump" happen to your business' The Lord Daresbury, Peter Greenall, Chief Executive, The Greenalls Group plc

'An easy and enjoyable read . . . you will almost certainly pick up some new ideas that will be of benefit not only in your work but perhaps in your personal life as well' *Salesforce*

'Let's just say that I started chuckling reading the introduction . . . stuffed with witty, practical advice on how to achieve great customer service' *Enterprise*

'Written with the passion and excitement it extols, it will inspire you to rate your own organisation. The best book yet on this vital subject, still so poorly understood in the UK' *Director*

BATTERIES INCLUDED!

Creating

Legendary

Service

BATTERIES INCLUDED!

NIGEL MAY BARLOW

RANDOM HOUSE
BUSINESS BOOKS

This edition published in 2001 by Random House

© Nigel May Barlow 2000
All rights reserved

Nigel May Barlow has asserted his rights under the Copyright, Designs
and Patents Act, 1988, to be identified as the author of this work.

First published in 2000 by Random House Business Books,
Random House, 20 Vauxhall Bridge Road, London SW1V 2SA

Random House Australia (Pty) Limited
20 Alfred Street, Milsons Point,
Sydney, New South Wales 2061, Australia

Random House New Zealand Limited
18 Poland Road, Glenfield,
Auckland 10, New Zealand

Random House (Pty) Limited
Endulini, 5a Jubilee Road, Parktown 2193, South Africa

The Random House Group Limited Reg. No. 954009

Papers used by Random House are natural, recyclable
products made from wood grown in sustainable forests.
The manufacturing processes conform to the environmental
regulations of the country of origin.

ISBN 0 7126 8068 3

Companies, institutions and other organizations wishing to make
bulk purchases of books published by Random House should
contact their local bookstore or Random House direct:

Special Sales Director
Random House, 20 Vauxhall Bridge Road, London SW1V 2SA
Tel 020 7840 8470   Fax 020 7828 6681

www.randomhouse.co.uk
businessbooks@randomhouse.co.uk

Typeset in Goudy and Gill by MATS, Southend-on-Sea, Essex
Printed and bound in Great Britain by
Creative Print and Design Group, Ebbw Vale (Wales)

This book is dedicated to my father
Peers Ronald Barlow,
a legend for kindness in his family

Why *Batteries Included!?*

WHEN I described this book's title to a friend he immediately set about, with some glee, classifying all his acquaintances as either having batteries included, or not. Though there is a more serious use of the expression in this book – the passion, energy and creativity that we all possess – my friend's experience gave me the idea that this was an excellent intuitive way of rating a system or individual providing us with service.

Great service is, after all, in the eye of the beholder. We are likely to rely on intuition and feelings at least as strongly as logic in judging the experience. Using this simple criterion, I found that when I went shopping with my 12-year-old son he could evaluate instantly whether a service encounter had batteries included or not.

When your people answer the telephone, do they sound as if their batteries are running down, or are they highly charged?

Do the systems you use to service your customers have batteries included – are they immediate, simple, fast and responsive – or is the power flow sluggish and unreliable?

Do your customers get a boost to their own energy when they deal with you? Is their experience so memorable that they will spread positive stories in the marketplace about you? *Batteries Included!* is all about helping you to say a vibrant 'yes!' to these questions . . .

CONTENTS

INTRODUCTION

BATTERIES INCLUDED! marries two of my great interests – some might say obsessions – of the past 15 years, Creativity and Customer Service. It's about creative approaches to your customer. In many ways this is a new book encouraging you to bring the full power of your attention to bear on an area that's critical for business success. In another sense it seeks to synthesise and apply to business the common sense we all have about intimate personal relationships, which seems to be so easily forgotten when we put our business hats on. It's both a 'how to' *and* a 'why to' book.

I believe we have too narrow a concept of what service really means. It's necessary to have a deeper and wider understanding of the impact of service on the quality of our lives than the one we use to judge our daily shopping experience. Service can be a means of improving the quality of human relationships we all enjoy. Expressions such as 'caring for the customer' and 'putting the customer first' have become hackneyed and tired in the business arena, but they still carry the seed of the much higher ideal of reaching beyond one's small self to empathise with and enrich the lives of others.

While this does not mean that making your customers' lives easier, more successful and pleasurable is going to bring world peace, save the whale, or create enlightenment, it does have the potential to improve the capacity for human understanding and quality of life. We are all customers of one another. We have many service experiences each day, which can either lighten our load or tarnish our enjoyment. Every time we order goods over the telephone, buy a pair of shoes or get our car fixed we take on the role of a demanding customer, sometimes forgetting that in our own profession the people we are dealing with are also customers.

This is not limited simply to business transactions. Today, priests treat their congregations as customers. One Swedish minister has even boosted church attendances by holding services at times when his parishioners have no excuse not to attend. And I was amused by the English vicar who put a large sign outside his church saying 'Last absolution before the M62'!

Hospitals are finally becoming patient rather than consultant-centred, and even the British educational system has been shocked by recent court cases brought by students who have realised that they are customers of the system, not merely passive recipients unable to judge the quality of teaching and examining.

Of course, successful businesses have long realised that their customers are both the bread and butter of today and the jam of tomorrow. A striking new piece of research even links high performance on the stock market with superior levels of customer satisfaction. For the period of the survey (the first quarter of 1995 through to the third quarter of 1997) Campbell Soup, Heinz, and Procter & Gamble were all in the top quartile in customer satisfaction and were also stock performance stars. Companies in the bottom quartile of customer satisfaction were generally losers in the stock performance stakes.

To find that these two measures are correlated is naturally not the same thing as saying that one causes the other, but in any event business has already realised that without delighted customers they will be struggling to stay in the game. Although *Batteries Included!* emphasises the human elements of great service, it's clear that money is here to be made as well.

Whatever field we are working in, the quality of service we give to others is the most powerful ingredient the receiver will use in evaluating our competence. Unless there's some major error of judgment, like removing the wrong leg, we often have little ability to judge a doctor's technical abilities, but we do know whether he or she is helpful, understanding and supportive. What is simultaneously most fascinating and frustrating about service is that it's an intensely personal, emotional and subjective experience. In other words, it's all about the quality of human relationships.

Batteries Included! . . .

Batteries Included! exists to help you rethink your service offerings and the quality of customer service your organisation provides. It sounds the death-knell of mere customer satisfaction by describing a new level of service to aim for – legendary service – where customers effectively do your marketing for you. The book uses a definition of service wider than the one current in business today, including Service with a big 'S' – service to the community and to the environment.

Based on the principle that real change comes from a spark of inner creativity and originality, the only relevant case study is your own. If you merely copy others you can hardly aspire to be truly different in the market-place. The world is full of lookalike companies that are under the illusion they are doing something different while their customers can barely distinguish them from their competitors. To take a retailing example, it's becoming increasingly difficult to tell one English high street from another as the same outlets always seem to huddle together as if there were some security in familiarity.

The *batteries* referred to in the title are the inspiration, passion and energy that need discovering or recharging to create a service experience for your customers which is unique, memorable and encourages them to choose and stay with your organisation rather than with your competitor. They are creative tools to help you rethink and reinvent the quality of your customer relationships.

There's nothing worse than receiving a Christmas present that says 'Batteries not included' on the box. Many management books fall into this camp because they describe all the ingredients of success without providing the batteries or thinking tools to implement sustainable improvement in your own enterprise.

Here is a list of the 'batteries' that can help you transform your service, and a brief reason why each may be critical to your business.

- Change the Box – because only by thinking differently can you truly differentiate yourself in the eyes of the customer;
- Learn from the Future – this will help you to visualise in story form the unique future you want for your customers;
- Develop Beginner's Mind – to allow you to become fully open to your customers' perceptions;
- Think *Both/And* – in order to develop the closeness of your relationship with your customers, and their positive feelings for you;
- The Power of Attention – to create a culture that makes your customers feel your attention is fully on them;
- *What If/ Why Not?* – helps you to bring your full creativity to bear on the customer's experience, and
- Recharging Your Batteries – provides you with checklists of ideas and actions to ensure all the batteries are fully charged.

The words in the subtitle – **Creating Legendary Customer Service** – are also chosen carefully. **Creating** means that only an imaginative and innovative approach will keep pace with the constantly changing demands of your customers, causing them to want to repeat this experience of doing business with you. **Legendary** addresses the fact that human beings' favourite means of communication is still telling and listening to stories. If the sum total of these stories is positive then you have created a legend that prospective customers are drawn to and existing ones stay loyal to through an emotional bond. In this sense your legend has become synonymous with your brand. **Service** is a term that needs more explanation because over-familiarity with a word wrongly assumes, particularly in the field of management, that we all share the same understanding . . .

What is service?

As customers we're all experts, aren't we? It takes only seconds to work out how we'd run this office, hotel or grocer's better if we were in charge. We know what good service is and wonder why those serving us can't do it just the way we want. But those of us who give service know it's not quite that easy in practice because customers have their own highly personal perception of what great service really means.

I have a very broad definition of service. Service is in everything that we do and is arguably the *raison d'être* for every organisation – service to customers, employees, investors, society and the natural environment. There's no point in a limited definition of service because customers make no such distinction. In their minds it's the sum total of all impressions gained from dealing with your organisation over time that causes them to evaluate you well or badly. So even the separation between products and services is largely irrelevant today; you can't obtain a product without service, however fleeting the contact may be. Service is everything you do with, or for, your customers.

However, we can usefully look at three main categories of service that are addressed in *Batteries Included!*

I. The experience that you have when you first acquire a product or receive a service.

This is the usual narrow definition of service, and is critical because of the power of initial impressions. If the experience is poor we're unlikely to want to repeat it. The examples most of us think of and hear about are perhaps more of the consumer rather than the business-to-business variety: what we experience in a restaurant, a bank or a car-dealer. It's not that this is unimportant in business-to-business relationships; the nature of these relationships is necessarily longer-term partnerships. For instance, it can take years to design, manufacture and supply an industrial component such as a car axle or bearing. For this type of business the following category of service is even more important . . .

2. The quality of service in an on-going relationship.

I have an acquaintance whose weddings are hugely successful, but who has less luck in continuing a satisfactory relationship! This is like organisations that woo you and give you great initial service, but are less responsive to your needs when problems arise. How do they support you as a customer when your car breaks down or your music speakers blow up? Do they stay in touch with you and automatically offer you upgrades and fresh accessories? How well do they honour their guarantees?

To continue with the marriage metaphor, do they leave you at the altar, having made their vows, or do you feel they are caring partners in your on-going experience with their product or service? Do they really know you – your past history, current and future needs and aspirations – or are you an insignificant statistic in their database? In short, do you feel it's a continuing relationship of equals where you feel valued? These are questions that organisations aspiring to legendary levels of service need to ask continually.

3. Service with a big 'S'.

This goes to the heart of what you are in business for. Service with a big S implies a higher sense of purpose for an organisation than merely making profits, or in current business jargon: 'delivering superior stakeholder value'. *Organisations are a resource to us, not we to them.* In a world that is hopefully shifting to higher standards of ethics and respect for human rights and dignity a business cannot pretend that it is a closed system, cut off from these influences. Service to the community and environment has moved much higher on the agenda of small and large enterprises alike, and customers increasingly judge you on how well you achieve these higher goals – as multinationals such as Monsanto, Shell and many others have recently discovered.

Service is everything

Let's separate the word service from its familiar noun 'customer' and think about the concept more widely. Life *is* service. Perhaps for you it's service to your personal goals and dreams, to your family and friends, and even in a wider sense to your community and environment. When you read this book you may have the immediate aim of improving your business service to paying customers and as a result gaining their loyalty and boosting your profitability. There's nothing wrong with this. My experience is that a profitable enterprise is more fun to work in, more stimulating and less fear-driven than a struggling one.

But I want to engage you in thinking more deeply and widely about the role that a passion for service plays in your own search for meaning. Beyond the basic needs to make a living are higher aspirations that make us more truly human: a need for achievement, the fulfilment that comes from creating a positive legacy from our efforts. Above all, the feeling of having given of ourselves fully, and in the process having made the lives of others a little better.

Does this make you feel uncomfortable? Is this somehow separate from and not relevant to the usual concerns of a business book? If so, it's hardly surprising. There's a great tendency for us to box off one part of life from another, whether it's dividing home from work, feelings from the mind or the serious business of running an organisation from the more joyful pursuit of personal interests.

In the same way the notion of 'service' is in danger of becoming narrowed down to a precise and measurable set of activities that organisations, especially commercial concerns, do with or for their customers to gain and keep their business. The label on my mustard pot illustrates this when it tells me that if I have any complaints I need to contact the customer service department. Too often service to customers comes into play only when there is a perceived problem.

Your business is a hologram. Every small part of a shattered holographic image contains the picture of the whole from which it has become physically divided. In the same way every part of your enterprise – people (employees or out-sourced), systems, and products – is seen as the whole picture by your customers. Each part reflects you in your entirety and will tell a positive, negative, or a somewhere-in-between story to each customer. A horror story or a positive legend.

Understanding how service contributes to our quality of life is a vital element in the customer service equation. *Without a sense that great service is a force for enriching the quality of our lives, service techniques will be swiftly revealed as mere trickery, customer care as a clever but unconvincing adjunct to the sales machine, and 'putting the customer first' as yet another empty management slogan*.

Think of how a great service experience – often involving a human contact where someone has really extended himself or herself to help you –

can make your whole day. And how a negative encounter can put you in a bad mood that you pass on to the next person you meet.

Here's where a commonsense principle comes into play – the law of attraction. We are attracted to experiences that we enjoy, and beyond that to the source of that experience. Put simply, we seek pleasure and avoid pain. *Our loyalty as customers is first and foremost an emotional response to how we feel we have been treated. Companies need to be loyal to their customers if they expect these customers to commit to them.*

It's critical to remember the power of the individual in judging service because so many enterprises are blinded by the fiction that they are dealing with 'a market'. *A market never bought anything – people do!*

In the drive for customer satisfaction many organisations have forgotten that what makes for great individual personal relationships is also what makes for great business relationships. A theme that runs throughout this book is the human laws of legendary service. It explores why these simple principles seem to be so easily ignored in our rush to re-engineer, downsize, flatten, automate and 'virtualise' our organisations, and how to realise their power in enhancing the quality of relationship we enjoy with our customers.

The writer's bias

This is not an academic book. Nor does it set great store by research in this most subjective of all business disciplines, though this is given due weight when it throws light on the often contrary nature of customer perceptions.

Like any field, business has forged its own language. I cringe at some of the mindless jargon that can distance organisations from their customers. The Customer Value Proposition, Exceeding Customer Expectations and Relationship Marketing are some of the most alienating catchphrases of the day.

But business is not isolated or separate from our personal lives. It's an open mouth that swallows influences from the worlds of psychology, philosophy, science, the arts and a humanity that continually pursues more happiness, knowledge, convenience and new experiences. Consequently I've used inspiration and quotations from many of these fields as well as business examples, to avoid the arid nature of management-speak. Great service companies try to remove all barriers that prevent the servers from being fully themselves at work. Management books tend to be a bit of a bore – it's OK to say it! – so I've tried to make sure *Batteries Included!* is laced with everyday examples and my own passions for music, philosophy, and science.

Have you ever finished all of a business book? Go on, be honest! A friend who is a successful consultant to major companies tells me, only slightly tongue in cheek, that he feels they are not designed for reading, but merely for owning and displaying prominently on one's boardroom table.

This is not entirely bad. In fact, it's potentially a great opportunity for those of us who write these books. But it fits with the pattern of the rest of our lives. You probably use only a fraction of your PC's capabilities, and most radio listeners spend 90 per cent of their time listening to only one or two stations.

My bias is that developing a true sense of service is one of life's most important goals. Forget for a minute the narrow notion of 'service' as it's used in business. One of the most profound reasons why we exist is to serve others, to enrich the lives of others and in so doing to give more meaning, joy, and sense of purpose to our own lives. At the risk of sounding pious, it's one of the reasons we are all here.

Love what you do

As customers we're naturally drawn to the passion and enthusiasm of those who love what they do. In the race to win and keep customers, it's often forgotten that giving great service can be a source of joy and happiness for the provider as well as the recipient. In the words of Albert Schweitzer,[1] a man who devoted his life to the service of others: 'I don't know what your destiny may be, but one thing I know. The only ones among you who will be really happy are those who have sought and found how to serve.'

What we need is less clinical professionalism and more unfettered enthusiasm. Recently I overheard a manager say: 'Accounting is not hard – except in the hands of professional accountants.' The same can be said of all of us who are customer service professionals. *Batteries Included!* aims to help you rediscover the beginner's mind of the inspired amateur and make the future an exciting field of never-ending possibilities. If you can drop the guise of the informed expert, so often rooted in present limitations, then you can create your own legend rather than merely following someone else's blueprint. Above all you can avoid the trap of mediocrity.

[1] 1875–1965. Theologian, musician and medical missionary. At 21 he resolved to live for science and art until he was 30, and then devote his life to serving humanity, which he did at the hospital he founded at Lambaréné, French Equatorial Africa, where he lived most of his life. His ethical philosophy is based on his principle of 'reverence for life'. He was awarded the 1952 Nobel Peace Prize.

When I take the train to London, this need for passion is brought home to me by an enormous piece of trackside graffiti that proclaims:

'I am a passionate soul
Screaming out in this tortuous mediocrity'

You need to be that passionate soul, a service obsessive. But has the Internet and e-commerce revolution so completely rewritten the rules of doing business that none of the old principles of service apply? And what do customers of the 21st century expect or even demand from their suppliers? The first chapter, New Millennium, New Trends, tackles these questions.

Chapter One

New Millennium, New Trends

'The old order changeth, yielding place to new.'

Alfred, Lord Tennyson (1809–1902)[1]

'In times like these, it helps to recall there have always been times like these.'

Paul Harvey, US radio personality

Exploring the Customer's New Needs will enable you to:

- Appreciate your customers as individuals
- Develop more intimate customer relationships
- Put the human touch in your e-commerce/Internet trading

WE are a demanding species. Yesterday's great experience is today's yawn and nowhere is this more true than in the field of customer service. Almost every survey shows that we are less happy with the levels of service we receive today than we were only a few years ago. A typical statistic from a 1997 report by the UK National Consumer Council tells us that 43 per cent of people surveyed had made at least one complaint about service levels in 1996 compared with only 25 per cent five years before.

The general assumption from this and similar reports is that service is getting worse. But is it? Or is it that our expectations have been unduly raised by the hype and blasé marketing promises that have surrounded the topic for the past 15 years? Don't we all have a tendency, individually and collectively, to remember fondly a past that has assumed a rosy hue with the passage of time? Believing all that's good is in the past is not a new

1 *Idylls of the King*, 'The Passing of Arthur', a sequence of poems based on Arthurian legend.

phenomenon. Listen to the Duke of Wellington[2] speaking in 1832: 'Few people will be sanguine enough to imagine that we shall ever again be as prosperous as we have been.'

If we could look at the matter objectively we would see that service *has* dramatically improved. People are generally more helpful on the telephone, deliveries are faster, recompense is easier to receive when we complain and many more service representatives have acquired at least some sense that they are there to help the customer rather than to deal with them at their own convenience. I can do my banking over the telephone 24 hours a day, send a parcel to the other side of the world in a fraction of the time it used to take – a reasonably friendly agent will arrive on my doorstep to pick it up – and airlines want to reward me for my custom with free tickets to a holiday destination.

So why the dissatisfaction? It's simply because we cannot see service – or much else for that matter – objectively. It doesn't matter to me as an individual that this telecommunications company has invested £10 million in more user-friendly technology when I can't speak easily to the person who could help me, or that this supplier has a 98 per cent OTIF (ON TIME IN FULL) delivery record when they lose the component I ordered. . . *and* don't bother to return my call when I contact them. I am not a statistic, at least not to myself, but an individual whose subjective view of the world demands more. And more . . .

Service hasn't become worse. It simply hasn't improved as fast as we expect and demand. Or, more precisely, as I demand because we live more than ever in the era of I. As futurologist John Naisbitt observes with co-writer Patricia Aburdene in *Megatrends 2000*:[3]

Threatened by totalitarianism for much of this century, individuals are meeting this millennium more powerfully. The 1990s are characterised by a new respect for the individual as the foundation of society and the

[2] Arthur Wellesley, 1st Duke of Wellington, British general, statesman and Prime Minister (1769–1852).

[3] *Megatrends 2000: Ten New Directions for the 1990s*, William Morrow, New York, 1990. Aburdene, an internationally recognised speaker and author, collaborating with Naisbitt on *Megatrends*, lectures on the impact of social and economic change on business and society and the importance of women as consumers and leaders. Naisbitt has been describing the future and its trends since 1968. A former executive of IBM and Eastman Kodak, he founded the Urban Research Corporation, which provided social and cultural forecasts for many leading corporations in the US.

basic unit of change. 'Mass' movements are a misnomer. The environmental movement, the women's movement, the anti-nuclear movement, were built one consciousness at a time by an individual persuaded of the possibility of a new reality.

Under-valuing the individual has been one of the great blights of organisational life. A man or woman may be a hero in his or her own family, but often suffers the belittling effects of being an infinitesimally small wheel in the large corporate machine in which he or she works. But as the new century begins, individual customers, at least, are starting to assert their power more and more. They are less happy than ever to be thought of as a 'market' or as a slice of the population that has been demographically segmented and labelled by companies who use their databases to assume they know what these individuals need, like and want. Again – there is no objectivity in service.

This realisation has driven large companies to invest heavily in initiatives such as one-to-one and relationship marketing based on the idea that in every transaction you are ultimately dealing with an individual rather than a category or market. This has had some success in *sales* terms, but a neutral or even negative effect on *service* as perceived by the customer.

However, the good news is that we appear to be moving into an age where companies *do* take the customer's experience more seriously. They have to because today's customers are better informed, have greater mobility and are more protected by legislation. And they are more fickle. This has led suppliers to take a serious look at the economics of customer loyalty (it pays!) and to begin to shift their pursuit of 'share of market' to what's been dubbed 'share of wallet', meaning, once you've got a customer, how can you develop the relationship so that he or she redirects more of the money spent with competitors to your pocket.

Both business and the public sector, whose customers are arguably greater in number and more difficult to please, are waking up to the fact that

- Great customer relationships are the only 'real' assets they have;
- The customer's subjective, personal rating of the service he or she receives is the single most important measure of success, and
- Customers are increasingly aware that they are being courted by many suitors.

One-to-one – what customers need in the New Millennium

The new needs that customers are expressing can be categorised into six fundamental 'I's – Individuality, Interactivity, Immediacy, Intimacy and Imagination.

The chart shows recognition of the customer's individuality at the centre. We are no longer passive consumers. We are more demanding, even 'vigilante consumers' as author Faith Popcorn would have it. Certainly we are often 'prosumers', an expression invented by futurologist Alvin Toffler in his (still) visionary book *Future Shock*, written in 1970. This means we take a more active role in, for example, putting together a meal in a self-service restaurant, co-designing our new bathroom, or being actively involved in choosing the colours, upholstery and features of a car. I want 'big business' to know that I exist; I have my rights and at least equal status in my transactions with it, the supplier.

The Internet encircles the other five 'I's, not because it's the *only* channel for relating to customers (as a scan through current business magazines would have you believe), but because it is adding a completely new dimension to the way in which we do business.

Why These 'I's?

Internet	– because it's fast becoming *the* primary service delivery channel;
Individuality	– because individuals increasingly want an experience that affirms that they matter, as well as merely acquiring a product or enjoying a service;

Interactivity – because customers are less passive and want to be more in control of their choices;

Immediacy – because the world has speeded up, customers are time-starved and want to feel you are there for them when they need you;

Intimacy – because only if you share the customers' experience and listen to their stories can you really provide what they want, and

Imagination – because customers want you to know their concerns, and actively to imagine and empathise with their situation.

Let's begin with the Internet, which is most valuable to customers when used Interactively, with Imagination, providing Immediacy, improving Intimacy and in a way that reinforces their power as Individual customers.

Internet

Tom Rearick, president and founder of the Atlanta-based Big Science Company,[4] predicts that the Internet '. . . will become a preferred medium for providing customer care.' He's not alone. A million words have been written, many in conventional media, about the impact of the Web on the way we do business, live, work and even vote.

The statistics are mind-bending. The number of users is doubling every 100 days. There's a panic as intense as the days of the great Gold Rush for buying technology shares. Perhaps, more significantly, we are realising the greater power of the individual to manage domestic matters, career and even education with a few clicks of a mouse. I don't intend to add many more words here other than to summarise the two main paradoxes in current thinking about the impact of the Internet on customer service.

[4] Rearick founded Big Science Company in 1998 to develop a corporate network publishing solution. The company is the developer of Klone Server, the first application server that understands plain English. It creates emotionally-intelligent, graphical characters that converse with web users and function as knowledge workers assisting customers with website navigation, product selection and purchasing, and problem resolution. Find them at www.bigscience.com

Paradox I		
Overhyped, Yes . . .	but. . .	The Hype's Understated!
The impact, usefulness and omnipresence of the Web in our lives is undoubtedly over-exaggerated		It is changing our lives and businesses in ways that will exceed our wildest imagination

We don't know what the Web will be when it grows up because we are all participants, willing or not, in the birth of the most exciting novel technology the world has ever known. Harking back to other new technologies, the inventors of the phonograph and the telephone had no idea how their new discoveries would be adapted and used. The Internet has already moved far beyond the vision of its original architects, yet is still in its infancy.

Probably the most powerful impact of the Net will be on our social structures and way of life. Voting over the Net will become the norm, home-working or telecommuting will become a reality for those who choose it and the news is good for the human rights movement. Actions such as the KGB's registration of every typewriter in the former Soviet Union to prevent the free flow of information will become impossible.

It doesn't mean that the censors won't try and impose old-millennium thinking – that nation of e-citizens, Singapore, has banned more than 100 websites and still seeks to impose state censorship. It won't succeed, which is either fortunate or unfortunate, depending on your point of view. But that's the reality as the Web's working facsimile of the human brain envelops the globe. Technology writer Kevin Kelly says that 'silicon chips linked into high band-width channels are the nervous system of our culture'.

Paradox 2		
Shop at Home . . .	but . . .	We Like the Human Experience
We will shop for everything on-line, from groceries to holidays, houses and cars. We can conduct a global virtual social life and even get married over the Net. Shops will disappear		We will still want choice and will often favour the shopping mall and human contacts. Indeed, the Web may introduce us to physical shopping channels we would never otherwise have discovered

In Douglas Adams's science fiction novel, *The Hitchhiker's Guide to The Galaxy*,[5] a button labelled DO NOT PANIC! appears from time to time at moments of great chaos. This would seem to be a useful button for many enterprises to press now if you subscribe to the view in the panel on the left. Thomas Blischok, managing partner of what was then accountant Coopers & Lybrand's retail division in Chicago evidently does. He says: 'Within five years, all commodity items will be delivered to your home and people will shop two or three times a month as a leisure activity.'[6]

Blischok made this comment in 1997, so if one believes him, the day when there are few or no physical banks, supermarkets, bookshops, florists, or any form of retail outlet is already here.

Virtual technology gives us an 'in-store experience' without having to leave home. Retail pundits tell us that we can even enjoy virtual ski runs where we can try out new boots on a perfect simulation of the slope we plan to visit.

But will it replace physical retail locations? Julian E. Markham, chairman of Glengate Holdings, naturally thinks not; he's in the business of developing offices and retail sites. He writes:[7]

Retail locations will be destroyed by a wholesale changeover to online service? The estimates of trading volume promulgated by the most die-hard promoters of online shopping think that by the year 2020 only 15 per cent of *total* retail sales will be achieved. Although this is a staggering amount, it must be compared to the present volume in America today of more than $3 trillion.

Markham's book was written in 1998 and the predictions he quotes may have come from a little earlier. However, commentators say that Web years are dog years – what might take seven years in another field seems to happen in one in the Internet economy.

Internet Speed
WEB YEARS = DOG YEARS
(7/1)

[5] Ballantine Books, 1995, ISBN: 0345391802.

[6] *Daily Telegraph*, 22 July 1997.

[7] *The Future of Shopping*, Macmillan Business, 1998, ISBN: 0333731808.

But if those encouraging us to shop in a bricks-and-mortar fashion feel smug in the knowledge that nothing can substitute for the smells of fresh coffee and bread, the Internet is already at their heels. Digiscents, a company based in Oakland, California, is already marketing a product that evokes appropriate smells from your computer to accompany the online experience.

How are we to think about all of this? And who is right? We can be certain of one thing: all predictions will be wrong. Wildly wrong. Especially those made by the experts. They have more to unlearn as commerce e-xplodes into a future none of us can guess.

I propose that the most useful way to comprehend what's going on is to adopt the language of paradox ourselves. In other words, both views are right on both sides of these apparently contradictory arguments. It's *both/and*, not either/or. (*Both/and* thinking is explored in more detail in Chapter 6.)

Here it means simply that e-commerce and the use of the Internet will continue to grow almost exponentially for some time *and* that more traditional service channels will grow, but they will need great transformation to offer a shopping experience that's a viable and exciting alternative to the speed and convenience of the Net.

Think of past predictions that we would stay at home for all our life experiences. The boom in VCRs in the 1980s promised to wipe out cinema-going. However, the reality has been *both/and*. In 1996, video rentals in the UK went up by six per cent on the previous year, and in the same year the Central Office of Statistics reported the number of people going to the cinema had increased by 23.7 per cent to 30 million. The cinemas have responded to the video threat by investing in multi-screens, better food and parking facilities and more comfortable seats.

Will it be the same with the Internet? Will our craving for the visceral experience of shopping be fulfilled as retailers are forced to make their outlets more friendly, accessible and fascinating to visit? Nobody knows and, if they say they do, don't trust them. My advice is not to be blinded by the numbers. So Dell's online customers spend 30 million dollars a day with the company? So American Airlines reaches 1.7 million interested prospects each week? It makes great reading, but remember to reach for the DO NOT PANIC! button, which in this case should help to calm us long enough to see the network for the chips.

Predictions of exponential growth are usually wrong. Here's Mark Gibbs, co-author of *Navigating the Internet*:[8] 'When Elvis Presley died in 1977, there

[8] SAMS, 1994, ISBN: 0672307189.

were 37 Elvis impersonators in the world. Today there are 48,000. If the current trend continues, one of every three people in the world will be an Elvis impersonator by 2010.'

Similarly, all predictions of the future based on projecting today's numbers forward will seem ludicrous when we have the luxury of looking back on them.

Patricia B. Seybold, author of *customers.com*,[9] brings common sense to these issues when she asks: 'What's the secret of a successful e-business initiative? . . . Who's really making or saving money on the Internet, and what have they done differently from those who have failed?'

Her answer is: *'It's the customer, stupid!'*

In other words, those who fall too much in love with the technology are likely to get burned, but those who have used it to make life easier for their customers have tended to succeed. And those who have made it a more entertaining, stimulating experience. We all seem to have an increasing appetite for entertainment, perhaps to soften the hard face of technology. Media writer Michael Wolf says: 'When consumer-focused businesses move to the Internet they must inevitably become entertainment companies.' For example, The Gap site not only advertises its clothes, but also allows customers to download music as a way of preventing them from clicking to a rival site.

This brings us full circle to the five fundamental 'I's – Individuality, Interactivity, Immediacy, Intimacy, Imagination – that introduced this section. The Internet may become 'a preferred medium for customer care', but this medium has to deliver many of the same human needs for service that customers have in dealing through other channels. Most of us don't suddenly shed our human skin when we try to do business online, thinking, 'I don't care if the system's slow', or 'I don't mind if I can't have two-way communication with this supplier', or 'The technology is so exciting that I don't care if it's far less reliable than my telephone or fax machine.' Or, at least, not for very long!

Again, Kevin Kelly summarises this beautifully when he says: 'The network economy is founded on technology, but can be built only on relationships. It starts with and ends with trust.'

The message is clear: don't exchange the old (existing knowledge of what

[9] Random House Business, 1998, ISBN: 0712680713, founder and CEO of Boston-based Patricia Seybold Group, a worldwide strategic technology consulting firm and computer consultant for 20 years. Her number-one rule of success in e-commerce is to make it easy for customers to do business with you.

keeps customers happy) for the new in the belief that e-commerce, e-tailing and interactive websites render it all irrelevant. If anything, the new technology means the opposite. We will have to sharpen our awareness of customers' experience because their expectations are sky-high.

The sections that follow each conclude with brief examples of organisations that use the Internet to allow for more Interactivity, more Intimacy, Immediacy and so on. Customers change, but perhaps not as rapidly in their needs for service as the current e-panic would have us believe.

Individuality

My company, Service Legends, conducted a fax survey of 250 clients, including around 50 main board directors, who said that above all other factors they wanted to be treated like individuals. This is as true for business-to-business, it seems, as consumer trading.

Individuality is at the centre of the Six Needs that legendary service providers must be aware of for the simple reason that every individual *is* the centre of his or her own universe. We feel most belittled in this sense of individuality when we are treated like part of a mass market, or a voiceless nonentity whose desires are merely 'processed' by a faceless organisation. This is reflected in research that reveals that 80 per cent of consumers who shop with UK companies do not believe their custom is highly valued. It's a short step from not believing my custom is valued to feeling that *I* am not valued.

Our greatest human need is to be appreciated (an acute observation by the great psychologist William James) so companies have got it seriously wrong if they expect unappreciated customers to repeat willingly the experience of shopping with them. Certainly we want a product or service that works, but even more we want to be made to feel that our individuality is recognised and affirmed – that we matter.

A tentative step in the direction of realising the needs of the individual was created in the late 1980s with the concept of 'mass customisation'. This means being able to service a mass market, but with many individual versions of the product. Many of us have now heard of the Personal Pair service from blue jeans market leader Levi's. This allows customers in a mass market (15-to-19-year-olds buy 200 million pairs a year) personally to 'design' their own jeans at a computer screen in a Levi's store, even down to answering the question: '**What name would you like on the leather patch at the back of your jeans?**'

Levi's Get Personal!

We are traditionally a mass manufacturer, moving stock in
large numbers. ... We have been extremely successful at this
over the past 150 years. But we did start to feel in the early
'90s that our customers long to be treated more individually.
Dirk de Vos, Levi's Europe Marketing Vice-President

A more dramatic form of mass customisation is that proposed by
Nicholas Negroponte, the director of the media lab at the Massachusetts
Institute of Technology. He talks about the newspaper industry being able
to produce the *Daily Me*, a version of the news specifically targeted to an
individual's interests. If your obsessions are, for instance, golf, computing,
and jazz, that's what your *Daily Me* will contain. The technology is already
there to achieve this, though again it is later than you think – those who
have access to their news over a PC filtered for their individual interests are
already beginning to drift from watching TV and reading newspapers
because they can help themselves to surf the world for whatever fascinates
them.

A subtle variant on the *Daily Me* is technology expert Kevin Kelly's idea
that what we really require is a *Daily You*, a paper that also covers the
interests of our closest friends so we will be able to converse with them.

One-to-one?

However, does one-to-one really attend to the individual, or is it a sham?
Customisation is not the same thing as *customerisation*, the latter indicating
that rather than tailoring or merely tweaking the offering, the customer's
individual likes and dislikes are placed firmly at the centre of everything you
do.

When I receive a cold mail shot starting with the words Dear Mr Barlow,
this is merely a primitive form of customisation. So, actually, are most of the
offerings created by the new pseudo sciences of relationship and one-to-one
marketing. In their brilliant *Harvard Business Review* article 'Preventing
The Premature Death Of Relationship Marketing', Susan Fournier, et al.[10]

[10] January–February 1998.

describe how mass marketing thinking still pollutes the practical implementation of real bonding with the individual.

Fournier remarks that, 'ironically, the very things that marketers are doing to build relationships with customers are often the things that are destroying those relationships. Why? Perhaps we are skimming over the fundamentals of relationship building in our rush to cash in on the potential rewards of creating close connections with our customers.'

These fundamentals of relationship building are a useful checklist to gauge whether you really understand customers' need for their individuality to be recognised. They include:

Understanding that it takes two to tango.

As with all good relationships, it has to be a two-way street. While companies build enormous databases on my buying preferences, how much can I influence them? They have my telephone number and can call me any time of day or night, but how easily can I contact them back? *And* speak to the *individual* I want to? I share information with them – what do they share with me? To connect with the customer's individuality, it's essential that you also present an individual face to him or her. Like relationships, it takes two. Organisations that value their customers' input are taken seriously only when they encourage real dialogue – face-to-face, online, or anyhow!

Appreciating the universal rules of friendship.

Oxford University professor of psychology Michael Argyle has identified these basic rules – they include providing emotional support, respecting privacy, preserving confidences and tolerance of other friendships. Most of these rules are conspicuous by their absence in the field of customer service.

Take, for example, respecting privacy. A Safeway supermarket in California recently upset a number of their customers by using their names at the checkout. This seems at first to be a clever way of acknowledging individuality by using the customer's name, but for reasons of privacy and even security some customers are disturbed by it. It's seen as an unwanted and even potentially dangerous form of false intimacy by the customer, even though the intention is benign.

Not surprisingly, these universal rules are extraordinarily close to what used to be called good manners. In fact, good manners is probably an expression that only those of us over 40 comprehend. I believe it's time someone invented a new word that doesn't have the stigma of formality attached to it, but instead encompasses sound principles of relating. I look forward to your suggestions.

Understanding CCS (Customer Choice Syndrome).

As a customer, my brain is addled by the choices facing me – I have to answer four or five questions just to procure a cup of coffee. There's even more complexity in the supermarket – in America, Coca-Cola is available in more than 50 product and packaging versions, Crest toothpaste in 55. And scanning the offers available from telephone companies could take the brains of a mathematician and the decisiveness of a Churchill to arrive at an even vaguely satisfying choice. I call this Customer Choice Syndrome, a new and potentially harmful source of stress.

Real Customer Choice

Real *choice* for customers in the future
will be not only choice of a much wider range
of *products* as choice of:
* Different service *processes or channels*
(for example technological or personal)
and
* Different service *experiences*

When companies bombard me with offers that claim to be tailored exactly to my individual needs – often as a result of trawling through their data warehouse, stocked with evidence of the consistency of my past buying patterns – something in me rebels. Especially when marketeers claim to know the details of my sex life from the contents of my supermarket trolley!

Certainly I want choice, but the effect of all these hyped offerings is to make me remember Bruce Springsteen's song about 50 channels on TV with nothing to watch.

The dazzling scale of alternatives – which give the illusion of choice between what are actually very similar offerings – has led to the stopgap solution of helping customers through advisers such as 'wardrobe engineers' to make good clothing choices and 'purchase pals' to guide them through department stores. It's stopgap because, without wishing to return to a Fordist or Soviet world of no choice, the final choice is really no choice – and why does the customer need such an array of lookalike products in the first place?

What self-service really means

So what's the answer? Legendary service providers will have to perform the balancing act of having an up-to-date customer database on my likes and dislikes, *and* the flexibility to use it – or not use it – while employing the principles of a good personal friendship. This means respecting my privacy, not giving me too many unwanted choices (which may create CCS) and, above all, allowing the relationship to be two-way.

This point is critical to respecting the individuality of the customer.

As customers we want to help ourselves, and to be helped in this process at the exact moment that we ask for help.

This is *not* the same as self-service, which in its earlier form was a way of cutting labour costs and transferring the workload to the customer. What is called for is the same kind of sensitivity that we display in the best of our personal relationships – a need for space to make decisions – even mistakes, but they're our own mistakes – and timely support and advice when asked for, or just occasionally, anticipated.

Who is getting this right? Perhaps, surprisingly, American Express, an organisation famed for its strong sales orientation. It appears to be tuning in to the individuality of the customer and the needs for the customer to serve him or herself. Alfredo Benedicto, head of Customer Loyalty (do you have one?) observes:

> 'We used to use database marketing to reach homogenous groups, treating people within those groups equally, but not recognising their individuality. We're now moving towards a one-to-one relationship with each customer. You can't have infinitely flexible products, but you can address your customers in such a personal way that you find out specifically what their wants and needs are, and respond to those. In the past, we were successful at selling things, but not necessarily at relationship building.'

**TRUE INDIVIDUALITY
NEEDS TO BE RESPECTED
IN THE PERSONAL <u>WAY</u>
CUSTOMERS ARE TREATED**

Benedicto is particularly insightful when he admits that you can't have infinitely flexible products, but rather that true individuality is respected in the personal *way* in which each customer is treated. Of course, acknowledgement of individuality is easier in a face-to-face situation. Like the British Airways stewardess I saw welcoming a young unaccompanied flyer on to the aircraft with the words: 'Oh, I knew we had a young girl travelling alone on the plane today, but I didn't know it would be *you*.' Does she say this to all the young passengers? I have no idea, but I was knocked out, as was the young girl, by the power of the individual attention she received.

Back at American Express, where most customer contact is over the telephone, giving customers more space to decide for themselves – the new form of self-service – is well understood. Staff are now coached to present opportunities to the customer in place of their former selling techniques. Benedicto remarks: 'The customer has to want to buy. … If British Airways is on strike, the dialogue might turn towards what happens if the flight is cancelled. So the customer decides to buy travel insurance. . . Our attitude is always, "Well, if you insist, you need it . . ." '

The crucial point is that respect for the customer's individuality has to be an instinctive response, like a reflex action in the body. You can't over-formalise or over-script this response. You can't bottle it. The feeling that my individuality as a customer is recognised, appreciated and responded to sensitively is a subjective judgment that flows out of the personal chemistry that is established. Here, attitude is more fundamental than skills or techniques. Your people's ability to connect with the individual self of each customer, backed by the systems to allow them to do this swiftly and accurately, needs to be the bedrock of all your coaching, training and leadership in customer care.

Finally, the idea of the global village, once thought to be a fantasy, has become a reality. This means that increasingly you are dealing with individuals from different cultures, with their own highly distinct sensitivities and ways of behaving. For instance, when Virgin Atlantic first put on flights to Japan, there were many things the Japanese customers were unhappy with, but their culture of supreme politeness stopped them from giving this feedback to the airline. Truly to respect individuality, your service providers need to be well versed in these cultural differences. There are fascinating and insightful books on the subject which should be on their reading list.[11]

---

[11] Fons Trompenaars, *Riding the Waves Of Culture*, Economist Books, London, 1993. Trompenaars grew up speaking French and Dutch and handled operations for the Royal Dutch Shell Group in nine different countries.

Individuality and the Internet

Individuality is best expressed over the Internet when

1. You're recognised when you log on (they know you);
2. The supplier has learned about you (unlike the hotel where you keep telling them the same information, but see no evidence of corporate memory);
3. You aren't bombarded with inappropriate mail or e-mail shots as a result of your connection, and
4. Your confidentiality is preserved.

A site to visit that uses individuality well

L L Bean: www.llbean.com
L. L. Bean keeps a record of what you've bought, building profiles on you as a customer down to your clothing size. They also know you as a customer because they provide information on their online site that helps you enjoy what you buy its product for – usually outdoor activities – to the full. This includes information on care and treatment of your hiking shoes and even which walking trails to take in a specific location. As an English customer it's a shame that it doesn't take international orders over the Web, but it does offer phone ordering.

Interactivity

Continuing the theme that organisations need to use the principles of good personal relationships in order to please their customers, it's clear that one of these requirements is *interaction*, an exchange that feels valuable to both parties. In rare cases this may be without words. I recall 1960s pop icon Marianne Faithfull describing the interaction in her long-standing relationship with Rolling Stones guitarist Keith Richards as 'mainly non-verbal'.

But take, for example, the everyday experience of acknowledging your neighbour, perhaps with a greeting or a wave. Without *interaction* he or she is a stranger on the street. Without interaction you are not in a relationship with him or her. And the more quantity and quality of information that passes between you, the stronger the relationship.

So it goes with commercial transactions. One problem of over-relying on technology is that there's less scope for a human interaction, therefore less chance of creating a unique bonding experience. Management writer Charles Handy observes how an over-emphasis on efficiency can lead to a vague feeling of dissatisfaction:

'Recently I discovered that I could book a cinema seat, choose the date and time I wanted, the price and location, give my telephone number and full credit card details all by punching the keys on my telephone and have every detail confirmed back to me by a computer voice, go to the cinema that evening, put my card into a machine and watch my ticket pop out – all done without any other human being. I was impressed by the efficiency of it all, but it took me a long time to do all that keypunching, and the call was long distance. Efficient for the cinema, not wonderfully effective for me.'[12]

What's happening here? Handy got what he wanted – and we've all experienced telephone rage at the automated system that is both unfriendly *and* doesn't work – but something was missing. The great complexity, with all the messiness, that accompanies human interactions. Thoreau was extremely prescient when he observed that 'men have become tools of their tools'.

There are three main categories of interactivity to consider in ensuring the kind of exchange that both pleases the customer and binds them more closely in a relationship with you.

1. Customers want to be in control;
2. Two-way communication. and
3. Enjoyment and belonging.

Customers want to be in control

Rakesh Sapra, United Parcel Service's manager of Interactive Marketing (again, do you have one of these?) recognises this. He says: 'Today, there are

---

[12] *The Hungry Spirit*, Arrow (Random House UK), 1998, ISBN: 0 09 92277 2. Handy has been acclaimed for his prophetic ideas on the changing nature of work and organisations.

very few passive customers. Our business-to-business customers are "hands-on" types who welcome being brought into the process.' He also observes that a top manager may not know – indeed may not be interested in knowing – the intricacies of the UPS transport system, but at least has the ability to track the shipment of his or her goods with the point and click of a mouse.

This feeling of control is a key aspect of interactivity – it may not help the parcel to arrive more quickly, but the customer feels happier in the knowledge that at least he knows where it is. The perception that I am *somehow*, however tenuously, involved in the transaction rather than merely a passive recipient makes me feel a more equal partner in the process. The interaction lessens the me/them split and helps me to feel that we are working jointly to deliver the end result.

An even more striking example of customer interactivity is the car-maker Rover Group's Personal Production Project. This allows a customer to walk into any UK or Western European dealership and to be able to order a 'made-to-measure' car. The process uses a multimedia selection and ordering system known as Discus. You can choose everything from the colour to the seat fabric, engine size and external trim. To bring your interactive choice to life you can then even view a video clip of the car in your chosen colour, together with the price and details of when it can be delivered. You have the feeling of driving the car even before you have taken delivery.

But perhaps the most significant shift here is not the technology, but the change in Rover's orientation in encouraging its customers to participate so actively in the ordering process. Stephen Gardner, Rover's international purchasing director, describes it as a *shift from supply-chain thinking to demand-chain thinking*. And the bigger the part that customers play in building their own product, the more likely they are to be happy with the outcome. It's another example of helping customers to help themselves.

Two-way communication

If you wave to your neighbour, but she doesn't wave back, you can't really say that any meaningful communication has taken place. This is one area where the creators of websites have realised that to draw the customer in there needs to be some interactivity rather than the passive thinking that uses the site merely as an electronic version of the brochure. Ski Europe, the US-based holiday company at www.ski-europe.com, has discovered that the likelihood of a visitor to their site booking a holiday goes up significantly with the number of interactions. The most effective way to draw the customer in is through a dialogue. The Vermont Teddy Bear Company at www.vtbear.com is also wise to this, providing quizzes and games on its site to prolong the interaction.

One simple pointer that helps you know an organisation is serious about the value of a two-way dialogue is that it has its telephone number clearly displayed, preferably on the first page of its site. It's surprising how many have overlooked this simple facility. Or possibly it's deliberate because they want to control who contacts them and how. Big mistake!

But perhaps the most powerful examples are those using dialogue for *learning* what is valuable to the customer and the owners of the site. Firefly is one of the best exponents of this art. It locates for you tastes, viewpoints and preferences in books, music and movies, and even people who share these interests that you might like to meet. It's used on barnesandnoble.com for book selection, for example. Smartness is an overused description in the high-tech industry, but appropriate here as *the more interaction you are involved in, the more useful and accurate the agent (as it describes itself) becomes.* Every time you log in, the agent 'remembers' – has learned – more about you and can help you more. It's joint learning as you also become smarter about how to use the system.

The most fascinating aspect of a two-way interaction that involves learning is that you may be able to actually *anticipate* a customer's needs. It may not have the prescience of a Jeeves who always knows what's best for his master, Bertie Wooster, but it's getting close. Firefly does this and, of course, so does amazon.com when it tracks the books or music you have ordered and updates you on-line with: 'If you liked "Mock Tudor" by Richard Thompson then you might also enjoy music by Fairport Convention, Lucinda Williams, Sandy Denny, Cry Cry Cry, and Bob Dylan.'

Of course, in the early dialogue you can experience some errors – just because you like Aerosmith doesn't necessarily mean you'll enjoy Bon Jovi, and Proust readers may not be hot on Zola. However, this is an acceptable mistake that another human being might legitimately make in conversation, and is, therefore, forgivable. The wonder of the system is that it learns and even for a proud category-hopper like myself it's more often right than not.

This is where hotels seem to have it so wrong – how many times do they ask for the same information, no matter how often you stay? What do they do with it? It's rather like a personal relationship where someone keeps asking you the same question and forgetting the answer – the corporate version of Alzheimer's.

You can apply this principle of interactivty to the way in which you read this book. Think of all the books we read and understand, but what percentage of the information in them do we actually remember and use? The answer is, of course, very little, and this is particularly true when we treat reading as a passive process. Look at the way writers and researchers use other people's books. Key passages are scribbled over and highlighted, Post-its stuck on at appropriate points, important pages are photocopied and sections are torn out with checklists, questionnaires and activities (for instance, you could apply this to Chapter 9). I encourage you to interact with this material and to treat *Batteries Included!* with just this degree of irreverence.

The value of a two-way dialogue that allows for learning is best encapsulated by Don Peppers and Martha Rogers in *Enterprise One to One*:[13]

'A learning relationship between a customer and an enterprise gets smarter and smarter with every individual interaction, defining in more detail the customer's individual needs and tastes. Every time a customer orders her groceries by calling up last week's list and updating it, for instance, she is in effect "teaching" the service more about the products she buys and the rate at which she consumes them.'

Again, this works like a relationship we have invested a great deal of time and energy in; we may change it, but it will take more effort than staying put and while in it we have the resources only for a limited number of other friendships of any real depth. Customer loyalty comes from helping the customer to invest in his or her own learning and participate in the buying process. Once you have spent time to make a particular supplier 'smarter' about your needs, it will take that much more energy to convince you to move your business elsewhere. As a supplier, how easy do you make it for customers to make you smarter about their needs?

Enjoyment and belonging

Most human beings have a desire to belong – to a club, interest group or a looser association of people who share an interest. In many cases this is a

---

[13] *Enterprise One to One: Tools for Competing in the Interactive Age*, Doubleday, 1999, ISBN: 038548755X.

positive choice they make as they want to share the sense of belonging and fun that they can have only with other skateboarders, golfers or Porsche owners, for example.

Games Workshop is a retailer of fantasy games and miniatures – elves, orks, dragons, space marines and the like – based in Nottingham. It also involves its young customers interactively in playing the games they subsequently buy. Any day at Games Workshop seems to be games day, with large table-top dioramas displaying opposing armies in complex contests such as Warhammer. As a parent you very quickly learn the combat strength of an ork and the efficacy or otherwise of your wizard's magical spells! Busloads of gruesomely dressed youths travel to large regional battlefests where it's impossible not to get involved.

The great thing about Warhammer is the outrageous enthusiasm of the young staff who obviously spend the evening painting the models and who seem to get as much of a kick out of the games as the customers themselves. In many ways the notion of a split between staff and customers disappears. Employees are sometimes indistinguishable from the customers and almost become the product itself.

This is not just for fun. Games Workshop has direct operations in nine countries and is a quoted company with annual sales of more than $100 million (£60 million). (Excuse me for a minute while I log on to test my necromantic skills in the Zombie Gross-Out A-Go-Go online contest. Understand this? Neither do I, but thousands of our offspring do.)

Interactivity and the Internet

An Internet provider that encourages interactivity displays the following features:

1. They draw you in;
2. They facilitate two-way dialogue;
3. There's learning for you and them;
4. They encourage you to stay and play, and
5. They provide a feeling of control by allowing you to give input to your own purchase process.

Sites to visit that use Interactivity well:

American Airlines: www.aa.com

This was the first major airline to develop a site that allows passengers to plan their trips and make reservations as well as discover up-to-date flight information. The interactivity goes as far as asking common questions like, 'How do I pack skis?' 'What's for lunch?' 'How far is the airport from town?' etc.

Kraft Foods: www.kraftfoods.com

The clever thing about this site is its Interactive Kitchen that finds hundreds of menus with ingredients you have in your kitchen. When I said I had only cheese, pasta and salmon, it offered me **306** different recipes!

Immediacy

There are three main categories of Immediacy that customers are demanding.

First, they want 'it' now – how quickly you can provide the service or product may be as much a determinant in the buying decision as the quality of what is supplied.

Second, there's a more subtle sense of immediacy, the feeling that the people giving the service are really 'in' psychologically, meaning they convey the impression that they are willing to respond swiftly, know what's required and care about the outcome. Finally, how immediate and on the ball is the response when there's a problem or complaint?

- Speed of service
- Is anybody 'in'?
- Response to problems

Speed of service

When Dr Roger Bannister ran the first four-minute mile in Oxford in 1954 he shattered a limiting belief held by much of the sporting world. Many medical journals had attested to the fact that it was humanly impossible to break the four-minute-mile barrier. *But what is most fascinating is that over the following 18 months more than 45 runners also ran a sub-four-minute mile!*

We make self-limiting assumptions about what is possible. So when lenders started granting mortgages – still 'subject to status' as they always were – over the telephone in 15 minutes, a similar barrier was broken. The rest began to stir themselves. The tortoises decided they had better become hares, whatever the fable said.

Now speed is (almost) everything. Food is fast, securities are traded instantaneously and electronically, spectacles are available from opticians within an hour and 'same-day delivery' has become commonplace. Carpet retailer Milliken now has a van in London that delivers carpet samples the same day the request is made. The sloth of our postal systems, particularly in the USA and Canada, has spawned a mega-industry of parcel delivery services which sell that scarcest of all resources, time. The 'made-to-measure' Rover car-ordering service described earlier promises the tailored vehicle in 14 days. Perhaps in the future we may be able to bill organisations that waste our time!

> 'If time is of all things the most precious, wasting time must be the greatest prodigality; since lost time is never found again, and what we call time enough always proves too little.'
>
> *Benjamin Franklin* [14]

The most sobering reflection is that quality has rarely suffered in this speeded-up world – in fact, it has often *improved*!

What are the new barriers to be broken? It's comfortable to reflect on the events of 1954 with the smug knowledge of hindsight, but what limiting assumptions are we making right now about how quickly a task can be accomplished for our customers? What's dangerous about an assumption is that we don't know we're making it until someone else points it out or goes ahead and overturns it. Of course, if *we* do it, it's innovation; if *they* do it, it's cheating!

How does the UK furniture industry hope to survive – let alone thrive – when it expects you to wait six weeks for a new sofa? Paying for the goods may

[14] US statesman, author, printer, writer, scientist (1706–90) famous for his wit and common sense in *Poor Richard's Almanac*. He believed successful people just worked a little harder than other people.

be immediate, receiving them is not. So when you are looking at immediacy you need to consider all the backroom operations that affect the speed the customer experiences. Here the problem is one between the retailer and manufacturer, and unfortunately the customer pays in waiting time.

Many businesses are investing in what has come to be called 'time-based competition'. Life insurance companies focus obsessively on the turnaround time of quotations and mobile communications businesses such as Orange will courier a new phone to you in an hour or two if you've lost your old one. But what helps to achieve this is firstly focusing on all the links in the chain that deliver that eventual service to the customer, and second, creating a culture where decisions are made quickly.

Behind-the-scenes immediacy means looking at every stage in the service process that eventually impacts on the customer. This can mean relationships with suppliers, delivery schedules and, of course if you're in manufacturing, speeding up every aspect of the production process. Time *is* money, not just to your customers, but to your own concern because research has shown that saving time in the delivery process tends to reduce costs. Quality may also even improve as a result. There are three essential checks to make in thinking about improving the immediacy of your systems:

Does it make a difference to the customer?

Asking people to focus on cutting time in essential steps is fine, but my experience is that this is worthwhile only if it really is valued by the customer.

Suppliers! Suppliers! Suppliers!

How often have you heard sales representatives complain that they would love to be able to serve you with the goods, but their suppliers were either late or forgetful in not including the item in their delivery? As far as customers are concerned, your suppliers *are* you and unless they work in partnership with you to speed up every aspect of the delivery process you will always be limping in the eyes of the customer. The immediacy with which your suppliers treat you is therefore transparent to your customers.

Challenge assumptions.

Just because it has always taken a certain length of time to process an order doesn't mean it has to be that way in the future. This may sound obvious, but we've already discussed the power of limiting assumptions, particularly when you are operating within an established 'box'. Pick a figure as your goal – say a 50 per cent reduction – and stick relentlessly to removing every barrier that prevents you from achieving this. Work backwards from the ideal rather than wallowing in today's problems. Recalling the four-minute-mile example, once one individual starts questioning the boundaries of what's possible, then many others do it, too.

Let's consider the kind of culture that can make quicker decisions for its customers. Often the larger the organisation, the slower the decision-making. I've noticed that my own small organisation can turn around documentation, proposals and reports in a fraction of the time that larger and intensively resourced companies are able to do. In this sense, small is beautiful because there is a culture of caution inherent in larger entities. This is particularly felt by the customer when he or she wants an answer to a complaint or a request for something out of the ordinary. No wonder Lou Gerstner, CEO of IBM, says: 'The challenge for us at IBM is how to incorporate small-company attributes – nimbleness, speed and customer responsiveness – with the advantages of size.'

What are the characteristics of a culture that allows for quick and immediate decision-making? Stanford University professor Kathleen Eisenhardt studied 12 micro-computer companies in which she identified a number of clear behavioural differences, that allowed one set of those companies to do things in two to four months that took the other group from 12 to 18 months to accomplish. We could call the slow decision-makers tortoises and the quicker ones gazelles. The slower ones often had communication by memos, lengthy reports and regular formal meetings and relied heavily on thorough analysis of quantitative data and future trends. They also delayed implementation until big choices were made.

The gazelles, on the other hand, were characterised by holding frequent but short ('noisy') meetings, considered many options simultaneously and relied heavily on intuition. The data that received most attention was up-to-date, real-time information rather than established industry reports, and strategy and tactics were fully integrated. In simple terms, they learned by doing.

If you want to be one of the quick it's worth considering how you can:

Challenge the level at which decisions are made.

As a customer you want the person in front of you to represent the full decision-making capacity of that organisation. In its extreme sense it might be unreasonable, but the challenge for organisations who want to demonstrate their immediacy to the customer is to ensure that real-time decisions can be taken in the vast majority of cases without the person having to check with his or her manager or supervisor. How far down should you push this decision-making ability? There is no hard and fast rule, except that if you work on the principle *further than you think*, you'll be getting closer to matching the customer's needs for speed of service.

Involve others in your planning.

If a plan has to be explained or sold to people who weren't in at its birth, they will rarely 'get it' with the same feeling of commitment as if they had co-created it. Involving as many people as possible in creating your customer-focused systems means that they become living exponents of the system rather than its mechanical operators.

Encourage people to use their own best judgment.

This is the essence of the US department store, Nordstrom's, instructions to its people, and a powerful tribute to the way in which that company trusts its people to do the right thing.

The more you can demonstrate that you trust your people to make the right decisions for the customer, the less bureaucracy and time-wasting they will experience. The risks are dwarfed by the benefits of saved costs and reduction of time spent by senior people in approving small requests. To what extent should you allow service representatives to be flexible in using their own best judgment? Again, the answer is simple – *much further than you think*.

Finally, it's worth remembering that if you're selling time you can often charge a premium for the service. To take an example, the one-hour photograph development service is about 50 per cent more expensive than the one-day service. The photographs are exactly the same, so what I have bought is immediacy. Putting yourself in the customer's shoes, think of any aspect of your service which if radically speeded up would:

1. Create what is effectively a new product?
2. Help you to stand out from the tortoise competition? or
3. Enable you to charge a price premium?

Customers want it yesterday. There are even examples of delivering a service before a customer requests it, such as Mercedes' use of satellite-linked technology to conduct minor repairs and diagnosis on your vehicle while you're driving along. Computerised monitoring systems in lifts allow the supplier to ring up and tell you there's a problem – or there's about to be a problem – even before you know it yourself. So perhaps the ultimate goal of immediacy should be to deliver before the customer has even asked!

Immediacy also becomes more critical when middlemen everywhere are nearing extinction. The current buzzword in business is *disintermediation*, which means cutting out the middleman or removing the layers between the buyer and supplier. Stockbroker Charles Schwab achieves this with online investing tools for the ordinary person. Direct Line Insurance in the UK was the wildly successful pioneer of cutting out the middleman, initially in the car insurance business. Perhaps the area where this will strike most and give customers greater immediacy – here implying both greater speed and lower costs – is in the field of banking.

The Forces for Disintermediation

1. More sophisticated investors and borrowers;
2. New entrants put pressure on margins;
3. Increased banks' cost of capital, and
4. Technology reduces transaction costs and banks' customer loyalty.

Michel Tilmant, Reinventing The Bank, *1998*

But the messages in the box above describing the need to reinvent the bank are applicable to most businesses. The race is on to remove any barriers between you and your customers before (a) they find their way around themselves, or (b) your competitors provide that facility. The threat is real – travel agents are only one example of a whole profession under threat as customers track bargains for themselves around the globe.

However, look at your systems and your leadership first. Don't simply do what has become fashionable and turn middle management into the 'bad object' or convenient scapegoat. It's the leaders who allow over-hierarchical, convoluted and bureaucratic systems to stand between them and their customers who are really to blame. And while you're at it, why not cut out the middlemen who cut out the middlemen – the consultants who make a living by telling you what you already knew, that some jobs no longer add value either to your business or to the customer?

Is anybody 'in'?

In a memorable TV sketch American comedienne Lily Tomlin asked: 'Have I reached the party to whom I am speaking?'

Often we speak to people who are just going through the motions, merely following a script that they intone listlessly.

> 'Have I reached the party to whom I am speaking?'
>
> *Lily Tomlin*[15]

My fantasy is that telephone operators and hotel receptionists, particularly in the UK, have been on a lengthy training programme where they are heavily drugged and brainwashed into repeating these formulaic responses, often ending with the helpless-sounding 'How may I help you?'. There's no immediacy here, rather an alienating distance that discourages the customer from asking for anything too difficult – like the request they called to make in the first place.

At London-based 7C Communications, which sells telephone services, advisers rotate regularly to give feedback to their peers on 27 different parameters, several addressing soft factors such as empathy, tone and speed of voice. They are judging the *immediacy* of attention that is sensed through the wires by the customer.

Experts in the field of telecommunications talk about the 'death of distance', the fact that collapses in the cost of global communications mean your colleagues can be in Taipei while you work from Dublin and you can be online or on the phone as and when necessary as call charges plummet. The death of distance means that knowledge workers, as writer Peter Drucker originally dubbed those of us who work with our brains rather than our hands, can be located in every part of the globe. Indeed, India, China and the new Asian economies provide a ready source of highly qualified

[15] Comedienne who brought Ernestine the customer-service deficient switchboard operator to millions in the US in the 1970s on cult TV programme, *Saturday Night Live*. Her attitude was that if you were impudent enough to complain about your phone service you might as well use two paper cups attached by string because the response would be 'We don't care. We don't have to. We're the Phone Company.' How many of us might make the same comment today about our Internet service provider?

outworkers for European and US companies through the immediacy of the new technology. And vice-versa.

What seems to have lagged behind is our *appreciation* of this immediacy of communication. Many still treat the telephone as a device that keeps them from being fully natural. Not so the most successful sales advisers in BT Telemarketing's giant UK call centres. Observing their best advisers, I'm struck by the quality of attention they radiate to their customers. They use body language and convey the same physical and verbal energy as if they were sitting side by side in a pub with the caller. They are really 'in' for their customers.

A few innovative companies have caught on to the idea of using actors to coach their people in the quality of voice modulation and projection, and physical movements for those who deal face-to-face with customers. In my experience it's talked about a lot, implemented little. Direct customer contact staff *are* on stage – it's more than a metaphor – and they are usually not given the skills to improve their performance. No wonder the applause is so restrained . . .

Immediacy of response to problems

'Turning complaints into opportunities' is one of the catchphrases of the customer service professional today. And should be, as is clear from the words of British Airways' Charles Weiser. He says: 'Though 50 per cent of those who chose not to tell the airline about their experience defected to other airlines, the majority of customers with problems who did contact someone at British Airways – 87 per cent – did not defect.'

Complainers stay, provided they are handled correctly. The silent ones are more likely to leave you because you are not 'in relationship' with them to the same extent. In an ongoing personal relationship you need to be able to make your feelings and opinions known *and* to receive a response. The bond becomes stronger when it has been tested. Trust is earned when shared difficulties are overcome.

In the same way, customers test the relationship when they give feedback and complain. The process of putting problems right has been labelled 'service recovery' and the commonsense economics of giving a fast, willing and no-quibble response has been understood, at least intellectually, for the past decade or so. But when I ask management groups whether they have a clear and fast recovery system that is readily understood by most people in their organisation, only a small proportion put up their hands confidently. Ironically, these same companies often have high-profile campaigns aimed at securing 'long-term customer loyalty' or 'customers for life'.

How well an enterprise responds to a complaint – a lost order, a defective part, an indigestible meal – is one of the most significant elements customers use to judge the quality of service. Colin Marshall, former chief executive of British Airways, would frequently read out letters from customers at staff conferences describing how their bags had gone to the other side of the world, but the individuals were still delighted with the service. Crazy people? No – what these customers were praising was the airline's helpfulness in putting the error right by offering loans of vital items such as clothing and even computers to help them out until luggage was returned.

While it's dangerous to build a strategy on this, a service disaster wonderfully handled can turn a statistic into a friend.

How easy is it for you to get an immediate response when you have a complaint? If it's a real slog, you probably won't bother – and most likely won't return as a customer either. How refreshing then to read on the packaging of food products in London-based sandwich and snack retailer Pret a Manger: 'If you would like to speak to me or one of my colleagues regarding anything to do with Pret a Manger please feel free to call on 020 7827 6300. Thank you. Julian Metcalfe.'

Immediacy and the Internet

Immediacy on the Internet means both speed of use and the feeling that the supplier is very much in touch with your requirements.

A site to visit that uses the concept of Immediacy well:

Amazon.com www.amazon.com

The immediacy of this site is expressed in the speedy response and delivery time of products ordered and by giving the impression that they are there with you at every stage of your transaction. This is achieved by:

- Each book having an anticipated delivery time, which is noted with the title;
- Confirming each order by e-mail within a few minutes, and
- Notifying you by e-mail when the book is sent and when it should arrive (nearly always sooner than expected).

And of course you feel they know you because all the fiddly data such as your credit card information, address and so on, are stored so each successive order is simpler.

Intimacy

Intimacy with your customers means much more than just being close to them. It means understanding their everyday experience of using your products as well as their present and future needs. But it shouldn't be thought of as a soft, nice-to-do measure. Becoming more intimate with your customers can boost both profitability and loyalty.

There's nothing more intimate than toilet training. US paper products giant Kimberly-Clark's diaper business launched its Huggies Pull-Ups training pants in 1991 and was soon selling $400 million (£240 million) worth per year. The product was born from assigning a small team, many of whom were intimate with the issue as they were also at the stage of toilet training their own children, to sit down in the homes of their customers to hear real-life stories.

Their conversations discerned that there was stigma attached to a child still being in diapers, perhaps more for the parents than the children, while maturity was associated with the transition to underwear. The result was Pull-Ups, a hybrid that carried the more grown-up message of maturity while still having the safety factor of diapers.

Most significant of all, though, are the comments of GVO's Michael Barry, who has conducted consulting work for Kimberly-Clark. 'The stress in toilet training,' he says, 'comes from parents' feelings of inadequacy and you'd never get people to admit that in a focus group.'[16]

A focus group, so beloved of Tony Blair's New Labour, is one of the ways organisations try to get closer to their customers, but the Kimberly-Clark example shows its limitations in achieving real intimacy. Intimacy means really getting inside the customers' hearts and minds, and experiencing with them *in situ* how they use your product or service and how it helps or inhibits their enjoyment of life.

Toolmaker Black & Decker used an almost anthropological approach in the early 1990s to study how their customers in the US – as represented by 50 male homeowners between 24 and 54 – used power tools on projects.

'The executives aimed to discover exactly why users favoured certain tools over others. Dissatisfaction was high. Do-it-yourselfers wanted a cordless drill with enough power to complete a good-sized job. They wanted sanders and circular saws that didn't kick up clouds of sawdust; safety mechanisms that would instantly stop saw blades from

---

[16] '*Story-Telling: A New Way To Get Close To Your Customers*', Fortune Texts Edition, 3 February 1997.

spinning when they switched off power and a hotline for questions about home repair problems. Never before had customers so clearly voiced their concerns.'[17]

Fred Wiersema

The result was new equipment that matched what they wanted. B&D's new line of Quantum saws, drills and power tools, relatively cheaply priced, surpassed its sales goal in 1994 and helped to fend off strong challenges from competitors such as Makita and Sears. My only footnote to this successful project is, don't women use power tools also?

Why don't more organisations conduct intimate surveys such as this? Arguably, it should be easier to create intimacy in business-to-business where representatives of your company may spend a great deal of time on the customer's site.

One barrier is that *it takes two to be intimate*! As a customer I am wary of the many organisations that seem to want to befriend me. They possess an alarming amount of data on my lifestyle and buying patterns, whereas they may be completely unknown to me. This is hardly the basis for an intimate relationship and if they approach me initially with questionnaires the friendship is unlikely even to start.

The omnipresence of questionnaires was satirised recently in the magazine *Private Eye*. A company called Burglars Inc. leaves a drop-in note saying: 'We called while you were in, could you please fill in the form and let us know when you're out so we can drop by again?'

Being intimate is a sensitive and delicate business, as we all know from personal experience. There are three practical steps to help you learn more intimately about your customers.

Intimacy

1. The approach
2. Sharing the customer's experience
3. Sharing of feelings – the emotional contract

---

[17] *Customer Intimacy*, HarperCollins, London, 1998, ISBN: 0006388396. Wiersema is former senior vice-president of CSC Index and a business strategist noted for his action-provoking insights and research on marketing and customer service.

The approach

Customers – corporate and individual – are constantly being courted by potential suppliers who 'only want to be friends'. So it's important in the early phase to demonstrate:

a) What's in it for the customer?
b) How might the information be used?
c) Confidentiality/building of trust.

When focus groups were new, people were flattered to be asked. Now you might have to pay, resulting in a certain degree of self-selection in whom you get. Developing intimacy is actually even more time-consuming and so it's important to get the relationship right at the very start.

Sharing the customer's experience

There are two vital tools here, story-telling and innocent witnessing.

Story-telling means listening to stories told *in the customer's own words*. This lessens the amount of filtering when you're trying to understand what's right, wrong, or so-so about the existing service or proposed new service. *If you use too many prepared questions and checklists the chances are that you will only learn what you already know.*

Intuit, a personal finance software company, used innocent witnessing in its Follow-Me-Home programme, literally watching over their customers' shoulders as they tried to install Intuit software at home. Not so much close to the customer as breathing down their necks!

From those observations came a blinding glimpse of the obvious – small business owners were using Quicken home finance software to keep their books, but this was based on the unnecessarily complex double-entry bookkeeping system required only by accountants. As a result the simplified Quick software was created and is now used worldwide.

The message? Real, close-up listening and watching without prejudice works!

Staying with the customer through the whole experience cycle

There's much talk these days about staying with customers throughout the entire period when they use your product. A great deal of service is focused on treating them charmingly at the acquire-it stage, but wise suppliers realise this is only the beginning of the relationship. Customers' loyalty depends greatly on how well you treat them during the maintain-it/use-it phase and even the moment when they come to upgrade-it/replace-it.

The Customer's Whole Experience Cycle:
Where are you strong? Where are you weak?

Acquire It	→	Use It/ Maintain It	→	Upgrade It/ Replace It?

For example, Brother make excellent electronic products. At the acquire-it phase of my relationship with them I was happy. However, the unremitting unhelpfulness of their so-called 'helpline' made me feel abandoned in the use-it/maintain-it phase of my relationship. So when it comes to upgrade/replace they're nowhere on my list of choices.

How intimate are you with your customers through each phase of their ownership experience? In practice, businesses tend to excel in one or other of these stages: a legendary service provider will need to stay close to its customers throughout their whole journey to ensure continuing loyalty.

Intimacy and the Internet

Intimacy on the Internet means feeling that you can use the technology to become closer to an individual you wouldn't ordinarily be able to connect with, and also that he or she can reach you with highly personalised knowledge of your needs, and perhaps a bit of humour, too.

A site to visit that uses the concept of Intimacy well:

Virtual Vineyards: www.virtualvin.com

Much of Virtual Vineyards' intimacy is provided by the personal way you can e-mail individuals at its site. The most popular is Peter Granoff, the resident wine expert. He becomes like the customer's personal sommelier over the Internet. The extra colour he adds to the dialogue is his description of trips he has made to particular wineries and even the surroundings where he tasted a specific wine. It's intimate because you can feel yourself there.

Imagination

'Know thy customer' is one of the commandments of modern business. However, this does not just mean having megabytes of information about past buying patterns. People feel that they are known if imagination has been used clearly to understand how their use and enjoyment of the service can be improved. Let's explore what organisations need to do to imagine what's important to the customer.

- Imagine the customer's experience.
- Imagination at work.

Imagine the customer's experience

Have you ever noticed that in petrol stations the number of the pump you have used tends to be invisible from where you queue to pay? It seems the strategic placement of pillars to block the customer's line of sight is an essential part of forecourt planning.

I once pointed this out to a cashier who shook his head in pity and declared that *he* could easily see the numbers from where *he* stood. It's just that he couldn't identify my car!

This is a clear metaphor for lack of *imagination* in the service process – the supplier's perception versus the customer's perception. Of course, we have not been short of slogans aimed at recognising the customer's point of view:

- Walk in the customer's shoes
- Think about the customer's perception
- Get closer to the customer
- Perception is reality!

'Imagination is more important than knowledge. Knowledge is limited. Imagination encircles the world.'

Albert Einstein[18]

---

[18] Mathematical physicist (1879–1955) awarded the 1921 Nobel Physics Prize for his work in theoretical physics. Of his part in developing the atom bomb he commented: 'If only I had known, I would have become a watchmaker.'

But in practice this is felt by customers to be the biggest gap of all – why can't they use their imagination and be sensitive to my experience? Computer helplines are the new villains. During a 10-minute conversation I recently recorded no fewer than seven pieces of jargon I didn't understand and I'm not completely PC-illiterate. Well, at least I didn't think I was before this exchange!

Here we are considering a blind spot that exists in ordinary relationships – why can't he/she imagine my viewpoint, my feelings? In service it seems we are all experts when we are customers, but if we move round the table to provide service we become blind to the other's experience.

> Using your imagination
> to understand the customer's experience
> *is* the job of service.

In a very real sense customers become 'other', our imagination is blunted and fails to reach out to embrace this 'otherness'.

Not so for Tony Barnfield, who runs The Nurses' Cottage Hotel in Sway, a village in Hampshire. This small hotel has won nearly every award going for service. 'Prepare to be pampered' is Tony's service imperative. His philosophy is to treat everyone as an individual – even his tax-man – to build a personal relationship with his guests and to experience what they experience during their stay with him.

So, of course, he keeps meticulous records of all his regulars and knows exactly what they've eaten every time they've stayed with him. He is, he promises, as enthusiastic about the food he serves as the cleanliness of the bathrooms or the view from the beds, so from time to time he sleeps in a guest bedroom to see what his guests see. Are the light switches at a convenient height? What's on view when the bathroom door is open? How does the sunlight, or moonlight, shine into the room?

Tony employs 13 staff part-time from Sway – some are students and some are older residents – and includes them in his Christmas greeting card to his customers. He treats his staff as individuals and wants them to be seen as individuals; he knows their abilities and makes sure they all play to their strengths. He also trains each one of them in his personal style of service.

This is not new. It's just rarely practised and acted upon, or if so, it's done by managers and not by front-line staff who also need to be encouraged to experience what the customer experiences. I suggest that before anyone is given any job in a service role he or she should have to undergo an apprenticeship where he or she plays the customer, preferably not on a training course with role-plays, but *for real*. Part of the budget for this would come from savings on mystery shoppers and (yet another) customer survey, because if you're hiring the right people they will give invaluable feedback *and* be encouraged to share their insights with existing staff. It's a bold request for newcomers, which is why supervisors and managers need to be involved closely and sensitively in a coaching role.

This should also include knowledge of the product. As a customer, I begin to lose confidence in a supplier when he knows less about his own product or service than I do. I became a loyal customer of my BMW dealer on the spot when, soon after I'd bought my car, I couldn't stop the alarm. I drove it to the dealer and immediately the service receptionist jumped out from behind her desk, rolled up the sleeves of her very smart Chanel-style suit, opened the bonnet, found where the key was sticking, and switched it off.

While I didn't expect her to fix the ABS braking system – though my confidence in her was so high I would happily have let her attempt it – it was a striking example of her knowledge of at least the basics of the product. How well do your people really know their own product? It doesn't take much imagination to see how this reassures the customer.

In this example the receptionist was providing responsiveness and a kind of assurance, one of the most important Intangibles (to introduce another 'I') that contribute to a successful service encounter. Forum Corporation, well regarded since 1971 for its research in analysing what makes customers happy or unhappy with service – its clients include 17 of Fortune's top 25 most admired companies – have identified five main factors: Reliability, Empathy, Responsiveness, Assurance, Tangibles.

Chart 1 shows the view from inside the organisation. Tangibles, which include factors such as operational efficiency, delivery, price, product quality, are the factor companies perform best on. But when you switch to the *customer's* viewpoint in Chart 2 describing what factors are used to judge the supplier, you will find tangibles the *least* important. In presentations I often flip backwards and forwards between the two because to really get the point you have to *see* it, i.e. that organisations put a great deal of time, effort and resources into what matters least to the customer.

Of course, this is a slight exaggeration as customers want it all! It's more important to me that my washing machine works than that the repairman smiles and passes the time of day with me. But in our unfair world the customer tends to *assume* the quality of the tangibles – without this you

How Well are Companies Performing on the Dimensions of Service Quality?

Mean Response

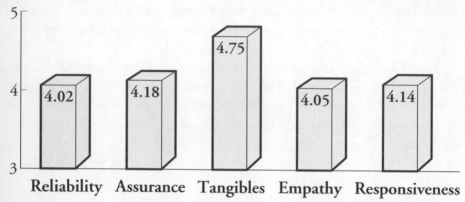

1=poor 3=average 5=excellent

Chart 1   *Source: Forum Corporation, Boston*

wouldn't be in business – and often judges you more harshly on the intangibles.

To create legendary service you have to make these leaps of imagination day in, day out to focus on the intangibles that customers regard as critical. Everyone seems to be selling intangibles today – car-makers are providing us with a lifestyle, computer manufacturers supply us with solutions, and even food is fashion.

Try tackling the answers to these five questions:

- What are the most significant 'intangibles' to our customers?
- Is everyone fully aware of this, or over-focused on the tangible element?
- Have you asked your customers?
- Have you simulated their experience? Recently?
- How can you focus your attempts to be different not just on product, but more on the customer's intangible experience?

How Much Did Each Dimension Influence
Customers' Overall Ratings of Service Quality?

Relative Importance

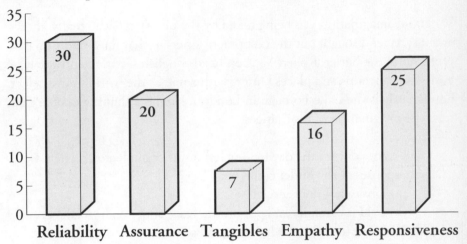

Importance ratings are based on multiple regression analysis.
All dimensions are statistically significant at p= .001.

Chart 2   *Source: Forum Corporation, Boston*

'We try to get inside our customers' heads.'
              John Honis, co-founder, Value Call International

Finally, amazon.com has used imagination to design its online bookstore to be as much as possible like a physical store. You can browse on 'tables' at the front of the shop, which give you information on specials and what's new, then go to a specific section where you find illuminating pieces written by experts or critics. If you have a more accurate idea of what you need, you can of course just type in whatever information you remember about the book and don't even need to get it exactly right for the search process (usually) to come up with the answer. This is all intuitively familiar to us as book browsers or hunters, which may be one of the reasons why Amazon has won over even some of the most hardened book sniffers who love the experience of rooting around a physical bookstore.

Imagination at work

When my imagination was being taxed by the question 'Who really knows about service?' I sought out the best practitioners in that most traditional of professions, the butler. Robert Watson heads English Gentlemen Butlers, a business that trains and places butlers with some of the world's most select hotels, such as the Lanesborough in London. He has a simple example that tests the imagination of his trainees:

A guest goes out for the day having left a suit crumpled on a chair.
The responses of the butler could be:
  (a) Ignore it – poor service;
  (b) Fold it carefully and put on the back of the chair – OK service;
  (c) Hang it in the wardrobe – good service;
  (d) Press and/or dry-clean and return to wardrobe – outstanding!

What I like about this example is that it's imagination in action – it's not a vague injunction to 'use your imagination', but a clear set of different *behaviours*, which the trainee can relate to. Do you have a similar clear set of guidelines for the difference between OK and outstanding service that your people can easily relate to?

But if you're encouraging people to use their imagination, it can't be over-prescribed; there's a healthy element of risk. One guest asked for a present for a friend who was fond of cigars. This time Robert sent out a young butler with the injunction to 'use his imagination'. The young man returned with an £800 cigar humidor! Fortunately the guest, who was obviously a person of means, was delighted.

Some people believe you should suffer for your art. Not the Stockholm Museum of Modern Art where you can pick up a free small folding stool to enable you to appreciate the most striking exhibits in comfort. What are galleries selling? Quite clearly an enriching, aesthetic *experience*, which for most of us means not standing and jostling with the crowd. The museum has self-service lockers for your bags, enabling you to avoid the hassle of the cloakroom queue. It's also designed to give you stunning views of Stockholm's harbour. Even great art is appreciated better if the mind has a break. And if you're selling what is ultimately an imaginative experience, it's nice to see imagination used in the process.

The Marriott in London's Grosvenor Square is a great hotel. Not because of its elegant wood panelling and liveried staff, but because imagination has been used to identify the small things important to the business guest that are invisible to most hotels. A card on the bed reads: 'If we don't serve room service breakfast on time, we pay for it.' They've used their imagination to understand that time (the intangible) is more important than the breakfast. The Marriott's breakfast isn't my personal favourite, but I'm more concerned that it arrives on time than the quality of the toast. I'm buying an intangible – time.

UK-based Nichols Foods does everything in its power to ensure that all visitors have a memorable experience when visiting its Wigan headquarters. Your car is fully valeted while you are in the meeting, even if you've come to sell them something – an imaginatively wide definition of who the customer is! Also, you are invited to rate the quality of the valeting, a nice touch that gets you to interact more with the company.

Finally, here's a quirky example of imagination run riot in the advertisement a friend saw for an ear-piercing business. It's interesting to imagine the alternatives to waiting!

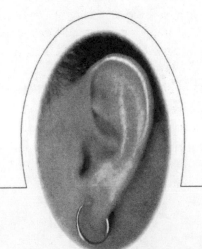

Ears Pierced - While You Wait!

Imagination and the Internet

Using imagination in your e-commerce and website means understanding

1. Simplicity and ease of use from the customer's point of view, and
2. Making use of the site a stimulating and interesting experience.

Some sites are more or less brochures on-screen, for example, Volvo in the USA. Others confuse with too many options, special offers and irrelevant information. (I've been unsuccessful many times in trying to load Real Player™ on to my PC).

Sites to visit that use the concept of Imagination well:

Vermont Teddy Bear Company: www.vtbear.com

This one's for fun, but it has mazes, puzzles, colouring pages, contests and pirate stories – and you can order teddy bears as well.

Harley Davidson: www.hd-stamford.com

Harley really knows its customer base and uses language and visuals that are empathetic to its fanatical followers. The site is even bold enough to start with the words LOYALTY. Harley owners are *loyal*. To the *core*.

Hog owners will appreciate the imagination that's gone into making a site that might have been designed by themselves.

For some penetrating questions, activities, and ideas relating to this chapter turn to page 240.

Chapter Two

What is Legendary Service?

'Our goal as a company is to have customer service that is not just the best, but legendary.'

Sam Walton (1918–92), founder of Wal-Mart[1]

'In the long run men hit only what they aim at. Therefore, though they should fail immediately, they had better aim at something high.'

Henry David Thoreau (1817–62), philosopher, writer, naturalist and social critic[2]

Understanding what Legendary Service means will help you to:

- Understand what it means to be a legend for service;
- Aim far beyond mere customer 'satisfaction', and
- Decide the first steps to take on the journey.

More real than Disney

ASK most people whether they'd rather work for an organisation that's highly respected by its customers, or one that has a reputation for being so-so, and the answer is obvious. It's more fun, as well as more secure, to work in a business that's successful and to whose name people respond positively

---

[1] A small-town merchant convinced that people would flock to a discount store with a variety of merchandise and friendly service, opened the first Wal-Mart in 1963 and in less than 30 years built it into a chain that made him the world's largest retailer. Walton also said: 'I had no vision of the scope of what I would start. But I had confidence that as long as we did our work well and were good to our customers, there would be no limit to us.'

[2] In *Walden* (1854).

when you're out at dinner or talking in a bar. So where do we look to discover the seeds of greatness?

I'm intrigued by the fact that hard-nosed business people whose everyday credo is 'show me and I'll believe it' become so inspired and excited by visits to Disney. What business is Disney in? Dreams, happiness, a fantasy factory. And why has it captured people's imagination so much when their 'real' world is selling financial services, drilling for oil, or retailing groceries?

A psychologist might tell us that it's because of a deep yearning for our youth, when the sun was always shining on Main Street. Or that it's a manifestation of the American Dream 1950s-style, when the world seemed safer, happier, the notion of endless progress and pleasure through technological wizardry was an unsullied vision of the future. Notice how it's hard not to use the language of myth when we describe Disney – wizards, magic and dreams. The fact that it makes enormous amounts of money doing so is what attracts so many managers to visit and try to learn its secrets.

The great value of Disney is that its success has allowed us to use the language of legend-building without too much fear of ridicule. To recast a familiar phrase, Disney isn't a Mickey Mouse business. Creating our own legend isn't either, but we need to explore the ingredients that will make it thrive in the so-called 'real' world, which is as much Grimm Brothers as Disney.

There are powerful reasons why a legend is such a valuable metaphor for business. First, legends are concerned with greatness, achieving something that seems impossibly far beyond today's horizons. It's the same with many corporate visions that seek to inspire customers to share their myth or legend.

Second, the greatest legends touch the heart and spark the intuition. There is a great deal of talk in business about passion for the customer, which is only possible when people's emotions are fully engaged.

Third, a critical part of the definition of a legend is 'stories to be told'. An organisation has achieved the status of a legend with its customers only when they spread positive stories about their experience, influencing others to join and stay with the same club. And finally, legends are timeless, passed on from generation to generation. Organisations can learn a great deal from the process of legend-building to improve their longevity.

Let's explore the metaphor of a legend further, relating it to the pursuit of fabulous service. There are a number of ingredients we need to take on our journey together.

Creating a Legend

- The Quest
- Code of Chivalry
- Heroic Acts
- Using Magic
- Finding The Holy Grail

There has to be a stirring *quest* to raise your fellow adventurers' eyes to a horizon that transcends the possibilities they see today. Imagine King Arthur inspiring his knights with the imagination to perform to a standard 'recognised as one of the best within our industry'. They might have returned from their adventures justified in the excuse that 'no one else has been able to slay that giant either – benchmarking against other knights shows I did as good a job as anyone else in my position might have been expected to!'

Most corporate quests, commonly called visions, missions, purposes, strategic intentions, challenges, long-term goals or objectives, are mind-numbingly similar and all too often uninspiring. This doesn't have to be the case. Sony's aim to 'experience the sheer joy that comes from technical innovation' is highly uplifting and couldn't be Aiwa or Bosch, could it? Similarly, Steve Jobs's vision of Apple Computer creating 'a bicycle for the mind' has inspired ease of use, familiarity and a strange form of man-machine bonding that has powerfully driven so much of Apple's activities for the past 20 years.

I have a small fantasy that tucked in between retail outlets such as Tie Rack and Sock Shop is a business called 'The Mission Shop'. This allows busy executives to go in and buy a cheap, off-the-shelf mission statement. 'To Be the Best', 'To Be Number One' or 'To Become the Customer's Preferred Choice' seem to be the most popular lines.

But if your quest is really going to be meaningful, it has to be:

- Far beyond what seems possible today;
- Emotionally charged, and
- Unique and authentic for your business, and recognisably so.

The Knights of the Round Table lived by an extraordinarily high *code of chivalry*, which included commitment to one's word and unfailing loyalty to King, Queen and comrades. The form that a code of chivalry often takes today is a set of values or beliefs about how a customer should be treated. One of the most famous is, of course, the principles that drive Stew Leonard's legendary dairy store in Norwalk, Connecticut:

Rule Number One – the customer is always right;
Rule Number Two – if the customer is wrong, see rule Number One!

This works for Leonard's dairy business, but may well be too simplistic for a larger organisation, which doesn't have the visible presence of a founding family guiding day-to-day operations. But whatever your code is, it's vital to remember that customers don't buy only your product or service, but also the values and ethos you stand for.

The core elements of a meaningful code of chivalry for the customer might be:

- Speak the truth – always meet your promises;
- Honour the customer, and
- Act in a spirit of generosity and kindness.

Heroic acts are the essence of legends. Retrieving the Golden Fleece may not be something that you are asked to do on a day-to-day basis, but by definition anyone who is performing to such an outstanding level that it could be called legendary is doing something that involves an element of risk and danger. Even if the danger is more a threat to your career than to your life. As we all know, trying to change something necessarily means creating enemies.

The enemies that we meet in organisational life are often psychological as well as physical. First, we have to slay the Culture Monster. People often blame the culture or the system for their inability to deliver what the customer wants. This monster exists very much in people's minds, and can be slain only by realising that people *are* the culture and have a greater capacity to change it than they realise.

As a hero or heroine you will also need to lift the Curse of Blindness. This is the inability to see and feel the world the way your customers do. One of life's problems is the difficulty of fully understanding the perceptions of another. This is one to think about when you get home this evening.

Finally, to create a legend we need to remove the Spell of Helplessness. This is the evil magic that binds many service representatives with the illusion that they have no power to act individually to help you as a customer. The significance of the individual in commerce has been haunted by the past ghost of scientific management, which made him or her feel like a tiny cog in the giant organisational machine. As the power of individual customers is now on the rise, they expect to be met with similarly empowered people serving them. If there's helplessness within the organisation this is what the customer will experience.

Writers often talk about the *magic* of Disney. They're not simply talking about witches and wizards in the cartoons, they're talking about the intangible but highly memorable experience of brilliant service that the organisation delivers in its theme parks. The reason it's magic is because few others have been able to replicate it.

In terms of building a service legend, magic means that you appear to anticipate the customer's needs. This is achieved by superb imagination and empathy which can appear to the customer like mind-reading, whereas in reality you have anticipated his or her likely reactions at each stage of your performance.

Many magicians today even explain how a trick is done and are then still able to perform it to their audience and fool them again. Similarly, many books have been written about the 'magic secrets' of great service companies such as Nordstrom, Disney, and others, yet people seem to be unable to repeat the spell. This is because the magic comes from deep in the hearts of those who founded and run these organisations. All real magic comes from within.

In legends the hero will often consult a famous magician, a Merlin whose advanced wisdom helps him in his everyday endeavours. But these days the magician may be young. When Archie Norman of supermarket chain Asda set about the heroic task of reviving the company's failing fortunes he consulted the young entrepreneur Julian Richer, who brought to bear the magic that he had woven in his phenomenally successful hi-fi outlets, Richer Sounds. Fashioning a team of advisers from outside your industry who can inspire your people to create magic – here meaning something not expected or understood in your own sector – is a smart move.

What is the *Holy Grail* you are seeking when you radically improve the service to your customers? For many the current definition is probably customer loyalty. However, I'm not convinced that loyalty is a topic in its own right, but rather the outcome of the phenomenal care that you put into your relationship with these customers.

Some believe that the grail is a historical artefact – a vessel, salver, or cup. The psychological view is that it is an alchemical process that transmutes not base metal to gold, but raises human life from the mundane to the higher plane of enlightenment. Similarly, the holy grail of service is to create a climate where employees are transformed from mere time-servers to heroic status, and customers from statistics to delighted advocates of what you do.

It can't be the result of a one-off initiative. There has to be commitment to a higher cause such as creating a better, happier and more fulfilled world. Meeting your budgets, reducing customer waiting time and complaints are the daily reminders of how well you are doing, but only a bone-deep conviction that you are part of something truly great will inspire your followers to heroic acts.

Perhaps the grail is never found. It's always just beyond the next forest or castle, but unless we reach for it the slough of despond – business as usual – awaits us.

Modern legends

The Phantom Menace – Star Wars Episode 1 is one of the great blockbusters of all time. But the continued success of the Star Wars films – or industry – should hardly surprise us. The director, George Lucas, acknowledges that a great deal of his inspiration came from that master synthesiser of world myths and legends Joseph Campbell, who writes: 'Throughout the inhabited world in all times and under every circumstance, the myths of man have flourished; they have been the living inspiration of whatever else may have appeared out of the activities of the human body and mind.'[3]

Myth is used here in its proper sense, not as untruth, but as a story-form method of conveying insight, wisdom and the performance of heroic deeds. All of us are living a myth or legend in our own lives, often unconsciously. We might, for example, be playing out the present-day myth of Superman or Superwoman, feeling we can cope heroically with all that life can throw at us. Unnoticed, this is a force that drives us in all our endeavours and it often takes a discontinuity in our lives such as an accident, failure or bereavement for us to see the footprint of our own personal myth clearly.

Industry is a process of legend building, particularly for those organisations that understand that their real coat of arms is formed by the values

[3] *The Hero With a Thousand Faces*, Paladin, Grafton Books, 1988. Campbell (1904–88) was an internationally known scholar, author and lecturer on the relationship between myth and our own psychological development.

embedded in their brand, values as intangible and at times as tenuously related to our day-to-day experience of 'reality' as the Greek myths of old. 3M is a legend for innovation, Nordstrom for service, Microsoft for prolific growth, Virgin for youthfulness and energy.

Great business leaders are also the heroes or heroines of their own legends. Sir Richard Branson might be characterised as a cheeky pirate, boldly assaulting the cumbersome fleets of his more traditional competitors; Bill Gates, in his early days, as the Little Tailor of Grimm Brothers fame who used his unshakeable self-belief and nimbleness of mind to slay the mighty giant, IBM.

Of course, in business no happy ending is guaranteed, but though organisations rise and fall at a rate that would have made the strategic planners of the '60s and '70s giddy, there is something more enduring that can perpetuate itself, the core myth or legend that entity is built on and which organises, often unseen, outer endeavours.

'Managing change', a favourite expression of management writers and consultants, is transient and superficial – even if it can ever be achieved successfully – compared with the new work of the leader, *managing the changeless*.

By 'the changeless' I mean the underlying values and beliefs, captured in story form, that explain to the world what an organisation really stands for. I use the term changeless because the great legends and stories that have captured life's profoundest truths and greatest inspiration – those in the Bible and the Koran, the Vedas of ancient India, Greek mythology, the Arthurian legends to name just a few – have survived unchanged and flourished in a way that the science of their times has not. Outer forms change, but the songs that convey the most insight remain the same.

Moving from the magical to the commercial, pharmaceuticals company Johnson & Johnson's credo has long been famous for embodying the company's relentless focus on the welfare of its consumers. I was impressed recently, when working with one of its UK subsidiaries, Janssen-Cilag, to find management re-inducting every employee into the timeless values behind the now admittedly dated words of the original.

Stories such as the company's immediate withdrawal of the drug Tylenol from *all retail shelves* even when a relatively small batch was discovered faulty has become one of the great ethical legends of modern business. Times and technology change, circumstances shift, leaders come and go, but legends are built by acting heroically from an unchanging code of conduct in much the same way that the fabled Knights of the Round Table performed their duties.

So what makes for a modern service legend? I'll leave the detailed definition of the term until the following sections, but the logic is:

- Story-telling is as old as mankind, and survives today as the most immediate and memorable means of relaying information.
- Customers tell stories – to their service provider and to other customers and potential customers – based on their personal experience or stories that have been passed on to them.
- The sum total of these stories can be a positive legend, a horror story, or a totally uninteresting and forgettable tale.
- If the legend is positive, customers do not need objective figures on customer satisfaction, reliability, consistency – they want to buy into the legend, and to stay with the reliable and changeless values that it represents.
- Everything you do with, and for, your customers creates the subject matter for the legend.

Creating a legend is not an overnight task. Every pore of the organisation needs to breathe the belief that service in its widest sense is its *raison d'être*.

Glad to be grey?

I come from a culture where the three highest superlatives are:

- Pretty good,
- Rather nice, or
- Not bad.

It's hard to be positive in this kind of culture, isn't it? I can find myself inadvertently insulting American friends with my response after being taken out for dinner by them. When they ask how it was, I reply enthusiastically: 'Not bad!'

'What do you mean, "Not bad"?' they respond.

I change into another gear . . . 'Uh, miraculous! Awesome. Amazing!'

Expressions such as delighting or wowing the customer are therefore quite high on my cultural cringe scale. But despite the mask of indifference, even the British have a secret desire to be lit up by a ray of sunshine that breaks through the grey clouds of most business encounters.

The difficulty of impressing us as customers is brought home by the story of an elderly lady who had never seen the sea. A well-meaning friend took her on a lengthy drive to witness this marvel. She stood on the shore for some time, gazing intently at the incoming tide, then turned to her host with the words: '*Is that all it does?*'

For all the endeavour that most organisations claim to put into creating great service for their customers, all too often 'is that all you do?' is the most likely response. It's increasingly hard to 'wow' us. What company does not have a Putting the Customer First or Service Excellence programme? And yet, as Barry Gibbons of fast food chain Burger King remarked: 'Even when we did it right, it was still pretty ordinary.'[4]

People everywhere, even the British (who may keep their delight to themselves), are seeking an experience that makes them feel cared for, supported and acknowledged. A whole industry has been built around the notion of customer satisfaction. However, it's rapidly becoming yesterday's industry as we ungraciously take so many miracles for granted and increasingly demand the impossible. Ready for the challenge?

Why satisfaction isn't enough

Standards change at an alarming rate. What was great service yesterday is a yawn today. Consider the miracle of flight. Fifty years ago most of us regarded it as an amazing experience that you could sit down, close your eyes and be transported in a hunk of flying tin in no time at all to a land where winter had turned to summer.

Today we are unimpressed with this marvel and are more likely to compare different airlines on the quality of personal service, food, or in-flight entertainment that we receive. Most of us travellers don't even know what model of aircraft we are flying in. But we *do* know whether the steward smiled and if we can hear the movie on our headphones. The new challenges that organisations are facing to make themselves stand out from the crowd are more to do with the intangible aspect of the experience than the hard, tangible element.

The New Customer Challenges box overleaf illustrates just how demanding customers like you and me are becoming. Almost every business group I have spoken to agrees that these are the challenges they are now

---

[4] Recognised as a 'Turnaround Champ' by *Fortune* magazine after his five-year stint as chairman/CEO of Burger King, he retired from big-company life in 1994 .

facing. If you are looking for a new agenda for change it could be useful to table one of these challenges as the topic for each of your creative sessions.

The New Customer Challenges

1. Choices are greater.
2. Expectations are higher.
3. People want more for less.
4. They want it yesterday.
5. The competition is getting cleverer.

Customers and consumers are for the most part resistant to being labelled 'satisfied' or 'loyal'. We live in an era where most of us are in a state of permanent dissatisfaction. Anyway, even 'satisfaction' does not create the intended effect of wedding me to one particular supplier, as is shown by recent research by business machinery manufacturer Xerox. It revealed: 'One discovery shattered conventional wisdom – its totally satisfied customers were six times more likely to re-purchase Xerox products over the next 18 months than its satisfied customers ... The only truly loyal customers are totally satisfied customers.'[5]

It's obvious from this that the notion of mere customer satisfaction is dead – we don't go back to an airline, restaurant or component supplier by choice merely because we are satisfied. It's just not the kind of language that individual customers use, although industry has created the fiction that if their own internally driven questionnaires show 92 per cent customer satisfaction, then what's wrong with me if I don't rate them as highly?

---

[5] Jones and Sasser, *Harvard Business Review*, November–December 1995.

It's clear that there's a need for something more than is currently on offer from most service providers. However, what is this 'total satisfaction' that is hinted at in the Xerox research? It's one of a host of new and rather vague 'beyonds' that don't do much more than express our dissatisfaction with the idea of satisfaction.

Beyond satisfaction

The most popular words used to describe service beyond merely 'satisfying' are:

- Exceeding customer expectations;
- Total satisfaction;
- Creating customer delight, and
- Wowing the customer.

Legendary service is a concept that captures the essence of these beyonds. All these expressions are driven by the notion that, like beauty, happiness for customers is in their eyes only and will be created by some experience that both pleases the mind and touches the heart. And if it does, it will inspire them to share their positivity with others. A legend is spread by word of mouth, or through the expanding bandwidths of our connected economy. It's the only reliable yardstick to judge that you have done a wonderful job for your customers.

Customers believe other customers far more than the huffing and puffing of your marketing and PR machine. If someone gives you a positive personal reference about a product or service, don't you trust that more than any other story? A striking example of the power of customers spreading a legend is the Saturn experience in the USA. Saturn to me doesn't stand out as a *product*, as an automobile – its stunning sales figures are almost entirely down to the power of the *service* legend. The company claims that more than 95 per cent of its owners try to convince friends, family and colleagues also to buy a Saturn because of the great – and unexpectedly great, given the track record of the US automobile industry – service experience.

Making a Legend Work for you –

Turn your customers
into your marketing department!

Within a Saturn owner's experience are undoubtedly a lot of wows and considerable delight. Expectations have certainly been exceeded. Whether or not this results in total customer satisfaction, to use the phrase described earlier, can perhaps best be judged by the missionary zeal of Saturn owners. The important point is that a legend has been created. You have turned your customers into your marketing department. The true value of delighting your customers is that they help to build your legend.

If it sounds unreal that people will buy a legend, remember that we live in a world that seems to value the intangible over the tangible. Who makes *real* money these days? Software, telecommunications and the information industry in general. The numbers are incredible.

> The market capitalisation of leading internet company Yahoo! has appreciated by 3,800 per cent since 1996 and is now worth 480 times expected earnings for 1999. Yahoo! is worth more than Texaco or Merrill Lynch. America Online, the largest Internet company, has risen by 34,000 per cent since 1992 and is worth 273 times expected earnings for the year to June. That makes it bigger than Ford or Disney. Both companies would be in the Japanese top 10 and AOL would be in Europe's top 10 ahead of Nestlé, Shell, or UPS.[6]

Yahoo! bigger than General Motors? It barely makes a profit and all it's doing is helping us to help ourselves because the Internet is so damn big. Can this really be a serious business? Even its advertisements – featuring purple nuns saying 'We meditate all day, and yahoo like crazy all night!' – suggest that we've moved beyond the Information Age into a creative age that is fast rewriting all of the old rule book. What rule book? These upstarts don't even know there is one.

Many of the new Internet e-wonders have confounded the analysts working with outdated models such as price (P)/earnings (E) ratios. How

---

[6] Roger Taylor and John Labate, 'Age of the Day Trader', *Financial Times*, 9 February 1999.

can you determine the P when there's a negative 'E'? And yet the 'P' is sky-high! Understand this? Neither do I, but it's become commonplace for organisations to acknowledge that all they have to sell are intangibles – reputation, brand values, innovation, business solutions, speed, smartness, convenience, or time-saving devices – and of course, the most powerful of all intangibles, customer service.

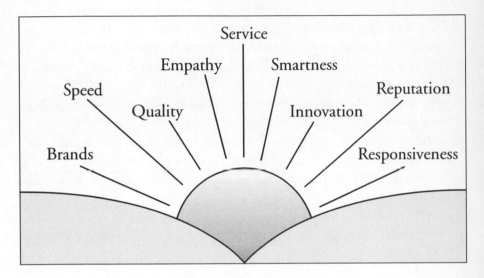

The Rise of Intangibles

Intangibles are where organisations put increasingly large proportions of their focus and energy.

People will buy the intangible that is your legend, as Saturn owners have done, if you have one to sell. Good products, or merely satisfying service, simply won't hack it today. Legends are told around the hearth, but today the hearth is global. In other words, there's no place to hide because positive or negative stories about your organisation flash around the planet in seconds:

'If you have an unhappy customer on the Internet, he doesn't tell his six friends, he tells his 6,000 friends.'

Jeff Bezos, founder and CEO, amazon.com[7]

---

[7] When Bezos learned that the Internet was growing at 2,300 per cent annually, he decided an on-line business was a future worth aiming for. He and his team spent a year developing database programs and creating the amazon.com website, opening its virtual doors in 1995. Based in Seattle his competitive strategy is: 'Obsess about customers, not competitors.'

Individual stories, positive or negative, are building your legend as we speak. If they are negative you may decry them as rumour or 'myth' meaning, in the current inaccurate usage of myth, unreal. However, it's real enough to drive your customers' buying decisions and influence them to choose or reject you.

Our world is increasingly transparent. Everyone can know everything, if not in three clicks, then soon after. All organisations are in the business of writing their own legend, whether consciously or not. And if your customers are so 'wowed' by their experiences with you, you will become a beneficiary rather than a victim of the oldest method of information sharing known to mankind – story-telling.

The benefits of harnessing this human need to tell stories to others about their experience are:

- Your customers will do your marketing for you;
- They will pay a premium – happily – for the promise of service your brand stands for;
- They will be as loyal as human beings can be, and
- You will gain a great deal more enrichment and fun from what you do.

Is this guaranteed? No, you have to write your own happy ending. Here's what to aim for in creating a positive service legend.

What is legendary service?

To become truly 'legendary' you must be:

- Famous for providing *exceptional experiences* that your customers will want to retell to other customers, existing or potential;
- Redefining the customer's expectation of your industry or sector as, for example, McDonald's originally did with food retailing and Virgin Atlantic has started to do with airlines;
- Aware that relationship is all. You may not exist *for* your customers, but you cannot thrive without them. And the only real asset your organisation has – whether you're selling financial services, designer clothes, or PCs – is the quality of this relationship with your customers;
- Creating a culture where your people find a real sense of meaning

through doing a superb job for your customers, and

- A recognised leader in service to the community and the environment – service with a big 'S'.

If this seems like a tall order, remember the words of the poet Robert Browning:[8]

> 'Ah that a man's reach should exceed his grasp,
> Or what's a heaven for?'

What follows is a more detailed description of the characteristics of a Legendary Service provider and allows you to compare yourself with this service heaven.

Action point: If you're like me you may tend to skip these kinds of activities and move on to skimming the text. I suggest that you do stop to take the time to evaluate how your organisation matches up, however subjectively, because only then will you really 'get' the size of the gap between where you are now and where you would like to be. This is relevant whether you are a small business, a global corporation, or even a professional working alone.

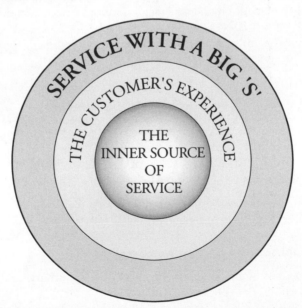

---

[8] English poet and playwright (1812–89) whose work is distinguished by its spiritual insight and psychological portraits.

Characteristics of a legendary service provider

The following checklist describes an organisation that consistently provides its customers with more than satisfaction: Legendary Service.

The Inner Source of Service

1. People act spontaneously from the belief that delighting customers is their real job.
    0% — 10 — 20— 30 — 40 — 50 — 60 — 70 — 80 — 90 — 100%
    In Your Dreams!   On a Good Day   Got It!

2. Customers feel they are true partners in a way that transcends Service Level Agreements, and operates on the level of the heart.
    0% — 10 — 20— 30 — 40 — 50 — 60 — 70 — 80 — 90 — 100%
    In Your Dreams!   On a Good Day   Got It!

3. We have a culture where people find real meaning in giving service to others.
    0% — 10 — 20— 30 — 40 — 50 — 60 — 70 — 80 — 90 — 100%
    In Your Dreams!   On a Good Day   Got It!

4. We have generated an unstoppable belief in our people that they can 'invent their own future' rather than be restrained by outside forces – the market, competition, industry regulations or management dictates.
    0% — 10 — 20— 30 — 40 — 50 — 60 — 70 — 80 — 90 — 100%
    In Your Dreams!   On a Good Day   Got It!

The Customer's Experience

5. We stay close to the customer at every stage of their experience – acquire it/maintain it/replace it.
    0% — 10 — 20— 30 — 40 — 50 — 60 — 70 — 80 — 90 —100%
    In Your Dreams!   On a Good Day   Got It!

6. We create memorable 'wow!' encounters that inspire them to spread the legend to other potential customers.
    0% — 10 — 20— 30 — 40 — 50 — 60 — 70 — 80 — 90 — 100%
    In Your Dreams!   On a Good Day   Got It!

7. We positively touch customers with the positivity and pride of all those who work in our organisation.
    0% — 10 — 20— 30 — 40 — 50 — 60 — 70 — 80 — 90 — 100%
    In Your Dreams!   On a Good Day   Got It!

8. We demonstrate superior levels of empathy for a customer's situation and needs.

0% — 10 — 20— 30 — 40 — 50 — 60 — 70 — 80 — 90 — 100%
In Your Dreams!   On a Good Day   Got It!

9.   We have created systems that are intuitively loved by customers. Far more than just 'customer friendly'.
      0% — 10 — 20— 30 — 40 — 50 — 60 — 70 — 80 — 90 — 100%
      In Your Dreams!   On a Good Day   Got It!

Service with a Big 'S'

10.   We are respected as a trend setter in serving the needs of the community.
      0% — 10 — 20— 30 — 40 — 50 — 60 — 70 — 80 — 90 — 100%
      In Your Dreams!   On a Good Day   Got It!

11.   We are famous for taking the lead in serving the environment.
      0% — 10 — 20— 30 — 40 — 50 — 60 — 70 — 80 — 90 —100%
      In Your Dreams!   On a Good Day   Got It!

12.   We are widely known for consistently making ethical business decisions.
      0% — 10 — 20— 30 — 40 — 50 — 60 — 70 — 80 — 90 — 100%
      In Your Dreams!   On a Good Day   Got It!

HEALTH WARNING!
I don't know an organisation in the world that is truly legendary, but some exhibit one or more of these characteristics. This list is constantly being updated and revised as I believe that the 'achievement horizon' is always beyond today's performance, and measuring yourself by today's winners is a sure recipe for being tomorrow's loser. I take full responsibility for having frightened you a little.

Scoring Code

- **0–25%** Go to jail. Do not pass GO or collect any money whatsoever, as your business probably can't afford it, but don't feel guilty about calling for immediate help.
- **25–50%** Work to be done. Perhaps pick the three items that you most need to work on and put them on the agenda for your next Away-Day/Team Meeting. Therapy not needed, but you're unlikely to be showing a clean set of heels to the competition. . . especially when they're in front.
- **50–75%** Pretty smart! We could all learn a thing or two from you. However, remember that today's successes can be the enemy of tomorrow's triumphs and focus on one aspect you score well on, and attempt to make it world-class.
- **75–100%** You probably don't think you need anybody's help. However, do share your successes with Service Legends at: nigelbarlow@servicelegends.com so that we can all learn from you.

The inner source of service (points 1 to 4)

I don't believe organisations that say they exist only for their customers. It's rather that they cannot exist without a good relationship with them. Realising this, US travel agent Hal Rosenbluth posted the sign 'The Customer Comes Second' around his offices. This means that you cannot become the number one choice with your customers without treating your own people even more as number one!

Of course, you have to do both, but the message is clear – if in doubt start with your own people. The inner is the basis of the outer and any attempt to 'wow' your customers without first having created a culture where your own people spontaneously live the value of service will be limited in its impact.

The word 'spontaneous' in the first point is vital. Customers quickly become resistant to scripts they feel have been imposed on the individual serving them. When you hear 'How may I help you?' intoned listlessly, it's as painful as listening to amateur actors who haven't learned their lines properly. Make no mistake, we can judge instinctively whether someone else really cares, or has merely been told to.

This is demonstrably the case with Virgin Atlantic staff – more than 90 per cent of them passionately advocate using their company's service to their family, friends and acquaintances, according to the airline's internal surveys. These people are proud to work for the organisation. It's not much of a stretch of the imagination to apply the legendary-sounding term 'crusading' to their activities on behalf of the company.

In essence, all the questions on the Inner Source of Service are to do with the conviction that what people do makes a real difference to themselves, their customers and the organisation's success.

There is nothing more infectious than the enthusiasm and passion transmitted to customers by people who believe in what they do. You can't bottle it, you probably can't train for it and you're unlikely to be able to copy it from elsewhere. A significant part of the work of leaders in the new millennium will be the creation of a culture of self-belief in their people. (More on this in Chapter 7: The Power of Attention.) Empowerment, accountability, a sense of ownership and similar buzzwords are really sub-categories of the belief that the individual self can make a difference.

> 'Vision becomes a living force only when most believe they
> can shape their future.'
> *Peter Senge*, The Fifth Discipline[9]

As customers, can't we feel and touch the energy generated by people who find meaning in what they do, and who believe in themselves and the product or service they almost become? And don't think this is an unreal fantasy. This inner self-belief generates the emotional response that is also money-making: customer loyalty.

Possibly the best recruitment line of all time was the one Steve Jobs used to lure John Sculley from his comfortable job in Pepsi to the much riskier one in Apple Computers: 'Do you want to spend the rest of your life selling sugared water, or would you like to change the way people think?'

This is an extreme instance of engendering belief in a greater cause, but it does pose the fundamental question 'What are we here for?' that needs to be answered if you are to engender 'unstoppable belief' in your people that they can create something great and lasting. In short, a legend.

The customer's experience (points 5 to 9)

We are all hungry for the new. This is certainly true in our role as customers, although if we're inside an organisation going through its umpteenth reorganisation we may have a more wary opinion of the effects of all this newness.

The key word in this section is 'experience'. Some experts argue that we are now in an 'experience economy' and that the service economy is history.[10] It describes how customers in our sensation-seeking world demand memorable experiences that make them say, 'Wow, that was great!' Forget reliability, quality, value for money and all the grey stuff. We're looking for colour, excitement and new stories to tell. Stop press! The current frenzy for titles beginning with 'E' continues unabated – Michael J. Wolf's latest book,

[9] Doubleday Books, 1990, ISBN: 0385260946. Senge is famous for his work on how organisations develop learning capabilities.

[10] B. Joseph Pine, James H. Gilmore, B. Joseph Pine II, *The Experience Economy*, Harvard Business School Press, 1999, ISBN: 0875848192.

The Entertainment Economy, argues that the driving force of the new world economy is entertainment. He describes how Las Vegas grows by 8.5 per cent a year and in Britain more people are employed in the entertainment industry than ever were in coal mining at its peak.

A striking example of how far customers' expectations have been raised is the experience of Rebecca Jenkins, a charismatic figure in the generally dour world of road haulage in the UK. Rebecca is managing director of the Lane Group, which numbers among its customers top retailers such as Next, C & A and The Body Shop. In the early 1990s the Lane Group had achieved a near-miraculous on-time delivery performance for The Body Shop of 99.93 per cent. Miraculous when you consider the increasingly chaotic state of Britain's roads.

One March morning she was travelling to a meeting at The Body Shop's headquarters in Littlehampton, Sussex, quite understandably expecting praise for her company's great performance. During a lengthy meeting the client gave no plaudits for the Lane Group's tremendous on-time performance. Rebecca finally reminded them of the great service experience she was delivering and was told that this was no 'experience' at all because The Body Shop expected more. The feedback shocked Rebecca. It was summarised in one tart criticism.

'You're boring!' they told her. They then went on to describe the nature of the 'something more' they required – a more intimate partnership in which drivers would give feedback to The Body Shop on how their customer could perform better and would engage in joint discussions on how to make their business together more exciting, interesting and effective. It now manages this relationship by a system of open-book accounting whereby the client knows exactly how much profit Lane Group makes on the contract. The boundaries between customer and supplier have become extremely porous.

> Are you . . .
> Efficient, but ***Boring***?

Rebecca summarises the course of action she took to become more intimate with The Body Shop as follows:

- We felt we had been given the right to challenge The Body Shop. There were many areas where they were causing us a problem but we had put up with it. Now we could challenge them strongly and set timescales for it to be put right.

- Both organisations had to be much more open. We needed The Body Shop to take us into their confidence in terms of strategic planning. How else could we provide the best logistic solution if we did not know their thoughts on UK stores activity, new products, and new store locations?
- We attended their daily staff meetings and joined in as if we were their employees.
- We got involved in their community projects and got them to support ours. We won best community project of the year, an in-house award usually for their own employees.
- We shared in the cost savings made on the contract and also gained a bonus for achieving various service and innovation targets.
- We worked jointly with them and put the first commercial vehicle operating on natural gas on to UK roads.

The story also illustrates the Lane Group's experience of how intimate you may need to become with your customers – how high the bar has been raised if you are to deliver what the customer regards as fabulous service. While not all organisations may be as demanding as The Body Shop, those likely to survive soon will be. And what they will be demanding is an intimate relationship as well as efficiency.

This is why there is a great deal of emotional language in the questions on Customers' Experience – words such as 'loyalty', 'wow', 'pride', 'empathy', 'intuitively loved'. The reasons for this are explained more fully in Chapter 6: Think *Both/And*, which encourages you to discover your organisation's service heart (or lack of it!). This emphasis is because feelings drive buying decisions more than logic, even in a business-to-business environment. Ultimately a human exchange is involved, meaning that emotions consciously or unconsciously colour our choice of one supplier over another. We tend to rationalise after making our choice to give comfort to our logical self, but instincts are always swifter, more immediate than logic. And certainly only an emotional bond will create the lasting customer loyalty that is the holy grail of focusing on the customer.

Naturally this doesn't mean that people will stay for very long with an organisation that supplies outmoded, unreliable, or badly priced services, whatever their positive feelings for the provider. Providing good products, reliable delivery and friendly service is essential, but only the entry point to doing business in a world where customers are more informed, have more choices and are more blasé about the wonders of technology.

The power of great service to win hearts and minds is rationally encapsulated in the research of J. D. Power & Associates, long-standing experts on customer attitudes in the automobile industry. Founded in 1968, the Los Angeles-based company has achieved international recognition for its marketing information in the areas of consumer opinion and customer satisfaction.

The bar chart describing the percentage of customers who return to the same dealer for their car illustrates that the service is even more significant than the product in influencing this decision. ('Good' dealer here means all the intangible elements of service – integrity, the attitude of the reception-ist, the responsiveness of the dealer to any problems with the car's reliability, etc.) A cynic might interpret this to mean you can produce lousy products and still keep customers if your service is great, but the key to long-term loyalty is to achieve the tricky goal of doing both. And if service outweighs product when we are buying something as tangible as a car, how

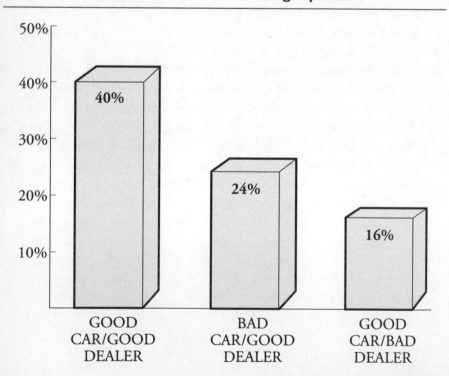

Percentage of buyers getting the same make of car as the one being replaced

Source: J. D. Power & Associates
1993 New Car Customer Satisfaction Index Study

much *more* critical is it in our mind if the product is intangible, such as an insurance policy, a ticket to a theme park, or a holiday package? So, if you're in any doubt about where to focus first, start with service!

Finally, all the questions in this section are to do with something beyond the norm. Is your service 'on a par with industry standards', 'meeting customer expectations', or 'benchmarked as among the best'? Forget it. Because your customers will.

Service with a big 'S' (points 10 to 12)

The last three questions relate to Service with a big 'S'. While Patagonia, the maker of outdoor activity equipment based in Ventura, California, is obsessed with the environmental impact of every stage of its manufacturing, and The Body Shop's environmental charter place them among the champions of service to the environment and the community, the same cannot be said of recent performances from multinationals such as Shell, Nike and Monsanto.

Shell's public relations debacle over the dismantling of the Brent Spar drilling platform was a 'leaking' of the inner culture of the company to the general public. Its perceived arrogance and lack of preparedness in handling public opinion became transparent. Ethics is also an important ingredient of service with a big 'S' – again Shell fell down on this due to its alleged involvement with the military dictatorship in Nigeria.

Integrity and the Bottom Line

Many organisations believe there is no correlation between integrity and bottom-line performance. They are wrong. Integrity and performance are not at the opposite ends of a continuum. When people work for an organisation that they believe is fair, where everyone is willing to give of themselves to get the job done, where traditions of loyalty and caring are hallmarks, people work to a higher level. The values around them become a part of them, and they think of the customer as someone whom they owe the finest possible product and service.

Industry Week

Nike's 69 per cent slump in earnings in the last quarter of 1997 is thought to be attributable partly to its alleged involvement in mistreatment of its Asian workers. Monsanto's aggressive tactics in trying to push what many scientists believe are under-researched GM products on to a wary Europe looks to be proving unsuccessful. There may well be a five-year moratorium on the growing of genetically modified crops in Europe, and the company's share price has suffered as a result.

The power of the Internet means that the positive legend you are trying to spread can turn sour in a nanosecond. Monsanto attempted a high-profile PR campaign in the UK professing the values of Food, Health and Hope. Its full-page spreads even listed the website of environmental pressure group Friends of the Earth to give potential consumers of its products the idea that they were approaching the GM issue in the spirit of balanced, rational debate.

However, lobbying groups of consumers now have access to the same technology as corporate behemoths, and organisations such as the Natural Law Party, the Soil Association, Friends of the Earth and Greenpeace combined loosely but effectively to spread the message of how inadequate the safeguards are with the new biotechnology. Many believe that after Monsanto's campaign the general public was *less* convinced of the safety of its new products.

What's this got to do with service? It demonstrates the need to think more deeply about what service is. It's no longer part of a closed system as your activities are increasingly visible to the world at large, and intangibles such as ethics are critical factors by which your customers will judge you. People 'buy' your values, or at least their perception of your values. Perceptions are changing so fast that there are those who believe senior figures from the biotechnology or genetic engineering sector will be on trial within the next five years.

Look at the increase in volume of ethical funds. A paltry few million dollars 10 years ago, they have now grown to billions under management. A recent survey indicated that seven per cent of customers will switch from a supplier if they don't like its ethics. I would suggest that this data is already behind the times. In an age where information technology means everyone can know everything and your business is increasingly transparent to the public, there's real commercial as well as moral danger in not placing high value on business ethics.

Ethics in a global economy

As companies become more global with factories, sales and marketing, and back-office operations in far-flung places, convincing socially conscious customers that they are not exploiting the disadvantaged, disturbing the environment or destroying a country's cultural heritage will become critical to the success of their product.

John Naisbitt, Global Paradox, *1995*[11]

Huge shifts in the world's values can sometimes be captured by small stories or examples. Yahoo! outstripping GM in value is one such instance, heralding perhaps the end of the industrial era and the real beginning of an information or creative age. In a similar vein, the arrival of environmental awareness as a key issue for consumers is captured in a story told by ecology writer John Elkington. In his excellent book, *Cannibals with Forks,*[12] he describes how he walked into a hotel past a crowd of demonstrating workers in the chlorine industry. He was part of a group presenting information on the negative environmental impact of this industry. He observed that the world had spun around: 10 years previously *he* would have been demonstrating outside with a placard. Now he and his colleagues were on the *inside* conferring with industry leaders. The world has turned inside out.

If you're worried that all this seems remote from the day-to-day world of serving sandwiches, systems solutions, or providing a hotel room, a powerful phrase that I learned in my travels to the Far East is 'It's later than you think.' If you're just beginning to think about the client's perception of your ethics, service to the community and the environment, then you're going to have to do some rapid catching-up. This new awareness of the canny and informed consumer expands daily with frightening immediacy. Frightening, that is, if you're not prepared. In early 1999 only committed Greens and some scientists knew about the genetically modified foods issue – six months later even the smallest corner store in the UK knew how important the topic was to its customers.

[11] Harper, 1995, ISBN: 0380724898.

[12] New Society Publishing, 1998, ISBN: 0865713928.

It's later than you think! ! !

Entrepreneur Julian Metcalfe's chain of innovative sandwich emporiums, Pret a Manger, displays a large sign in its outlets:

Pret creates hand-made, natural food, avoiding the obscure chemicals, additives and preservatives common to so much of the 'prepared' and 'fast' food on the market today.

Also to hand for all customers, from an unobtrusive wall rack, is its 'Passionate About Food' pamphlet – 'What we sell. Why we sell it'. It gives a brief background to the company, how its food and drinks are chosen and prepared, the company's contribution to shelters for the homeless, its use of recyclable paper rather than plastic or Styrofoam. Isn't it refreshing when organisations are upfront about what they believe in – provided, of course, they can deliver?

Service with a Big 'S' – Where Are You?

────────	───────	──────────	────────────
Ignorance	Denial	Compliance	Commitment	Legendary

The scale above helps you to evaluate how focused you are on Service with a big 'S'. It ranges from ignorance – unlikely, these days, because of the explosion in legislation – to legendary. You can apply this scale to ethics, the environment and community issues.

The most crucial distinction here is between commitment and a legend-creating attitude. Commitment implies that you put your resources into exceeding the requirements of the new legislation. Legendary means something more. It means that you are *known* for this commitment and openly make this part of your brand in the way that Patagonia and The Body Shop have been proud to do.

Or, as in the case of Nichols Foods, the UK-based food distributor based in Wigan, Lancashire, you create a culture where everyone has two jobs.

Nichols employees work for the company and are also expected to work for social projects in their community. They're encouraged to take the time to do this and receive benefits for this service. For example, if an employee receives a Duke of Edinburgh award he or she receives extra days' holiday. Chief executive Gary Unsworth believes the skills and benefits the employee receives by doing charitable work improves his or her own self-development, and has good knock-on effects for the company.

US supermarket giant Wal-Mart is another organisation intent on establishing its credentials as a service legend. When Wal-Mart Green Co-ordinator (do you have one?) Paul Estrada heard that a river in San Marcos, Texas, needed cleaning up, he and dozens of associates tackled the problem immediately. They used Wal-Mart's environmental approach to adopt a seven-acre section of the river. As a result, they are not only keeping the river safe and clean for future generations to enjoy, but are also protecting the homes of several endangered plants and animals.

This is a striking example of the Wal-Mart environmental and community pledge – service with a big 'S' – in action. The company's commitment reads:

'At Wal-Mart we believe it is our responsibility to be a part of the collective effort to protect and preserve our natural resources. That's why we have developed a four-part company-wide commitment to:

- Provide environmentally improved products to our customers;
- Look for better ways to build and operate Wal-Mart stores and offices;
- Support and encourage local community and environmental activities, and
- Support educational programs for children.'

However, despite the fact that founder Sam Walton was a retailing visionary, Wal-Mart may be a flawed role model for Service with a big 'S'. Its success in offering the lowest possible prices while profiting from vast sales volumes (almost 140 billion dollars, (£87.5 billion) a year in sales in 1999), may have been partially achieved in some cases at the expense of questionable working conditions for its Third World suppliers.

Bob Ortega's book *In Sam We Trust: The Untold Story of Sam Walton and*

How Wal-Mart Is Devouring America[13] highlights the exploitation of children in clothing factories in Central America. Wal-Mart are, of course, not alone in this: Charles Kernaghan, who exposed a factory in Honduras that exploited workers making clothes for Wal-Mart and other US retailers, also found workers making 15 cents (12p) an hour and children as young as 15 in one Nicaraguan plant.[14]

So what's the problem? Wal-Mart's low-cost formula obviously works for many consumers, and its assault on European retailing – starting with an effective bridgehead in the highly conservative German market – looks set to replicate its success in the US. But just as companies such as Monsanto totally underestimated the health and higher-perceived ethical standard of European consumers, Wal-Mart would do well to ensure its low-cost offerings are supported by higher ethical standards.

Thinking more widely about your whole offering as it is perceived by customers and potential customers is an essential prerequisite for business today. But remember that spreading a positive legend is a two-edged sword. Though technology allows for our brand and the values it stands for to be communicated instantaneously, we have to be prepared for how dissatisfied customers may take us on at our own game and spread a counter legend.

Every customer is a potential story-teller with access to more or less the same technology as a multinational. Authors of websites such as 'Wal-Mart Sucks' – run by Richard Hatch, an unemployed toy collector in Bangor, Maine – may be seen as angry loners with nothing better to do, but business would be wise to realise that we are entering an age where the individual has the power to influence many minds.

Using the checklist

I'm often asked by companies to help managers 'think outside the box'. The essential starting point, though, is for people to know what box they're in. No one gets up in the morning and thinks 'I'm going to do a lousy job for my customers today', but a blind spot exists because you are the box.

Therefore, the first activity is to use the checklist in this chapter to evaluate what your box is now. The questionnaire is valuable as a way of comparing perceptions. So why not give it to your customers and your people?

[13] Times Books, 1998, ISBN: 081 296 3776.

[14] CNN Interactive, CNN.com, 11 November 1997.

The all-important next step is to compare gaps between your own perceptions and those of your people, and the inner perception with the customer's view. It's important to do this open-mindedly, remembering that perception is reality. Set up meetings or discussion sessions where you explore *why* the gaps exist before you start thinking of actions to address it.

One tip is to focus on each of the characteristics separately – the task will seem too overwhelming if you try to tackle the whole picture at one attempt.

Language is important. You could try removing the term 'satisfaction' from your vocabulary. It probably appears in customer satisfaction ratings, mission statements and the day-to-day language people use to describe the customer's experience. Try substituting words like 'wow', 'delight' and 'the customer's experience'.

Also, remember that legends are built up out of many individual stories. Rather than trying to force-fit your customers' experience into your own convenient bar charts or pie diagrams, institute story-telling sessions where you bring in clients to describe in their own words the story of what it's like doing business with you. The trick is to listen without evaluation, perhaps the hardest feat a human being can accomplish.

Hold sessions where you encourage the people in your business who have most direct customer contact to tell stories also, and then consider what kind of a legend this is building in the marketplace.

Finally, it's important to elicit good stories from your own people as well as problem tales. Customers have a tendency to dwell on the negative, which can have the effect of making your people feel defensive. Given the right encouragement, they will almost certainly have positive stories to tell.

For some penetrating questions, activities, and ideas relating to this chapter turn to page 242.

Chapter Three

Change the Box

or How to Differentiate Yourself by Being Different

'Most organisations reward individuals and groups that choose to re-invent the wheel.'

Bjarne Stroustrup,
computer scientist at AT&T Laboratories

'Discovery consists of seeing what everybody has seen and thinking what nobody has thought.'

Albert von Szent-Gyorgy (1893–1986), biochemist
and molecular biologist awarded 1937 Nobel prize

Changing the Box helps you to:

- Change expectations of customers in your industry or sector
- Differentiate yourself by creating a new service experience
- Apply creativity to your customer relationships.

To lead a life freer from limitation is a strong desire for almost everybody. Otherwise we may be faced with the prospect of thinking 'Is that it?', to quote the title of Bob Geldof's autobiography. We can become blind to the greater possibilities available to us.

Imagine you exist in a world that only knows two dimensions. Then someone suggests that there's a third dimension. 'Where is it?' you say. 'Show me.'

He points out that it must exist because when he causes vibration at point A in the diagram below he can feel the effect at point B. This proves nothing to you because the 'box' you live in is firmly grounded in what you consider to be *the* reality. This madman is as much of a heretic as Galileo when he supported the Copernican view that our planetary system is heliocentric (centred around the sun) rather than geocentric, having the Earth as its centre. Galileo's heresy was not finally forgiven by the Vatican until 1993.

For all intents and purposes, you *are* the box you exist in. A three-dimensional view is pure heresy. But if you could suddenly see your world from this three-dimensional perspective you would realise that:

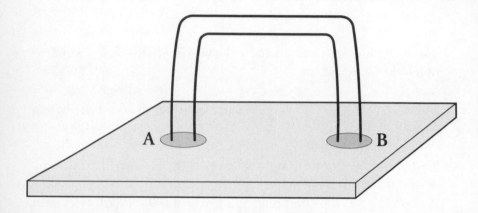

- You had made self-limiting assumptions about the nature of your world;
- You could make creative connections between parts of your world that previously seemed unconnected – in this example, points A and B;
- Many more possibilities and choices would be open to you, and
- You would have certain distinct advantages over those still restricted to the two-dimensional plane.

This is a metaphor for seeing the world differently. In similar vein, there's much talk about creating new paradigms in business. The word is rarely used in the way that Thomas Kuhn intended when he wrote his book *The Structure of Scientific Revolutions*.[1] For him, changes in paradigms were as fundamental as the shift from a classical view of the world – millions of billiard balls interacting predictably in time and space – to a quantum-mechanical perspective – the physical universe seen as the result of fluctuations of an underlying field. These days any slight shift in management thinking is dubbed a new paradigm.

Why is this important to understand? Because most attempts at business

---

[1] The University of Chicago Press, Chicago, 1962, ISBN: 0226458083.

change are merely a tinkering with the existing system. To re-use our first metaphor, they are still minor differences in a flat plane. Thinking 'outside the box' implies that the box – a two-dimensional box in our metaphor – is the basic reality and all we can do is make token excursions outside it.

This may be why so many organisations seem to *differentiate in exactly the same way*. If you could blind-taste different businesses in the same way that you can compare the products of, say, Pepsi with Coca-Cola, could you distinguish between one bank and another, between oil companies, hotel chains, or car manufacturers? Except at the very extremes of the scale, dire or wonderful, it would be an interesting challenge to tell them apart. Yet many are beckoning to their customers: 'Come to us. We're not like the others.'

Unfair? Probably, but then customers usually are. Uncannily they often have the mindset of the person who has seen three dimensions because they are not so locked into the intricacies of your industry as you are. They don't know what's impossible. They expect more. Unfair? Yes, and that's why thinking outside the box won't be enough to address their needs. If you want to be a legend you have to *change* it.

We know that mere customer satisfaction is no longer enough to guarantee that customers will return to us. However, while it's easy to say that we need to move beyond expected standards of service, it's not that simple in practice. The greatest limit on possible achievement is an invisible, self-limiting 'box' we draw around ourselves.

To demonstrate this more specifically, here's an old puzzle with a new twist.

● ● ●

● ● ●

● ● ●   S1

The task is to join all nine dots in S1 with four straight lines without the pen leaving the paper. People trying this puzzle usually scrabble around with various possible solutions, but then realise that they've been setting themselves a boundary or limit, for example, they've *assumed* that you can't go outside the box. Those who realise this find there are many solutions, the most common of which is the four-line diagram in picture S2.

This is where most people finish their search. They've either worked it out creatively for themselves, or seen the answer, which is featured in books on the subject of creative thinking. Business people call this 'thinking outside the box'.

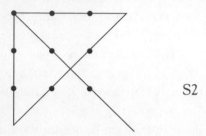

S2

However, the world has moved on. A four-line solution is only slightly better than none at all because there are more radical ones available if you challenge the prevailing assumptions and change the box itself.

S3 shows an answer first developed by a nine-year-old girl. She said that if you have the correct writing apparatus – a word she could not even spell – you can do it with ONE line.

S3

Many adults express shock, or even slight anger at this solution. Surely she had cheated? But it's worth remembering that one person's innovation is another's cheating. All she had to do was redefine the opportunity. Most people attempting the puzzle set themselves the self-limiting barrier that a line is thin and the dots are far apart.

These three stages of thinking are a metaphor to describe how we think about change and, in this instance, altering our approach to customer service. If table S1 – business as usual – summarises your approach to business, you're barely in the game. Many organisations see S2 as their aim,

S1 – Business as usual

- OK service – no worse than the rest;
- Greater focus on product quality than the service experience;
- One priority among many, and
- Adequate to stay in business – at least for now.

S2 – Good service

- Service spoken about as a high business priority;
- Satisfying and occasionally delighting the customer;
- Eager to copy what the competition is doing, and
- Possibly winning well-known service awards.

S3 – Legendary service

- Uniquely achieving what only you can do;
- Redefining the expectations of one's industry or sector;
- Joyfully living deeper service values;
- The value of service drives everything else in the business, and
- Customers spread the legend by word of mouth.

but only performing as described in S3 will be enough to make you stand out from your competitors. If you aspire to legendary service you will be acting dynamically on the belief that good enough has never been good enough. Only 'one-line answers' will do.

The kind of thinking that creates a one-line or legendary solution is open, fresh and even childlike in its simplicity. Here is some focused advice on what you need to do to 'change the box' in your thinking:

- Redefine the expectations of your industry;
- Focus on the potential, not the expected;
- Get customers to help you change your box;
- Steal from other people's boxes;
- Learn from other fields, and
- Banish the grey.

Redefine the expectations of your industry

This is a tall order, but the benefits are enormous if you can escape from the gravitational pull of what's currently expected by customers dealing with your sector. You are not dealing merely with people's perceptions of your company, but also their view of your whole industry, whether it be banking, building, software support, public transport, automobile retailing or the travel industry, to name but a few.

One player that has successfully challenged the stereotypical view of its industry is GM in their Saturn car operation:

> We knew from the beginning that if Saturn was to succeed we'd have to do more than just sell a good car. We'd also have to change the way cars are sold, the way the people who sell them are perceived and the way customers feel about the experience of shopping for a car.
>
> *Stuart Lasser, Saturn dealer*

Try substituting the equivalent examples from *your own business*.

Change the way *pensions / coffee / automotive components / financial services* are sold (substitute your own example).

In October 1997, an unlikely alliance was formed when Wells Fargo Bank combined with Starbucks Coffee Company to offer a cocktail of services under one roof, making a more social and relaxing experience out of the normally boring visit to a bank. These centres also feature a variety of other businesses including photocopying and dry-cleaning.

Charles Schwab's online broking services have revolutionised the way investments are bought. In one sense they have really given power to the people by enabling customers to cut out the middleman ('disintermediation' in current management speak) and play the stock market for themselves. *Schwab has presciently anticipated the demise of middlemen everywhere by providing the tools for customers to help themselves.*

There's no more striking example than that of amazon.com, who have changed the way in which books, that most traditional of all products, are sold, probably for ever. Even those of us who enjoy browsing in bookshops have fallen for being able to press a button and order a book while simultaneously being able to send a copy to friends anywhere on the globe.

Change the way the people who sell them are perceived.
What do people think of life insurance salesmen, restaurant staff, brokers, exhaust repair mechanics, etc.?

There's usually a stereotype in customers' minds and it's often not a positive one. What can you do to shift perceptions? This was the issue faced by Rebecca Jenkins when she took over as managing director of the UK haulage business, Lane Group. Most people's image of truckers was of wild men who lived in their cabs and ate Yorkie bars. Rebecca revolutionised *the way in which these people regarded themselves* by insisting on cleanliness, smart uniforms and the direct involvement of the drivers in the company strategy and in giving positive feedback to customers – demanding companies such as The Body Shop, Next and C&A.

The message is clear – upgrade your people's image of themselves and this will be transmitted spontaneously to your customers. In service this often means reviving a sense of pride where the person giving the service is not subservient, but regards him or herself as an equal with the customer. I love the small card carried by staff at Ritz-Carlton Hotels, which says: 'We are ladies and gentlemen serving ladies and gentlemen.'

No sense of servility here, but rather an acknowledgement of equal status with the customer.

Customer perceptions will alter only if the change comes first from the service provider. None but the most old-fashioned and despotic of customers really likes fawning obsequiousness from traditional-style hotel staff. In the words of Eleanor Roosevelt:[2] 'No one can make you feel inferior without your permission.'

---

[2] *Catholic Digest*, August 1960. Roosevelt (1884–1962) undertook extensive political activity as wife of polio-stricken Franklin D. Roosevelt and was his social adviser when he became US President (1932).

Give your people permission not to feel inferior and this will positively change the way the customer perceives them, too.

'No caffe latte?
And you·call yourselves a bookstore'?[3]

Change the way customers feel about the experience of shopping for *groceries / air travel / books*, etc.

As writers Pine and Gilmore announce in their new book, we are now in the Experience Economy.[4] For many of us shopping is not one of life's great

---

[3] Cartoon by Shanahan, The Cartoon Bank. First appeared in *The New Yorker*, 27 June 1994.

[4] *The Experience Economy*, ibid.

joys. If you are going to compete with amazon.everything – as it soon will be
– you have to offer a stimulating, entertaining and worthwhile alternative.
This is what Barnes & Noble and Borders do with their in-store coffee
shops, and the pressure on them to enrich the experience with poetry
readings, concerts, lectures, hand-written staff recommendations of books,
and so on has been heightened considerably by the greater efficiency of their
online competitors. (In Barnes & Noble's case, this includes themselves as
they have a thriving Internet bookselling service.) But it's hard to taste the
beans over the Internet, or to bump into a friend with quite the same degree
of intimacy.

It's strange how long this idea has taken to percolate from the US to
other parts of the world.

In the UK, ritual humiliation from surly servers is the order of the day.
It's amazing how the average English person can make the innocuous phrase
'How may I help you' sound like a curse. How tremendous, then, to walk
into a branch of Richer Sounds, leading hi-fi retailer, and see that not only
are all the staff friendly, but also every sign in the store is designed to convey
a positive message. Instead of saying 'No dogs allowed', they have a polite
notice that says, 'Guide dogs welcome', which implies simply that other
dogs are not. Are shoplifters deterred by signs that say 'Shoplifters will be
prosecuted'? I think not. Richer Sounds shops have one that says: 'Free ride
in police car – for shoplifters today only.'

It conveys the desired point, and makes honest customers laugh. As
founder Julian Richer says: 'We like amusing signs because we think that if
we can get customers to smile, we are halfway there.'

Even more enticing is the example of the Wound About shop that sells
mechanical toys in San Francisco. A stand outside the store does not give
you the usual list of 'don'ts', but is headlined 'Guide to Fun' and reads as
follows:

☞ Please do touch the merchandise
☞ Feel free to play with anything in the store, except the employees
☞ If you break it . . . relax, we know you didn't mean to
☞ Because we care . . . share demo toys with others!
☞ Food and drinks allowed – enjoy!
☞ Speak any language – except foul
☞ If you're under 18, you must be with someone older
☞ Our toys carry a lifetime guarantee – the lifetime of the TOY, not YOURS
☞ All sales are final (more or less)

☞ Most importantly, our employees are instructed NOT to say, 'Have a Nice Day'.

While the service experience didn't quite live up to this stunning menu of possibilities, it's a courageous attempt to change the way we feel about entering a shop. The message is 'Welcome, come in and enjoy yourself'. A few hundred miles down the coast in Santa Barbara I experienced the other extreme in a shop selling jewellery. I counted no fewer than 17 signs that shouted 'No!' at the customer, the complete opposite of everything at Wound About. The crowning glory was one above the service desk that said:

'We reserve the right to refuse service to anyone for any reason.'

Does your reception/retail outlet/factory/website shout 'Yes, come in!'? If it does, you're removing the 'box' or barrier that exists between you and your customers. If 'no', intimacy will be that much harder to achieve.

When I am shopping for books, my personal search engine, and for me the only viable alternative to the Internet, is called Catherine, the manager of my local bookstore. She gives me good-humoured banter and personal recommendations in a way that even amazon.com's sophisticated preference-finding technology can't emulate. 'So that last Richard Ford novel I recommended was a bit too sophisticated, eh? Here's one with smaller words and more pictures, which you might be able to manage' is a typical quip.

The point is that as a customer I want different *channels* available to me. The ease, convenience and likelihood of finding the book I want is a great appeal of the Internet, as well as the fact that I can order from any geographical location, 24 hours a day. But when I have time for human interaction, I'll visit a physical location.

Focus on the potential, not the expected

Successful service organisations deliver more than the expected. They have a healthy focus on what marketing people call the latent or potential needs of the customer. That means those things the customer has not yet asked for, or even imagined, but is delighted to have when offered to him or her.

The Expanded Service Offering Box

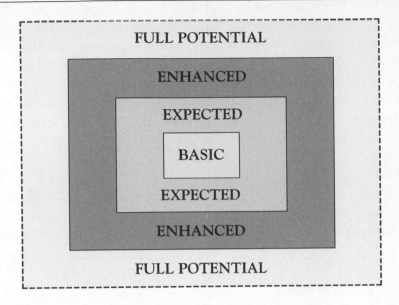

The first step, of course, to changing the box is to know what box you're in. A useful model is the Expanded Service Offering box, inspired by Professor Theodore Leavitt's Total Product Concept.

Using the familiar example of the hotel experience, the *basic* service offering is to provide shelter and a certain level of helpfulness. The *expected* offering these days is a telephone, television, room service and a degree of friendliness. The *enhanced* service offering might be to provide secretarial services, fax machine in the room, health club, massage, and staff who are happy to bring emergency toothpaste and aspirins to your room.

As for the *full potential* service offering – the sky's the limit. Limousines to the airport, guided tour of the local area, staff willing to go out of their way to fulfil even the most impossible requests at short notice, and so on. The outer circle is indicated by a dotted line meaning the horizons are unlimited, or limited only by your own imagination and choice.

The greatest opportunities for differentiation are obviously in targeting your efforts on the outer reaches of the model. All hotels have beds, rooms, and nearly all supply television sets and telephone as standard. Legendary service providers are continually working on the enhanced and potential aspects of service. Hotels chain Marriott has worked well on the enhanced circle. It has recently created 'The Room That Works', with all the right plugs, jacks and attachments for the travelling business person who is likely to spend hours working in the room with a laptop.

Where do you spend your time and effort? For most businesses it's a classic case of Pareto's Principle, the 80/20 rule. Eighty per cent goes on the basic and expected offering. However, something like 80 per cent of delighted comments from customers will be because you have done something extraordinary in the outer boxes, the 'enhanced' and 'full potential' offerings. My practical suggestion is to list all the activities you are involved with and next to them put a code categorising each as part of either your basic, expected, enhanced, or potential service. Then work out what percentage of your time and effort you spend on each category.

The answers are usually striking. Although it's true that if we don't perform the basic 80 per cent of expected functions well we are likely to be out of business – a friendly hotel where the plumbing doesn't work is hardly likely to create delight– customers take this for granted and will be really excited only by the focus you put on the outer boxes. *And yet that is usually where we spend the least time and effort.*

So try considering:

- How *not* to do so much on the basics – this may mean delegating, sharing or ignoring certain activities, and
- How to focus more on the new and unexpected areas at the fringes of the model.

The difficulty in making this happen is that the basic and expected aspects of what we do tend to use up the majority of our time. While working with financial controllers in Nestlé I was told that they were often stereotyped as 'bean counters'. This made it more difficult for them to provide a great service to other functions in the business as they were expected merely to crunch the numbers. However, they know they could fulfil their potential by also giving strategic advice and interpretation. You *become what people expect you to become.*

Of course, there is a *both/and* here. In some businesses the delivery of the basic or expected is so erratic that it can seem like a luxury to focus on higher things. Remember to do both well.

'We are proud to do the small things well.'

Ken McCulloch, *managing director, Malmaison*

Virgin Atlantic is a striking example of how focusing on the outer can make a real difference, particularly in the case of its Upper Class service, which has won just about every transatlantic award. This features a limo service from home to airport, and lounges where you can get your hair cut, shoes cleaned, nails manicured and even a massage or reflexology. At around $6,500 (£4,000) from London to Los Angeles this may be the most expensive haircut you've ever had, but passengers are delighted. Virgin has also addressed the most limiting box of all – that rather unpleasant one in which your airline food arrives – by serving people proper food in their lounges *before* the flight.

One final point. The Expanded Service Offering model is not static, because raised expectations mean that what was enhanced yesterday is basic today. For instance, satellite channels on your TV and a trouser press in the room may have been futuristic a few years ago, but they are now just the basics. The trick is to keep re-imagining what the outer reaches of the customer's experience could be. Try adding some refreshing surprises every week. Novelty is memorable while sameness is quickly taken for granted.

Get customers to help you change your box

The blind spot from 'inside' the box is the view that customers are somehow 'outside'. However, great service providers have realised the need to eliminate this boundary and allow customers to be intimate, to share space in the same box.

If you can turn your customers into a fan club they will do your marketing for you. Not many organisations have quite such a visible or noisy set of customers as Harley-Davidson. They are not selling just a bike, but a sense of belonging or even a new image:

> 'What we sell is the ability for a 43-year-old accountant to dress in black leather, ride through small towns and have people be afraid of him.'[4]

The partnership you form will help you to change the box, if you're listening and applying what you learn. Computer executives in the 1980s were at first disturbed by the number of ad hoc user groups mushrooming

---

[4] Dave Ulrich, Jack Zenger, Norm Smallwood, *Results-Based Leadership*, Harvard Business School Press, 1999, ISBN: 0875848710.

everywhere. For example, there are literally hundreds of Apple User Groups in the USA. It took even relatively open-minded Apple people some time to see that the limits of their own box were expanded by this fan base, and for them to support and encourage these groups. If consumers club together to discuss your product, there are undoubtedly risks, but these are enormously outweighed by the advantages of having enthusiasts who end up using your product in many ways that you hadn't even envisaged. The closer you can draw them in the more you will learn.

Those with the Smartest Customers Win

'Firms that encourage customers to talk to each other, to form affinity groups and hobby tribes, will breed smarter and more loyal customers while creating smarter products and services.'

Kevin Kelly [5]

Customers often identify with other customers of your offering. It may seem unlikely, but not impossible, that there will be a joyful fan club of High Street bank users or purchasers of oil additives. Many products and services seem to attract user associations that exist for consumer protection and defence against being overwhelmed by the corporate giants they are dealing with.

But you could try learning from real fan clubs. Fairport Convention was one of the most successful folk/rock acts of the late '60s and early '70s, and are still going strong after 30 years. The annual highlight for their fans is the Cropredy Festival, which has been held in a field in Oxfordshire every summer for 27 years. The group may not have regarded these fans as customers, but in many ways they are just that. The two-day festival is entirely fan-orientated, with musical requests and announcements between acts about the fans, rather than the group itself.

The wonder of the festival is that the locals really welcome it because the group has built a close relationship with the community. A whole sports centre has been built by the Scouts from their collections at the festival. Their job is to clear the rubbish from the site. The Sunday after the festival features a traditional cricket match when hung-over musicians take on the locals.

---

[5] *New Rules for the New Economy*, Viking Penguin, 1999, ISBN: 014028060X.

The music is excellent, but above all it's the *experience* that people are buying. For the group there is also the long-term profitability of keeping a loyal fan – or customer – base. Most tickets are sold through the group's own mailing lists rather than expensive advertising, and sales of music and concert tickets for other acts that are part of the Fairport's extended family are also highly successful through this channel.

The attraction for many fans is feeling intimately part of the family. Send an e-mail to one of the group members and you'll probably receive a personal reply. Contrast this with the anonymous arm's-length relationship customers have with most of their suppliers. Playing golf with your key customers is OK. But making the experience of doing business with you part of a lifetime commitment is one of the real secrets behind gaining customer loyalty. Allow them to become family, to *enter* your world and, they will want to share the journey with you. How do you turn your customers into a 'sect' that they love to belong to?

Steal from other people's boxes

You can be different only if you escape from customers' stereotyped expectations. 'Changing the box' means being a shape-shifter, eluding neat categorisation. Look at this description: 'It is a curious and stylish hybrid. Part sushi bar, part Viper Lounge, part Blade-Runner style.'[6] What on earth is it? It's a London restaurant called Itsu, the latest brainchild of entrepreneur Julian Metcalfe, whose chain of Pret a Manger sandwich bars was launched in the 1980s.

Itsu breaks the categories. It adapts the technology used in some Japanese restaurants of a miniature conveyor belt called a 'revolver', but applies it to an unusual variety of food. Although there is a strong Eastern influence – avocado crab with glass noodles, and spinach with deep-fried taro root – the restaurant also offers an eclectic range of desserts such as crème brûlée, and mango and green peppercorn brandysnap.

The system of the revolver does away with waiters, so how can this be a great service experience? The answer is clear: there are no waiting lists (Itsu refuses all reservations on principle) the food is reasonable value, and there's no hanging around. Metcalfe claims to be able to deal with a simultaneous influx of a hundred customers.

The service offering is clear. In Metcalfe's words: 'There are times when

[6] *London Evening Standard*, 5 March 1999.

all you want is to eat well and go.' In offering this he has shrewdly divined the unspoken need of many Londoners. His new hybrid venture not only escapes from appearing like any other restaurant, but has also borrowed creatively from the technology of Japanese restaurants and the style statements featured in futuristic movies.

What is Steven Jobs selling now? Apple's world-beating and highly customer-friendly computer, the iMac, is campaigning on a fashion ticket. Advertisements show the iMac in attractive bright colours with the slogan 'Collect All Five Colours'. The message is clear – it's now within the range of possibility for many people. The perceived limitation of computers as unaffordable and complex technological artefacts has been broken. The slogan also makes a subtle point that in buying into the world of the iMac you are joining a club. It's the unspoken psychological aspect of belonging to a lifestyle that's as fashionable as an Armani suit or a Cartier watch. Apple has stolen from the world of fashion and gained many customers who had never used a computer before.

The managing director of Virgin Atlantic, Steve Ridgway, also believes in the value of plagiarism. He cites his airline's drive-through check-in as an example of 'learning' from McDonald's. Not only is this hassle-free, but it cuts check-in time from four-and-a-half minutes to 45 seconds.

Learn from other fields

One way of 'changing your box' is to apply thinking from other apparently unconnected fields. One of the most exciting to learn from is the world of new physics which is genuinely changing the box, or existing assumptions, about how we see our relationship to the physical universe.

The Newtonian view – called classical physics – is of a universe made up of particles or billiard balls, whose speed, mass and interactions can be predicted by precise laws. But the new quantum field theory is that of underlying fields of energy leading to the revelation that a particle also has the qualities of a non-localised wave. This phenomenon is called wave-particle duality, a striking example of *both/and* thinking. Looked at under certain conditions, the entity behaves in classical terms as a particle, but from another perspective it's part of a wave that obeys completely different laws. Light, for example, is composed both of individual photons and displays the phenomenon of a wave. The two realities co-exist.

So what? Organisations are physical systems and, as such, are subject to this apparent paradox of being both localised in time and space, *and* perfectly correlated outside these apparent boundaries. For example, I might order a washing machine through the Internet (exhibiting more of the qualities of a quantum-mechanical transaction), but it still has to be delivered through a classical channel by the representatives who turn up to install it. In the gold rush to the new Yukon of Internet service this has often been forgotten: your organisation is both the (almost) timeless and spaceless cyber-space connection and the very physical, classical presence of the delivery man. The customer will judge you by *both/and*.

I recently ordered by telephone a washing machine from a leading UK retailer, whose 'quantum' systems seemed to be excellent. However, the delivery men, were amazingly obdurate in their attempts *not* to get it through an entrance that was awkward, but by no means impossible. They told me that they were sub-contractors and, in effect, not fully responsible. Eventually I hired two passing builders – they managed it skilfully in less than 10 minutes.

There are two vital lessons to learn from this experience. First, really to wow your customers you have to be great in the quantum – your telephone and Internet connections – *and* the classical channels – the physical delivery. One colours the customer's judgment of the other. Second, the customer will perceive anyone involved in the delivery chain as representing you: sub-contractors, deliverers, security staff, your suppliers and so on. In short, the customer ultimately judges you quantum-mechanically by viewing all aspects of your service as being part of the underlying 'wave' that serves them.

The blind spot from inside your organisation may be that you do not see this wider 'field' that your activities project into the business environment. But your customers do.

Customer service is not just something that your customer service department is responsible for. It's *everyone's* prime concern. They are all part of the 'wave'. Each moment is connected to a wider reality for the customer – for instance, understanding that a customer isn't retained for life by one excellent moment of truth, but will create his or her own judgment of your field, positive or negative, by a *series* of events. And some of these events may be triggered by people who don't work for you in a classical sense, but are part of your field quantum-mechanically – your 'outliers', outsourced, or sub-contracted people. This triggers a critical question: *when you out-source, do you ensure that these people express the same values you want your customers to experience?*

Customers are not interested in the billiard-ball view that these people over here are us, those other balls are our suppliers and ne'er the twain shall meet. A very literal understanding of what goes into creating a service 'balls-up'!

The metaphor of new physics therefore also highlights the importance of ensuring that *everyone* involved in the customer's total experience is fully *au fait* with your mission, standards and operating values.[8]

Banish the grey

It's about time that computers started shape-shifting. Any colour you like, as long as it's grey? Fordism has ruled in the computer industry until recently. Hopefully we will now see not merely new shades of grey, but many exciting, colourful and attractive new designs.

How would you rate your own business on greyness? It's the colour of most organisational boxes and the danger of greyness is being experienced even by mighty retail giants such as Marks & Spencer.

This is clearly captured by the visit of Anatole Kaletsky, a journalist for *The Times*, to the M&S flagship store in London's Marble Arch:

'Having left my daughter in the pulsating teenage party which seemed to be continually in session at Top Shop in Oxford Circus, I was immediately struck by the visual contrast. As I rode up the escalator through Marks & Spencer's cavernous, almost undecorated, neon-lit interior, I realised that I'd not seen a shop this drab since I lived briefly in Moscow 10 years ago.'

Where should M&S start looking to banish its perceived greyness? Well, it could start with the world of colour, or even learn from Top Shop. But can you imagine having a party at Marks & Spencer? The company's executives might argue that this wouldn't be right for their kind of customer. Unfortunately, their kind of customer seems to be more scarce these days.

Naturally there's a balancing act here because you need to steal, cross-

---

[8] *Note*: For practical purposes, I have not used the image of wave/particle duality in all its scientific precision. Telephone contact, at least that through wires, is still arguably classical. But with the introduction of fibreoptics, satellite communications, etc., the image is becoming more literal. And remember that 'it is later than you think' – 1998 saw the discovery, in its most infant form, of quantum teleportation. This is the ability to 'teleport' a particle through quantum-mechanical rather than classical means, implying that 'Beam me up, Scotty' is at least a theoretical possibility.

pollinate and integrate other influences while still maintaining the distinctive core of your own offering. I'm not sure I'd like to be cheered up by Disney-style characters or loud rap music while I'm selecting long-lasting underwear. However, something has to be done because the box is no longer appealing. And it has taken a great shock to make M&S management realise it is in a box.

In sharp contrast is the customer revolution that has occurred in retailer Asda. It's not surprising that Asda has recently become a key acquisition in Wal-Mart's campaign to take over Europe. Perceived until recently as down-market, Asda has taken the route of banishing greyness through its colourful and passionate drive to relate to its customers. One hardened shopper says:

'I went in sceptical, I came out a convert. You're met at the door by a woman who greets you. In a culture where people are conditioned to avoid eye contact even *after* they've been formally introduced, this was a small revelation. There was no Muzak. There was *real* music. When I was there they were playing Van Morrison!'

'The prices were really cheap, but most importantly I made five contacts with different store members who were all excellent. I asked four different shelf packers to point me in the direction of a product. Each made *human* contact – eye contact – with me. Each took me to the product I was searching for. More surprisingly, each one waited with me and asked if there was anything else they could do, even though they had been in the middle of another job when I took them away.

'The cashier greeted me with "Hello there" and made a human contact with me, not the vacant one I am more used to in supermarkets. She chatted about the apricots I bought.

'If it's raining they have a brolly patrol – they'll accompany you to your car with an umbrella. I bought two small bags of groceries and asked for a packer and someone to help me to my car. No comment was made about the small size of my load.

'Yet again, the packer made contact with me as she helped me to my car. She was friendly in a genuine way and cracked: "I expect you were hoping for a young stud to carry for you, and you got me!" I didn't tip and there was no lurking around or special attention in order to get a tip.

'This was a huge superstore. My experience is normally one of going into a daze and feeling completely isolated when entering a supermarket. It was an unusually good experience. I came away cheered up and impressed.'

In simple ways the Asda staff converted a potentially boring shopping trip into a more human experience. There are at least half a dozen pointers on great service in this brief story, which you would think their competitors could steal and implement over the course of a few weeks. That doesn't seem to have happened. If you're in a box, you may be the last people in the world to realise it. Another dimension? Just a fantasy!

Therefore, the most obvious strategy to 'change your box' is to seek help from others who aren't trapped by the same limitations. The customer design fanatic Steven Jobs of Apple Computers regularly uses poets, artists, historians and other creative people to help banish the greyness that is endemic in much of the computer industry. The original Macintosh design team was a mix of artists and engineers with a strong sense of aesthetic principles as well as techie know-how. Jobs has continued this practice because his aim is always to focus the best of human talent and creativity on any project.

The message is clear – banish the grey by learning from those who see in colour.

Creative approaches to customer service

Changing the box requires a creative and imaginative approach to the customer. What follows are six ideas that you can use to give your own business a positive jolt. These examples are unlikely to be transferable to your own business in exactly the form in which they appear, so treat them as inspiration to change your own box rather than as a precise checklist. For instance, there are many different ways of interpreting the first point, 'Live with them'. It could mean to you a wide range of approaches, from brief one-day visits to adopting the whole lifestyle of your customers in far-flung parts of the globe.

- Live with them
- Mirror your customers
- Bring them into your world
- Know your product (everyone)
- Anticipate latent/potential needs
- Educate your customers

Live with them

When Toyota planned to enter the Californian car market it sent some application engineers to live in Laguna Beach with the simple mission of finding out what Californians were like. Did the US car-making giants in Detroit even recognise that Californians are a separate breed? Evidently not, as illustrated by the subsequent dominance of Japanese and Korean car makers in the Californian market.

Key Question 1: Have the people in your organisation with the core responsibility for designing for the customer spent sufficient time living with the customer's experience with all its day-to-day complexities and messiness?

Key Question 2: If the answer is 'yes', have your people been adequately coached in innocent listening and observation skills, which do not discount *any aspect* of the customer's experience?

Key Question 3: If the answer to both is 'yes', have you given sufficient recognition to the stories they tell about the customer's experience?

Mirror your customers

If you're retailing music, you may have some unusual personnel problems. What do you do with a store manager of 27, when most of the music-buying population is about 12 and the manager can have problems relating to the style of service, let alone the musical taste expected by younger customers? Live bands in the stores, wall-to-wall videos of the latest rap hit played really loud are not generally welcoming to buyers of, for example, Neil Diamond's Greatest Hits, or Barry Manilow compilations.

The music-selling staff *are* the product.

Key Question 1: How consciously do your people's style and manner mirror those of your customers?

Key Question 2: To what extent does the make-up of your staff – proportion of women, ethnic minority groupings, etc. – reflect your customer base, or those you would like to have as customers?

Key Question 3: What do you need to do to make your customers feel at home when they do business with you?

Key Question 4: Are many of your customers female? If so, do your male staff know how they like to be treated?

Bring them into your world

With Patagonia, makers of outdoor activity and adventure equipment and clothing, a great deal of customer research is conducted literally outside the windows of its California office. The customers are therefore brought into their world in more ways than one – they are physically close and also actively sharing their enthusiasm for the company's outdoor activity products.

Perhaps the most consistent example of bringing customers into your world is still the legendary Carl Sewell, owner of Sewell Village Cadillac in the US. He insists on showing customers his sparkling-clean service bays, an area regarded as the underworld of most car dealers. This naturally changes the box by giving the customer confidence that the inner workings of the business are managed with the same attention to quality as the expected flashiness of the sales showroom.

Key Question 1: How can you break down the barriers between the customer's world and yours?

Key Question 2: How often do you bring key customers in front of those people who can most influence the customer's experience for the good, and in a forum where people can really interact with the customer rather than listen passively?

Key Question 3: How can you bring customers into the behind-the-scenes parts of your business that are critical to delivering great service, but which are usually out of bounds?

Know your product (everyone)

It's a great reassurance to customers that you know your own business. This may seem obvious, but with a lot of old knowledge and skills vanishing, it's often not apparent these days. For example, there is a simple test to tell what handle size your tennis racket should be based on your individual hand grip. Out of six sports retailers in my home town of Oxford I discovered that in five of these outlets no one had a clue about these basic principles. Naturally, I bought my new racket from the sixth retailer where it was clear that they were experts on, users of, and enthusiasts for their own product. They actually dissuaded me from buying the most expensive racket on offer because there wasn't an exact fit for my hand size.

In many retail outlets these days staff receive intensive training on how to take money and operate the computerised till, but almost zero in knowing the product.

A full knowledge of the product often means being able to make fair comparisons with competitor products. The training of BMW franchise owners is intensive on this point. In some cases they seem to know more about the pros and cons of rival cars – such as Volvo, Mercedes and Audi – than their competitors' sales people. But you don't need to be an expert about the competitors' products to be helpful to the customer. Richer Sounds stores regularly carry brochures from rival retailers Argos and Tandy, which they use to help the customer find what they want elsewhere. Richer's principle is: 'If you can't make the sale, you can still give the service.'

Key Question 1: How much training resource do you put into helping your people to know their products and services inside out?

Key Question 2: How can you give even the backroom people hands-on experience of using the product?

Key Question 3: If your product doesn't match the customer's needs, how prepared are you to sacrifice the sale by giving information on competitor products to make the customer happy?

Anticipate latent/ potential needs

Simply going by what the customer tells you may prevent you from creating anything new unless your dialogue is actively targeted – see the earlier section on Customer Intimacy. While there are famous ideas of new products emerging from customer feedback, including 3M's serrated sellotape dispenser, don't rely on customers actively to generate ideas about improvements in service. Too often they are busily engaged in making you get it right today rather than generating fresh ones for problems that haven't yet been anticipated.

A legendary service provider will always be serious about focusing attention, time and resources on those needs that the market hasn't yet articulated. Inventor and entrepreneur Dyson's phenomenally successful bag-free vacuum cleaners weren't brought to the market because focus groups told manufacturers that their life would be infinitely better if they didn't have to change the bag on their cleaners. Dyson, a serial inventor, says he created the new cleaner out of intense irritation at the inadequacies of old-style vacuum cleaners.

But once presented with the alternative, customers realised that they'd been conditioned by the more traditional manufacturers to accept an inferior technology as 'the box'. Worse than that, the makers were protecting a multi-million-pound business in replacement bags for traditional vacuum cleaners. Dyson anticipated and delivered an option that customers weren't aware they wanted until the opportunity was presented to them.

Key Question 1: Are you happy with the amount of focus you put on perfecting what already exists compared with imperfectly introducing the new or unknown?

Key Question 2: What more can you do to anticipate needs the customer hasn't yet expressed?

Educate your customers

When you order goods through a smart system such as amazon.com, one of the great intangible benefits you receive is that not only do these providers learn more about your likes and dislikes, but you also become more educated about other products you might find similarly useful but might not have known how to ask for, *and* the process of how to discover the information.

In other words, you become more proficient in your own self-service skills. They've helped you to help yourself.

Gary Unsworth, managing director of Nichols Foods, whose customers are the UK's leading vending and retailing companies, puts attention and money into educating his customers. In 1987 he took six of them to Colombia to teach them about the coffee business at its source. They were all customers for Nichols vending machine coffee. Unsworth makes a point of not talking business on these trips – he's more interested in the education and the relationship he builds, rather than short-term sales.

He says: 'I try to build a relationship and to help educate my customers.' Not surprisingly, Nichols gained significant business in areas other than coffee from the Colombia trip through the development of these relationships.

Unsworth is serious about his customers' education. How does he justify the expense? 'We can grow only if our customers grow,' he observes.

Key Question 1: Do you and your customers learn something new each time you serve them?

Key Question 2: What can you do to share learning experiences with your customers that will help them to grow their business even if it doesn't directly help you sell to them in the short term?

Key Question 3: How serious are you in investing time, money and resources to help educate your customers?

Out there, in worlds far apart from your own industry, are exciting, vibrant, inspiring role models. You can try to perfect the box that you're in, but there are upstarts everywhere who don't realise it's against the rules to change the box, stretch the parameters, add colour and playfulness to their business, and can achieve it all like the beautiful simplicity of the one-line solution to the nine-dot problem. Or, to use the metaphor of the two-dimensional world that began this chapter, you can look for those sources of inspiration who believe there's another dimension. They don't believe anything *has* to be a mere commodity. They're bound to be wacky, original, and even a little crazy. But they've seen that other dimension and their customers are fast becoming believers, too.

'The whole history of progress is written by freaks . . . there's no comfortable, happy, conventional person who has given anything to the planet. You can only do it with blood and tears.'

Gilbert and George, controversial modern artists,
The Independent on Sunday, *3 October 1999, p. 21*

For some penetrating questions, activities, and ideas relating to this chapter turn to page 244.

Chapter Four

Learn From the Future

'It was *déjà vu* all over again.'

Yogi Berra (1925–), baseball legend and wit

'Wealth in the new regime flows directly from innovation, not optimisation; that is, wealth is not gained by perfecting the known, but by imperfectly seizing the unknown.'

Kevin Kelly, technology writer[1]

Learning from the future will help you to:

- Escape the 'gravitational pull' of today's thinking;
- Create an inspiring picture of the future you want for your customers, and
- Communicate this story.

Learning from the future is a logical contradiction. How can we learn from something that hasn't happened yet? Try putting your sense of logic aside for a while – we live in turbulent times where logic isn't always the best tool for understanding what's really going on. In this chapter I'm appealing to your intuition and creativity to visualise the future through the powerful tool of focused story-telling.

Have you ever been fascinated by films or stories where people could visit the future? The value of a time machine to your business would be inestimable. Unfortunately this invention hasn't arrived yet. In the meantime, our imagination is the best technology we have for exploring the unknown, however imperfectly.

---

[1] *New Rules for the New Economy*, Viking Penguin, 1999, ISBN: 014028060X. As executive editor, Kelly helped to create *Wired*, which has been called the '*Rolling Stone* of computers'.

Business leaders and writers have put a great deal of effort into trying to predict the future. This often takes the form of trend-spotting. The great success of writers such as Faith Popcorn with her stimulating books *The Popcorn Report* and *Clicking on the Future* and John Naisbitt, author of *Megatrends* and its more recent versions, can be attributed to our craving to know what happens next and also to our fear of being left behind.

But while it's wise to be curious about these trends – there's an elephants' graveyard of corporations who didn't take this activity seriously enough – our guesses are rarely correct. The main difficulty is that we tend to extrapolate from the past or present into the supposed future, imagining that tomorrow is a linear progression from today, even if we allow for substantial changes in the numbers and improvements in technology.

This is true even for those who are not required to be accurate in their predictions – watch *Star Trek* and see how the dress styles and technology have changed considerably, but there seems to be little social or psychological innovation. The writers have taken us largely unchanged into a *different-looking* future, but it's really the present spiced up with special effects.

The only thing we can say with certainty about the future is that it will be quite unlike yesterday or today. Change does not take the form of a smooth transition from the present to tomorrow, but is a series of jumps or 'discontinuities', invisible to even the most astute observers. Indeed, those with the most experience may have the greatest difficulty in seeing ahead because they have the most to unlearn.

History is rich with examples of this, such as the statement reputedly made by the Astronomer Royal in 1957 that putting a man on the moon posed so many technological problems that it would take about 200 years to overcome them. In varying degrees we suffer from the myopia created by experience and expertise, especially if this knowledge has brought us great success. Letting go is harder.

Extrapolating forward from today limits thinking because:

- It's coloured too much by what you already know, which is likely to be what *everybody else knows also*. Or what they already knew several years ago!
- It assumes the future is like the present projected forward in time, whereas change takes place in a series of *dis*continuities or leaps that we are blind to from the standpoint of today.

The definition of successful benchmarking

STEALING GOOD IDEAS!

How good are we at learning from what's going on around us, let alone learning from the future? The current vogue is to study – to benchmark or compare – read about or visit other organisations in the hope that you will be able to compare your performance and transfer useful best practice into your own. Successful benchmarking means at the very least 'stealing' a few good ideas. When unsuccessful it's been dubbed industrial tourism. What happens to all those European business people who visit Disney and create no visible improvements to their own company when they return? Should they be made to repay the cost of their trip?

Learning from other organisations' experience can inadvertently hold you back. This is because when they are prepared to open their doors you will be getting to grips with its recent *past*. Remember that by the time you read about a company, say, in the *Harvard Business Review*, or see its story on video, the examples or case studies will almost certainly be past their sell-by date. Frequently the information will be three to five years old and in any case, the real magic of originality tends to be sanitised or even to disappear by the time you have the chance to learn about it.

Perhaps listening to your customers better, having your corporate ear closer to the ground, will help you anticipate the future more accurately? Well, yes and no. Customers tend also to be rooted in their present and past experience of you. Though they know what they want from you now – and you would be foolish not to learn from what they are saying – they are similarly driven by short-term thinking and may not be able to articulate clearly what they would like from you tomorrow. To summarise:

Creating the Future

Customer Listening + Benchmarking =
Maintaining the Present

Creativity + Imagination =
Creating the Future

In other words, if you try to base your predictions of the future (the unknown) on your knowledge of today (the known) you are likely to be (a) wrong, and (b) too slow to create anything new, fresh and different that will make you stand out from the crowd. *Customers will hardly flock to you because you know just what everybody else knows and perform in the same way as your competitors.* Legends are created by those organisations who visualise a better and *different* future, and learn and apply what it takes to realise that vision. Rather than merely predicting the future, they attempt to *create* it.

Create your own trends

'Invent your own future' is a phrase now popular in management circles, though in practice not applied with enough energy or imagination. Truly original minds don't usually create from outer observation of what's going on in the world, even though they do tend to be curious, knowledgeable and intuitive about the direction of change. They tap an inner source of creativity and originality, which enables them to *create* trends rather than merely respond to them.

Let's take two examples that illustrate this point, one to do with a product, the other with service. When Sony was developing the device that was to become the world-beating Walkman, the trend was towards bigger and heavier audio machines. Remember the 'ghettoblasters' of the late '70s?

When British electronics engineers first caught wind of the technology Sony was working with they *yes, butted* the whole concept – surely there must be a few zeroes missing from the data on power output, and who on earth would want a device that puny? Well, only a few hundred million customers, it seems!

After the event, we can be wise and 'spot' the trends – customers would welcome portability, convenience and a new lifestyle statement. But it's important to understand that major changes come from ignoring the present and inventing a distinctly different future that customers didn't know to ask for until they saw it. And of course the next trick is to build on the world-shattering innovation with constant improvements – Sony had created more than 300 versions of the Walkman between its invention in the late '70s and the turn of the century.

Mention customer service and one of the early heroes of the current revival is undoubtedly Stew Leonard. The success of Leonard's family dairy and grocery business in Norwalk, Connecticut, was in tune with the 'experience economy'. Making grocery shopping, so often regarded as a chore, *an experience*, allied with fanatical attention to value for money and receptivity to customer feedback are the visible signs of the service legend the Leonard family has created.

A live singer welcoming customers, staff dressed as farmyard animals and cartoon characters to entertain young children and take the pressure off parents doing the weekly shop, a prominent dustbin-sized customer suggestions box that is emptied and acted on *daily* by management, enthusiastic customer focus groups who give up their time weekly to contribute ideas to improving the shopping experience, are just some of the elements that have made the business a legend. And the business is phenomenally successful in commercial terms. It's unbelievable how little of this learning has been applied by other food retailers, even after they have made their customary 'service excellence tour' visit.

But all of this stemmed from an *inner conviction* that the customer needed to be treated in the same way we would all want in an ideal world. The idea is so simple that the owners of most companies won't – don't – give it sufficient airtime. The evidence for this is the stultifyingly average experience of food shopping most of us *still* go through.

> *The key message is if you want to be like everybody else, read about the trends and copy them. If you want to be different – a legend that stands out from the crowd – realise that you can create your own trends by living out the inner conviction of the future you would like to have for yourself, your people and your customers. Quite simply, you need to write your own legend.*

Big-band leader Glen Miller was once interviewed by a journalist who suggested that surely his ambition was to create a big band like the other great acts. He replied that no, this wasn't his aim; he wanted to create a band that was like no other. More recently, an artist from a rather different genre of music, Jerry Garcia, remarked: 'You do not merely want to be considered the best of the best. You want to be considered the only ones who do what you do.' Translating this back into business terms, these two legends weren't interested in being the best in class, but in creating a new class of their own. With the true wisdom of the fool, the satirical *Mad* magazine captured this line of thought when it described itself as 'Number one in a field of one'.

So how do you 'learn from the future'? And in a way that will recharge your batteries, regenerate your enthusiasm and commitment to create your own trends? There's only one organisation I've visited that really seemed to be in tomorrow's service Heaven today. I'd like you to meet Datalearn, a world-beating supplier of commercial and educational software, which I can only describe as legendary. Here's the story of my recent visit.

Datalearn: site visit – October 1998

This morning I have a meeting with Tom Morgensen, chief (he won't call himself CEO) of Datalearn. The company has a turnover in excess of £2 billion and is based in the countryside not far from London's Heathrow airport. It sells training and educational software to business, public bodies, schools and universities around the world, as well as having its own Internet browser, The Learning Guide. What drew me to the company were reports, written and verbal, about its ground-breaking service to its customers in a field not noted for customer orientation or after-sales support. In fact, Datalearn's success has been built on overturning many of the industry's assumptions.

- Customer loyalty is not the prime concern – loyalty to customers is the driving principle, the customer's long-term commitment stemming from their experience of being intensively cared for;
- After-sales service is thought of as sales after service – taking a longer-term view of customer relationships is the natural means of creating more business. A recent article described how 'Datalearn will do anything to keep a good customer', and
- Delighted customers are seen as the company's real marketing department. More than 90 per cent of customers urge friends, family and colleagues to subscribe to Datalearn's services.

In addition, the company has used its technology innovatively to blur the boundaries between server and served. Its proprietary software systems allow customers access to Datalearn's inventory so they can discover exactly when and from where they can order new products and upgrades to existing ones 24 hours a day from anywhere around the globe.

Video-conferencing helplines are available to customers with this facility, and Datalearn even has a profitable revenue stream from consulting to its larger customers on the best systems to install for internal and external communications.

Morgensen later told me how much being on video improved the attitude towards the customer of even his best helpdesk people. 'If someone's looking you in the eye you tend to respond more positively, even if the questions sound naïve,' he explained.

It's 9am and the driver sent by the company arrives on the dot. He introduces himself as Frank, shakes my hand and asks me if I had a good flight. He's casually but smartly dressed, and friendly. As I settle myself in the car I notice there's a selection of newspapers and magazines, including the *Herald Tribune*, the *Telegraph*, the *Sun*, and *Business Week*. In front of me is a small thermos of either coffee, tea or hot chocolate, all clearly labelled.

'Help yourself,' he says. 'It's a 25-minute journey, and ask me about anything you want to know on the way.'

I helped myself to tea, scanned the headlines in the *Tribune* and asked him, 'Do you work for Datalearn, Frank?'

'Oh, no, Mr Barlow.' He laughed. 'I'm self-employed. But I do a lot of work for them. They asked me to attend a two-day session which all people connected to the company – part-timers as well – have to attend. It helps you to understand their products and their . . . what's the word. . . philosophy.'

'Philosophy?'

'Yes, their attitudes towards their own people, and particularly to their customers. I enjoyed it – they paid me for the day as well, and I met a lot of the new people, and Tom as well. You know, the chief.'

The rest of the journey passed quickly as I engaged Frank in conversation about the company. He seemed to know a lot about it. My last question was about Datalearn's attitude to customers.

'Oh, it's not just an attitude,' he replied enthusiastically. 'It's real for them. They say it's about bringing joy to their customers. And making money as a result. You'll see.'

He dropped me at the end of a short driveway. Frank told me that if I'd been driving my own car, I'd have found it cleaned – and valeted if I desired – by the time I returned from my meeting.

'Do they do this for all customers?' I asked.

'For all visitors, I think,' Frank replied. 'And then they ask you to rate the quality of the cleaning. Most people appreciate it.'

As we walked up the short pathway to the front entrance Frank said, 'Hi' to a middle-aged man who was digging up a small border. The man looked up from his work, and came over to say hello. 'You must be Nigel Barlow,' he said. His accent was Dutch. 'I'm Jos', he went on, 'marketing captain. Welcome to Datalearn.'

He smiled broadly and added, 'Everyone in the company spends a day a month on the gardens or doing some maintenance on our building. Some call it Beautification Day. But I can't stand that label. I like getting out in the air for a change. Enjoy yourself!'

He turned away to answer the mobile phone that had been ringing in his overall pocket. I smiled at the idea that the marketing director – or, what had he said, 'captain'? – was receiving a business call while wiping earth from his muddy left hand.

'Does everyone do. . . that?' I asked Frank.

'Yes, even Tom. It means that they all feel responsible for their own environment. And if something's not right, they can fix it for themselves.'

Wryly I recalled how one of my clients, Chief Executive of a UK financial services company, would handle the same issue. He would tell his secretary that the front walkway to corporate HQ needed weeding, she would tell security and they would call maintenance, who might be able to 'look at it' some time next week. The thought reminded me how powerless many senior managers are when it comes to everyday changes, unable even to influence getting a good quality coffee machine into the building!

My musings were interrupted by a warm greeting from a striking black woman, elegantly dressed, who had risen swiftly from behind a small reception desk to shake my hand.

'Hello, I'm Sandra. A warm welcome, Mr Barlow. Hotel OK?'

'Yes, thank you. Do I have to sign in?' I asked.

'No, but you do have to sign *out*,' she replied. She pointed to a wooden table on which a large open book similar to the kind country house hotels leave out for your comments.

Frank said goodbye, refusing a tip.

'Everyone is very smart here,' I said, impressed by Sandra's designer-chic appearance.

'Oh, you should have seen me last week. I was in denims every day,' she smiled.

I asked whether there was a dress code. As we spoke one man passed us in a cream suit, another in Levi's.

'Well, kind of. It just has to be relaxed and elegant.'

'And who decides what is . . . er, "relaxed and elegant"?'

'You do. The individual. We all agreed the principle – fought over it for some time, I should say. But once agreed we think we're grown up enough to decide for ourselves.'

OK, I thought to myself. You're doing all right on the hygiene factors – style, greetings, environment, and liberal staff policies – but what are you like in the real cut-and-thrust world of commerce? I was soon to find out.

Sandra, who I realised from the slightest of accents was probably French, led me through a lobby full of flowers, with unusual artwork and sculptures that looked as if they had been selected for a private home rather than a company building. I found out later that they had been – Tom was an avid art collector and this was where he kept much of his artwork rather than at home.

My consultant's instincts were aroused. Something was missing. 'Don't you have something here like a Mission Statement, or Company Values, or a Customer Charter?'

'No, we don't. Isn't that a bit . . . what's the word . . . old-fashioned?' she replied. 'It's all in *here*.' She touched her heart. 'Well, it might seem corny, but if it's not inside, we can't really live it, can we? Tom will tell you. Probably at great length!'

There were a dozen or so large and informal photographs of people playing sports or relaxing with their families. Sandra explained that these were principal customers who often visited Datalearn. Staff members were expected to recognise as many as possible. Of course, these tended to be the major corporate clients, but on an adjacent wall were 30 or so photographs of children and students also using Datalearn products.

Sandra took me into the back of a first-floor meeting room, light and airy, where about a dozen people were having a very animated conversation at a round table.

'Tom wanted you to see this first,' she whispered as we sat down a few feet away. 'It's a Customer Day. It's where our people get together. They suggest – or argue – changes that need to be made for the customer's benefit, then the managers have to come back at four o'clock to tell them how they're going to make sure the ideas are implemented.'

'How many of these days do you have?'

'One every week, every Monday. We do it so often because we're not just dealing with gripes from customers, but also getting their input into the design of new products and ways to serve them. A week is a long time in our business. It's the one event Tom and the managers rarely miss, even with their travel schedules. Enjoy yourself. I have to go now,' she said.

'That's Tom over there.' She indicated a tall man in an open-necked cream shirt sitting almost opposite. 'He'll take you from here. Have fun!'

After all the build-up, Tom was something of a disappointment. Tall, pleasant-looking, but not particularly the charismatic Branson type I'd been led to expect. He wore blue jeans, had slightly greying curly hair and was listening intently to what a young man to his left was saying with great passion.

The young man, of Chinese origin, looked very young to me. His title was head of manufacturing. He was haranguing Tom and others at the table with a story of how customers were suffering delays in shipping because telesales people weren't inputting order information accurately into their

PCs. Later I was told that the shortfall in on-time delivery against target that month was 0.45 per cent – most orders were shipped accurately and on time, an average 98.7 per cent, but the year's target was 99 per cent and it was evidently a high priority.

Sitting just behind the young speaker was an elderly man, thoughtfully watching him. A mentor-like figure, I found myself thinking, and discovered subsequently that I was almost right. The meeting concluded with smiles and handshakes, Tom announcing that they would reconvene at four with some answers after they had thought about the suggestions and co-opted a member of the telesales team into the discussion.

Tom came to greet me, and introduced me to other members of his team. The young man who had been displaying such passion and apparent anger only a few minutes before was warm and approachable. His name was Sun, which he told me was a common name in the Chinese province he came from.

I was bursting with questions for Tom. As we walked to his office, I asked, 'Why was the manufacturing manager so angry about customer delivery numbers? Isn't that usually taken up by sales, or your marketing department, or even customer service?'

A glint in Tom's eye pre-warned me of his answer. 'I think you know what I'm going to say, but I'll say it anyway. The customer is everybody's business. The difference is we don't just say it. We do something about it. I think you've just witnessed that.

'Secondly, we don't *have* a customer service department. We're all it.'

I mentally contrasted this with the reality of most organisations – once you have a customer service *department* there's a tendency for the rest of the business to assign ownership for too many customer issues to that area. In terms of keeping your customers happy, it's often too late by the time they are put in touch with customer services.

We had stopped in the wide corridor, and I looked at a large open area where 30 or so desks were laid out, not in neat rows, but in a loose circle. I was struck by how different all the desks were and that every operator had an extremely comfortable chair, some like high armchairs and many of them were different styles, though all in colours that were in harmony with the light shades of the others. Though the atmosphere was relaxed there was a feeling of focused intensity in the air and I noticed that the people were animated in their body language.

'Our customer communications area,' observed Tom proudly. 'As you can see, half of our operators are using video connections to customers. I didn't like Sun calling them 'telesales' because we receive more calls than we make. And anyway, that's not our philosophy. I'll discuss that with him later.'

He showed me into his modest but comfortable office with a good view of the entrance. A small water fountain played in one corner, and I noticed that the desk was half-covered in mementoes, photographs and paper. Wait a minute, I thought, doesn't the wunderkind of the future have no office – an open door equals an open mind and all that – and a paperless desk? I put this to Tom.

'I need a room,' he said, 'otherwise how can I think? But it goes for everyone here – they can all book any of the offices on this side of the building whenever they need privacy or thinking time. But there are no phones in here – they're on the hot desks outside.'

Aha! A topic I could latch on to – 'hot-desking' – meaning no one has a pre-assigned office and so they just take their laptop and essential paperwork to whatever desk and telephones are available on the day. 'Do you practise it?' I asked.

'No, not really. People need a sense of ownership in their own space – that's why they choose their own chairs, as you will see in the communications centre. And they bring pictures to make themselves at home. Given that they spend a third of their lives here – why shouldn't they be comfortable?'

'Indeed', I replied lamely, heartened by the fact that Tom's desk was nearly as messy as my own.

The service legend

I probed Tom with a mixture of information-seeking and sharper-edged questions. Why did so many people talk about his company in such glowing terms, both customers and the press? How was business? What were the figures on customer loyalty? How did he go about creating a really customer-orientated culture? What was the company's policy to dissatisfied customers?

The usual questions and, in the main, the usual answers. I'd already noticed that Tom was no charismatic leader, but as our conversation continued I became intrigued by two things. First, that my host evidently relished every question – ones he must have faced countless times – with a freshness that seemed as if he were hearing them for the first time. And also that there was a quiet certainty in the way he answered them, with a gleam in his eye that told me we were discussing his favourite subject.

If ever I asked him a question he hadn't heard before, he carefully made a note in a small spiral book I noticed he'd been carrying. 'My computer!' he winked, saying these were good points he didn't know the answer to, but that they should stimulate interesting discussions in his Legendary Service Customer Team.

Aha! I thought. Caught you out this time. Why have a customer team when the philosophy was that *everyone* was effectively their own customer service department?

He thought about this for a moment, then replied: 'Everything needs a focus. You see, I've spent a lot of time studying – and living – the change process, and I've realised that change is *discontinuous*. It comes in leaps and bounds. For instance, the Internet hasn't gradually crept upon us. It's jumped into our lives in one bound. Forty per cent of our business now comes through the Internet and, of course, our browser allows us to profit from being part of the Net.

'Continuous improvement is a myth. It happens in fits and starts. You need structures not for their own sake, but to remind you what's important. As a result, the membership of the team changes about every six weeks. And there's always a customer on it.'

'OK. That's a good point,' I said. 'You've obviously thought intensively about what's good for your customers. But have you also thought about service in a wider sense, for instance Datalearn's service to the community and the environment?'

Tom smiled brightly. 'My hobby horses,' he exclaimed. 'Well, much more than that, as we're really passionate about our impact on society and on nature.'

He told me about the company's 'Green Team' that was currently spending two days with a supplier to help that company reduce emissions of noxious gases in the production process. It was also working on a joint strategy to reduce the amount of paper and packaging that flowed between them by 50 per cent.

His stories, too, of the company's involvement in the community were fascinating. Almost everyone in Datalearn seemed to be involved in some project, whether it was raising money for an old people's home, teaching computing to the unemployed, or organising day breaks at the seaside for the disabled. The list went on. 'It's all voluntary, by the way,' he added, 'but rather irresistible to most people who get carried along in the swing of things.' I wondered what would happen if a company recruit refused to take part in such activities, and suspected that Tom and his team would find a way of seducing him or her into a suitable activity.

For the first time the chief looked at his watch and I realised time was nearly up. I would love to have explored the table in the office that seemed to display many of Datalearn's products – CDs, videos and manuals.

But Tom seemed to want to ask the last question. 'You haven't asked me the *really* big question,' he said softly, but his manner had become more challenging.

'You mean the *real* consultant's question – where's your organisation chart?' Both of us grinned in the knowledge that if there was one, it was 'in there' as Sandra had gestured earlier. However, I realised Tom was serious, and that I didn't have a clue what he meant.

He filled the silence before it became uncomfortable. 'Where is the *real service heart* of this organisation? What are we here for? Why do we care so much about getting it right for our people and our customers?'

'That's three questions,' I teased.

'Well, I have a problem with consistency, as I'm sure you've noticed. Lucky my people don't!'

He continued: 'I could say to you that the real service heart is in the heart of every one of our people. Or something smart-ass like that. Or the fact that all our major customers – schoolchildren or company executives – get free training on our main lines of software if they request it. We may have to do it in groups, but our people will always spend extra time with individuals if asked.

'Many customers come here to our coaching rooms, so it makes it logistically possible. In fact we don't simply have customer chat rooms on the Web, but also an ongoing – 24 hours, if required – facility for customers to meet each other, exchange experiences, ideas and gripes. A physical chat room.

'They can pull any one of us into these discussions to get a response. We believe in being approachable and intimate with our customers, not in bombarding them with too many surveys and questionnaires. "Real time relating" is what we call it.

'Then the fact that all managers – yes, we still call them that providing they *do* manage – spend 30 per cent of their time talking and listening to customers and user-groups. Or even that our website has won awards as the freshest, most enjoyable and quickest source of ordering a product, both inside our industry and, in fact, in any industry.

We even encourage people who are unlikely to buy from us to visit and learn from a selection of several hundred topics on our site without paying a penny. We find if we're in relationship with them, many will buy our products, which they can download immediately themselves. It's like magic.'

Tom was obviously proud of these achievements, so I let him continue.

'And that every potential employee spends three days in meetings and interviews before we offer him or her the job, and has to be familiar with all our main products *before* starting. This helps to give us an attrition rate of only seven per cent.

'But at the core of this is something which for once we have written down. Now where is it?' He rifled through the papers under his desk until he found what he was looking for – a simple A4 sheet that read:

> ### Datalearn's service heart
>
> **'Our work is to enrich our customers' lives by creating joy for ourselves and them. Through this we make money for ourselves and our stakeholders.'**

Not earth-shattering, I thought. Seen some like that in California. A bit too good to be true. And so this is the real service heart? I felt let down, as if someone had promised me the secret of immortality and given me a book on aerobic fitness.

But as he talked through the true meaning to him of almost every word in the statement, I became gradually infected with his unstoppable enthusiasm. We'd gone well over the allotted hour, but there was no holding him now. I learned that every potential recruit had to write – or draw, or make a videotape according to preference – what this statement meant to him or her. In Tom's words: 'There's no right answer, but we've developed pretty sharp antennae that tell us if they've really "got" it, or are just playing along.'

I tried a half-hearted attempt at accusing Tom of creating a kind of cultish culture.

His reply was astonishingly frank. 'Well, not all aspects of cults are bad, you know. There's a powerful sense of identity, a buzz and a feeling of pride. It's only when they stop people thinking for themselves and feel they're somehow superior to the rest of the world rather than in service to it that they get out of hand. Otherwise I'm all for cults. Good ones manage themselves more or less.

'Sure, I'm the "chief". People give themselves their own titles here, and I call myself that because I feel a strong identity with my "tribe". But I don't have any five-year plans because so much changes in five weeks that I encourage my people to come up with new products and business practices. "Encourage" is wrong. Hell, they do it anyway. I can't keep up with every development in this field, try as I do.'

I raised an eyebrow. 'That old "empowerment" thing?'

'We don't use that word much. I think "involvement"' is a more accurate description of what goes on here. "Empowerment" implies I have the power or knowledge to give away in the first place. I don't. Perhaps the most revolutionary thing we've done here is to give *all* our people some shareholding in the company. "Ownership" is a buzzword in business, usually meaning real commitment to the organisation's objectives, but in my experience the only way you get ownership is when people *are* owners.'

Tom had risen and I realised that he had to meet his people to respond to the morning's Customer Day input. I was still wrestling with the notion of joy, which was strange for an organisation which must be, under the surface, an extremely well-oiled money-making machine.

As if reading my mind, Tom said: 'We're not perfect, you know. And the minute we start thinking we're even getting close is the time we should break up this company.'

I nodded. I had two quick final questions. 'Whom do you benchmark yourselves against?'

An expression of slight distaste showed on the 'chief's face for the first time. He looked slightly incredulous that I had even asked the question. 'Why, against ourselves, of course. And mostly against our future self, becoming all we can become, as judged by our customers. Benchmarking keeps you in the past – we love the idea of learning from the future!'

I didn't think I'd pursue this one as I guessed the answer could take some time. I was now on my feet too. The hour and a half had passed swiftly, leaving me with as many intriguing questions as answers.

'One last question.' It had been nagging at me since I'd sat in on the Customer Day meeting. 'Who was the elderly man sitting behind Sun in the meeting? His mentor, or something?'

'Yes, and no,' Tom replied. From his tone of voice he obviously held this man in high esteem. 'That's Pete Jackson, one of our first and largest corporate customers, working for . . .' He named a well-known international financial services house and added: 'He's also a mentor to Sunny. I imagine he thought he could have made his points more persuasively today and will be having words with him. We have four customer mentors in the business and we pay them for the time they spend coaching our people. Sometimes I wonder if they've got a real job to go to as they seem to like hanging around here so much! We learn from him too – he gave us the idea of appointing a head of customer intimacy.

'Pete loves sitting in on our Customer Days – he's here most Mondays. He says he learns a host of ideas he can take back to inject into his own culture. And he's not always as polite and quiet as you saw today – he often puts on his customer hat and mostly we listen. Not always, though. The customer isn't always right and we don't kowtow to him. It's a mature relationship – what most people are talking about when they say the word "partnership" but don't know what the hell it means in practice!'

He shook my hand warmly. We were at the head of the stairs now and he handed me back to Sandra, who was going to spend the rest of the day showing me various facets of the business. Part of me was longing to get my hands dirty – as far as any consultant ever does – in the manufacturing facility and to see how the real people at the coal face responded to this service heart philosophy. But something told me that I would find not clones, but people who shared a powerful belief system. Enthusiasm of this kind is infectious.

I was dying to see the customer response session and the angry young man – perhaps counselled by his more temperate customer mentor – but my flight to Holland was leaving. I was shown to the visitors' book, which left plenty of space for comments, many of which were inspiring and humorous, and had obviously been penned by customers. There was also an envelope for me, which contained a computer game looking uncannily like the one my 12-year-old son had been saving for. I quickly checked the back of the cover and realised that it would run on his Apple Mac.

Sandra said she hoped I didn't mind that she'd spoken to my assistant to find out what I'd enjoy taking back with me. She told me she was going to spend the early evening in her 'other job' for the company, official story-teller. 'What's that when it's at home?' I asked. She told me that this meant presenting at key briefings, executive meetings and training courses examples of both the customer's experience – good and bad – and those of Datalearn's own people in working with those customers. 'I've always loved telling stories since I was a child. And now I get paid for it! But in case you're thinking this is a soft option, I am fairly numerate too, and we do talk about numbers when they help to tell the story.'

As I said my goodbyes, Frank was there to greet me, asking me if I'd had a great day. 'Weird people, huh?' he said coyly.

I nodded, but as I sat in the car I was trying to remember a battle-cry of Steve Jobs, the manic but brilliant founder – and currently saviour – of Apple Computers. He had talked about creating 'insanely great' products. Why not, I mused, an 'insanely great' service culture? Why not create a service legend?

I reflected on the words of the service heart statement and realised that though not a customer (yet!) I had been greatly enriched by my contact with everyone at Datalearn. But joy? Not something an Englishman could own up to!

I realised that there was something I hadn't asked – a single question about the company's products, marketing strategy and competitive situation. If I worked for Andersen or McKinsey I'd have been shot for forgetting to cover these basics. But somehow I didn't seem to mind – I left excited and inspired with many practical ideas I could convey to my own clients.

Writing your own legend

The case study you have just read may have provoked all kinds of reactions – you may have been left feeling incredulous, stimulated, inspired, impressed or even irritated. You will see the six 'I's – Internet, Individuality, Interactivity, Immediacy, Intimacy and Imagination – are either exemplified or hinted at in the text. But don't aim to visit Datalearn – *because it doesn't exist. Yet!* If you're offended because you thought it was a real company – more than 50 per cent of the people I've given it to to read have done the same – allow me to explain my reasons for inventing it.

For a vision of the future to be useful it has to be believable, but only *just*. Any meaningful picture should stretch the mind or provoke some emotional response, including both excitement and discomfort. This is a fine balance – if it's too fantastical it's easy to dismiss, but if it's too similar to today's reality then it can hardly be called a vision.

I introduced Datalearn by saying I was going to tell you a story, and that is exactly what I propose you do with your own organisation. If you aspire to be truly different, writing your own future legend or case study of the future is a powerful tool for focusing people's creativity and commitment on the necessary steps to bring the vision to fruition. It's in this sense that it's possible to learn from the future. But before we explore how to write your own future story, let's reflect on the uses of the Datalearn story.

First, it's peppered with practical ideas you can steal, adapt and modify for use in your own business. If you think it's all too perfect, remember that's intentional. An ideal picture is necessary to lead you in the direction of realising your own ideals.

Second, many aspects of Datalearn are taken from existing legends of service. For example, the extreme no-quibble returns policy is inspired by a story that forms part of the Nordstrom mythology. It tells of man who returned defective car tyres to the company and received a refund. What's the story here? Nordstrom has never stocked this kind of product! Did it actually happen? Almost certainly not, but the story effectively uses exaggeration to make its memorable points, that (a) the customer is always right and (b) if the customer is wrong, you still make him or her *feel* as if they are right!

A certain suspension of disbelief is essential for creating stories that positively transform attitudes. What similar stories can you extract from Datalearn and suitably tailor to your business that will inspire your people?

Creating the story

This is ideally done as a group activity, because a shared view of your desired future is more likely to gain validity and ultimately acceptance. *The more diverse the group the better.* A wide range of minds – different levels of the organisation, different backgrounds and gender – is more likely to create a meaningful story. Less diversity in background will tend to a narrower view of the future and probably one that is wrong. Here are the suggested stages:

> 'New ideas come from differences. They come from having different perspectives and juxtaposing different theories . . . New concepts and big steps forward, in a very real sense, come from left field, from a mixture of people, ideas, backgrounds and cultures that normally are not mixed.'
>
> *Nicholas Negroponte*[2]

Fly a kite!

Most surveys reveal that people think the future is going to be rather like the present, only worse. This kind of thinking has prevailed for hundreds of years – Italian pundits of the 17th century were convinced that the world

---

[2] Co-founder and director of the innovative MIT Media Laboratory, a research centre that focuses on the study and experimentation of future forms of human and machine communication. A pioneer in the field of computer-aided design, he is also co-founder and columnist for *Wired* magazine.

economy was about to grind to a halt because of over-population and shortage of resources. *Plus ça change!*

The only way to overcome the gravitational pull of 'now' is to start with the future. Think of the future state you desire as a kite that you are pulling towards you. It's more useful than thinking of change as being like a rock you are straining to roll forward. As in the myth of Sisyphus, who was condemned for all Eternity to push a stone up a hill only to see it roll back whenever he neared the summit, working from now to the future can be depressing and limiting.

'The universe is change; our life is what our thoughts make it.'

Marcus Aurelius Antoninus (121–80),
philosopher and Roman emperor

In *starting from the future* be prepared to throw away all project plans with their milestones and deliverables. *Start* with the dream. Take your team to an unusual setting, away from the limiting realities of day-to-day operations. It may take great nerve and courage, but paradoxically *the higher you fly your kite, the more easily obstacles will disappear.*

Use the six 'I's

Add any future needs you believe your customers will have. And it's useful for individuals firstly to write in note form their own views of the future. In terms of team dynamics this will encourage the most effective ideas and not just the loudest voices to be aired in the discussion that follows.

Push beyond what seems possible

One of the warning signs that your ideas are not original enough is that they're likely to gain general acceptance. If nobody is stirred or shaken by the ideas they are likely to be yesterday's ideas. When physicist Niels Bohr observed that a colleague's theory couldn't be true because it wasn't crazy enough, he meant that it didn't push beyond the boundaries of what was already known and create the shock that genuinely accompanies new thinking.

The kind of thinking needed here is 'Why not?' or 'What if?' rather than 'Yes, but'.[3] If it's desirable, but outrageous, great! Don't censor at this stage. If what you would like to see for your customers is merely an incremental improvement on present performance, your competitors are probably already doing it.

Remember that what's possible in the future is always a big step – or at times a giant's leap – ahead of what the majority believe. *The leader's role is always to conceive the next impossibility to aim for.* Good leaders don't shy away from the job that should engage them most, creating a compelling vision of the future, which lifts people's eyes. In legends, giants do exist!

Put the customer at the heart of your thinking

So many visions of the future are inwardly-focused rather than customer-focused. Remember that you are looking to attain service that is legendary *as seen from the customer's perspective.* What will the customer of the future need, want and expect? And how will your organisation have to be transformed to make the customer's experience the centre of all you do? Will it merely satisfy them and what will it take to create a memorable experience?

Write your story

It's often practical for one or two people to do the actual writing – ever tried writing a mission statement in committee? – reflecting the thinking of all contributors. Make it as real as possible: names, numbers, settings, dialogue and so on.

Finally, check what you have written against the following criteria:

- Does it convey vital ingredients of the legend you would like your customers to be spreading?
- Is it genuinely futuristic?

---

[3] If you need further guidance on this, dip into Chapter 8: *What If? Why Not?*

- Does it communicate enough emotion/passion for the customer?
- Does it make you feel slightly incredulous?

Communicating the story

The primary focus for the story or stories you have created is within the organisation. This doesn't mean it can't be used outside as well. Marriott Hotels ran a series of successful one-page advertisements expressing commitment to their associates' (as they call their employees) sense of empowerment. It built on real stories of heroic service, such as receptionists rushing to the airport with a guest's forgotten passport, and so on.

But woe betide the organisation that tells these stories externally before it's built the internal reality to back them up. Many in the UK remember the Midland Bank's 1980s advertising claim to be the 'Listening Bank'. It's just that someone had apparently forgotten to tell their managers!

So how can you use the story of the future you aspire to, particularly in customer service terms, within your own enterprise? There are many channels.

Strategy planning sessions

The story can be used to create a powerful vision of the future which may then be backed up with harder targets – milestones, deliverables, key numbers, etc. For example, if you want to create on-site as well as online customer chat rooms, as in Datalearn, what are the practical steps you need to take?

Presentations

I remember a particularly powerful address – surprisingly from middle-management level – by a manager in a road rescue organisation, that told the story of how he would like his patrolmen to live, work, act and be rewarded in the future. He described how their daily life could be with specific details, the kind of vehicles they'd be driving, the tools available to them, how they would enjoy celebrating success together, and so on. The picture was inspiring to the right (the more visual or emotional) side of the brain for a rather cynical bunch of people. Several years on, at least half the story has become a reality.

Therefore, whenever you're talking about the future, use parts of the story you have created. When people can *see* the story of the future unfold in their mind's eye, your vision becomes a living entity.

Training courses

Painting a *'What if?'* scenario of the future you would like to have for your customers can be followed up with personal commitments to achieve that goal. The problem with many training events is that people are too burdened by the customer's current problems to see very far into the future. When delegates are asked to role-play the ideal future they would like to see for their customers, it doesn't have to be a fantasy. In a direct emotional sense they convey their present dissatisfaction as well as painting a vibrant picture of a more inspiring future. It's important to follow this with logical actions, but change begins when the heart is touched. The humour that is rediscovered also melts much of the resistance to the new.

Team meetings

In the same way that we've described the process for writing a story for the whole company, individual departments and functions should be encouraged to develop their own scenarios, aligned with the main legend. The more intimate the story is to our own sphere of influence, the more likely we are to take it seriously.

Play-acting

I once ran a conference for the senior management team of a Swedish company. For a number of reasons this organisation was in some turmoil about the future direction it should take. It had ambitious growth plans, but possibly lacked the financial muscle to back them up. Rational discussions on the issue had ground to a halt, and so my colleague Ian Taylor proposed a high-risk strategy that would invoke more emotion.

We asked them to put on a play using the metaphor of a well-known legend, myth or fairytale to describe the future the company was heading for. Dramatically, a group of senior managers used The Emperor's New Clothes as the storyline. A board member appeared dressed in nothing but a few Swedish banknotes.

The atmosphere was electric. Their message was that the company's share price was inflated and not backed up by enough tangible resources. And as in the story of the naked emperor wearing his new suit in public, a little boy from the press would soon point his finger to say that the Emperor wasn't wearing any clothes!

The chairman and other board members really got the message in a way that no amount of intellectual debate could have conveyed. The play had conveyed in a visceral way the future – in this case an undesirable one – and allowed the company to think backwards to measures it needed to take today to prevent this from happening. In a very practical sense it had learned from the future.

(Not the) final word

Try this process of creating your own case study of the future with those who are likely to be supportive, because for many it will be easy to mock. No one is an expert on the future, but predominantly rational thinking assumes it will be a sequential unfoldment of the present. It almost never is.

Every innovator has experienced waves of 'Yes, buts', that threaten to engulf his or her ideas. And if they are really ground-breaking there is likely to be a tsunami of objections. So you're in good company! Remember that many people are more comfortable with the status quo and are happier staying with a mediocre present (the known) rather than exploring a different future (the unknown).

Find your friends and supporters, and don't be surprised when the majority of people are better at raising objections than giving support. If you experience hostility and sniping from critics, reflect on *how* you are introducing the ideas. Conviction moves mountains.

If you are to be truly different and learn from your own best possible future, it's clear that your organisation *is* the case study. There are no role models, there are no perfect legendary service providers who we can look at to emulate. Of course, many of the examples in this book exhibit one or more of the characteristics of the ideal, while acknowledging that none is perfect and the horizon of achievement moves all the time. It's a never-ending story.

Great leaders, philosophers and spiritual teachers have so often used the story form for communicating their messages. The alternative is the vague exhortations contained in so many mission statements, such as 'putting the customer first', 'becoming the customer's preferred choice', and so on. And while numbers – 95 per cent on time delivery, for example – are essential for tracking how you are doing, they don't motivate many people to aim for something great. There aren't too many bar charts in the *Odyssey*.

For some penetrating questions, activities and ideas relating to this chapter turn to page 246.

Chapter Five

Develop Beginner's Mind

'In the beginner's mind there are many possibilities, in the expert's there are few.'

Suzuki-roshi (1905–71), Japanese Zen priest

'The only joy in the world is to begin.'

Cesare Pavese (1908–50), Italian poet and novelist

Developing beginner's mind will help you to:

- Understand your customers' Moments of Truth
- Become fully open to their perceptions
- Creatively shock yourself into a fresh start

ONE of the first questions people learn to ask about their own business is: 'What business are we in?' This is not a theoretical question. It determines where you focus your resources, time and energy, and the end result that the customer experiences. Using beginner's mind can help you to reframe what you're really offering to the customer:

'We're still in the entertainment business – at 25,000 feet!'

Sir Richard Branson[1]

This is not an empty slogan of Branson's because he's put his money where his mouth is. It's exemplified by beauty and massage treatments for Upper Class passengers, seat-back video and games systems for all other passengers, and great energy and flair in the attitudes of the staff. Virgin Atlantic is clearly in the business of delivering an *experience* as much as a comfortable flight.

---

[1] Branson chose the name Virgin 'because it reflected an inexperience in business . . . and also a freshness and slight outrageousness' (the *New York Times*, 28 February 1993).

Typically, Branson approached the airline business with fresh thinking. He knew almost nothing about it, *except* from the standpoint of being a dissatisfied customer. This gave him the great advantage of a 'beginner's mind', enabling him to make the transformation of the customer's experience his prime focus. To reinforce this, Virgin makes a point of recruiting as few people as possible from the airline industry to ensure its staff don't carry mental baggage from their experience with similar companies.

Like most beginners, Branson didn't know what was impossible. Contrast this with the attitude of many other airline chiefs too well grounded in the history of the industry to be able to change. As Professor Gary Hamel wrote in the *Harvard Business Review*:

'Experience is valuable only to the extent that the future is like the past. In industry after industry the terrain is changing so fast that experience is becoming irrelevant and even dangerous.'

While this point is easy to grasp intellectually, it's much more difficult in practice to escape from the clutches of the past. In other words, to develop an open, or beginner's mind where you see what customers want clearly *now*, unfettered by yesterday's experience.

Let's see what it takes to move our perception beyond the influence of past experience. What can you see in this image?

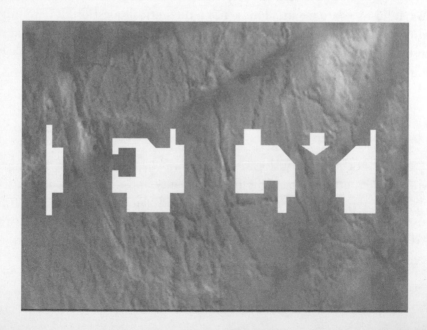

At first, many people see a jumble of shapes. Some see an arrow, or a tap, or a head. Try squinting or bending or looking at it with a sidelong glance. Eventually you will see the word FLY.

Several points come out of this experience. First, most people either see it or they don't. If they don't, it's usually necessary to give clues to help them.

To look at your own service through the customer's eyes is as difficult as switching this image inside out. We hear a lot about understanding the customer's perception, or even walking in the customer's shoes. It's easy to say this, but *very difficult* in practice because it means a complete switch of our perceptions.

Another problem is that once you've seen one solution, you stop looking for other, perhaps more interesting answers. This demonstrates the problem of experience – it has become an inhibitor to change and innovation.

This was brought home to me graphically by a client in the hotel industry who said: 'One month in a job and you go blind!'

By 'blind' she naturally meant that we stop asking difficult, curious questions, challenging assumptions about the way in which things are done and, even worse, losing the ability to think for ourselves. Einstein once remarked that it was amazing how people lost their curiosity after a formal education. Also their sense of mystery: 'The most beautiful thing we can experience is the mysterious. It is the source of all true art and science. He who can no longer wonder or stand rapt in awe is as good as dead, a snuffed out candle. . .'[2]

One month in a job and you go blind!

Mystery soon disappears for many after a few weeks spent in an organisation. A paralysing malaise of organisational life is that individuals often feel helpless to institute the kinds of changes they saw were necessary when they first took on the job. Customers end up experiencing too much inert expertise and not enough inspired amateurish helpfulness. We often forget that the word amateur comes from the Latin *amare*, meaning to love. To have the attitude of an amateur means greater enjoyment in what you do.

[2] *I Believe: 19 Personal Philosophies*, Allen & Unwin Publishers.

Too much attachment to the past may also make us blind to changes in technology. Writer Douglas Adams talks about the innate suspicion of people over 40 towards the Internet:

'I suppose earlier generations had to sit through all this ... with the invention of television, the telephone, cinema, radio, the car, the bicycle, printing, the wheel and so on, you would think we would learn the way these things work, which is:

a) everything that is already in the world when you're born is just normal;

b) anything that is invented between then and before you turn 30 is incredibly exciting and with any luck you can make a career out of it, and

c) anything that is invented after you're 40 is the end of civilisation as we know it until it's been around for 10 years, when it gradually turns out to be all right, really.

Apply this list to movies, rock music, word processors, and mobile phones, to work out how old you are.'[3]

Newness is all around us and yet we seem quickly to lose the ability to welcome its mystery with an open mind. We – that is probably anyone over 15 – already have a great deal invested in our own expertise.

To understand beginner's mind it is necessary to explore how perceptions are formed. Why do we lose our freshness? Why don't we see what the customer really wants? How can we continually reinvent our view of what business we're in?

The mechanics of perception

Nearly 30 years ago the BBC ran a series of documentaries presented by art historian Sir Kenneth Clark. It was entitled *Civilisation*, and covered the story of our modern world in a few hours. If you went out and made yourself a cup of coffee, you'd have missed the Renaissance.

With similar speed I'd like to address some findings of modern cognitive psychology so that we can get to grips with the nature of human perception and put this knowledge to good use in managing customer relationships.

[3] 'A Hitchhikers Guide to the Internet', The *Sunday Times*, 29 August 1999.

The visual, the mechanics of perception, illustrates how data from what we perceive is not received without judgment by our processing apparatus. The brain is not a blank sheet that faithfully reproduces an objectively accurate picture of the world. In a nanosecond we filter, select and match the input with our subjective receiving device, our *frame of experience*.

The mechanics of perception

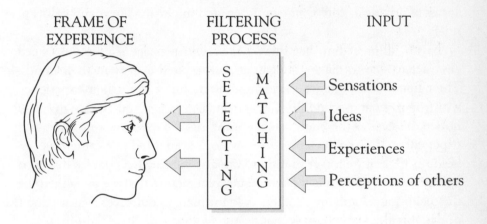

Our past experience influences what data becomes conscious to us. At a fundamental level this is a survival mechanism. Is that car really going to pull out of the junction in front of me? Is that person I've just had an argument with likely to hit me? Our antennae are constantly scanning the environment for these signs, alerting brain and body to prepare for action if a threat seems imminent.

In less dangerous situations, the same process of *selective perception* is still going on. Is this idea going to be useful to me? Should I believe this person? Will I enjoy this experience? Selective perception is the individual's bias, informed by past encounters, knowledge and preferences.

An amusing example of the quirky nature of human perceptions is the story of an elderly Australian woman who was asked: 'Would you like to visit England?' After a moment's thought she replied: 'No, I don't think I want to go there – isn't that where all the convicts come from?'

Think about how quickly our brain constructs a story about someone we are introduced to for the first time, or even when we observe a stranger sitting on a train or in a restaurant. I have often asked groups to introduce me after I have been working with them for half an hour or so. I might ask them to tell me how old I am, my education, my last real job, my marital status and number of children, the car I drive and what my dream car is.

It's amazing how people can construct a whole life history – often completely wrongly, but it makes sense to them – from tiny visual and verbal clues. No one ever says that they can't do this because they don't yet know me. Indeed, many say they would have made the same guesses within the first minute or two of meeting me. Some groups are even so certain of the answers that they will venture, for example, the names and ages of my daughters when I don't have any. I'm also intrigued to find that I come across as driving a Volvo, and am interested in playing chess and golf (I'm not).

This is all great fun, but there is a serious message – customers need almost zero *data* to make a judgment and to build a story in their minds. Their frame of experience selects and filters input from their experience with you in a nanosecond. In fact, customers – or you and I – don't usually notice the steps as the brain makes a meaningful pattern or story out of our experiences. If we compare the filtering box of our mind to a camera we are holding, it's as if we forget that there was any intermediary device involved and all we are left with is the end result, or a picture that we imagine to be the real thing. Our mental camera is so intimate to ourselves that we don't notice this filtering occurring. For us, the picture *is* reality.

The conclusions we can draw are:

- Perceptions are unique to the individual;
- Perceptions are created by experience; and
- Perceptions are 'real' for the perceiver.

So to know your customers it's necessary to switch off your own frame of experience and tune into how they perceive you *in their unique terms*. Remember, also, that their experience is not a purely cerebral affair – each experience will also connect to an emotional reaction, a reality that may cause them either to salivate or spit when they merely hear the name of your business. Or of your *industry*.

It doesn't matter what industry you work in because whatever great things you're trying to do now, your customers' frame of experience is likely to be tainted by the not-so-great past of your whole sector. Another reason to make a fresh beginning is to understand more fully your customers' perceptions. The most powerful way of doing this is to explore how, when and in what ways these perceptions form into what has been called the customer's Moments of Truth.

Moments of Truth revisited

The expression 'Moments of Truth' was coined by Jan Carlsson during his term as CEO of Scandinavian Airline Systems (SAS). He described how a customer's picture of a business is built up from very few contact experiences. In the case of an airline this might be the punctuality of planes, initial greeting from staff, clarity and fairness of pricing structure, the flexibility when you need to change flights and so on. Carlsson successfully switched his staff on to the understanding that from one or two critical incidents a customer would build up a mental image about the whole airline, positive or negative, depending on how well these incidents were handled.

For example, an unclean passenger cabin can easily trigger the perception that the maintenance engineers are equally sloppy. Not a logical link, certainly, but one that many customers will make. Perceptions often defy logic.

My definition of a Moment of Truth, building on our earlier discussion of the nature of human perceptions, is as follows:

> **Moments of Truth are specific
> mental snapshots which customers take
> of our business and use
> to run their own personal film
> of how well we are servicing them.**

Let's understand this more practically through the example of visiting a hotel. What's the first Moment of Truth? Most groups I ask suggest parking, the demeanour of the receptionists and so on. *Wrong!* The first moment of truth occurs well before you enter the door and it's outside the box that most hotels perceive. What have you heard about the hotel/hotel chain before you booked? And how friendly and helpful were they when you booked?

Then there's the hotel map or travel directions. I suspect that there's a special school of hotel cartography that delights in designing obscure or misleading directions. The guest-to-be is already making up her mind about you well before she encounters reception. I often find that the directions I receive are a product of too much inward focus – they're clear from the perspective of the hotel, but not as clear to someone who doesn't know the area.

Next, there's the greeting, offer of help with bags, cleanliness of the room, punctuality of room service, helpfulness of housekeeping, and so on. *All are distinct snapshots, blended swiftly together in the customer's frame to create a film, tailored to an audience of one, telling the story of the customer's unique experience.*

How many of these snapshots – Moments of Truth – does the customer need to play this film in his or her own mind? My customers say it's only one or two. Many make their judgments in the first few minutes, or even seconds.

Although it's a truism – and one that salespeople regularly trot out – that 'you never get a second chance to make a first impression', how many businesses have really absorbed this message? Marriott Hotels have it, focusing on the first 10 minutes of the customer's experience with alert bellhops and receptionists who are trained to make eye contact if the customer moves within a few feet (speaking distance) and to ask: 'How may I help?'

Marriott is on the right track, but its 10-minute focus is too long. *Three* minutes would be more effective as customers make their judgments – sometimes subconsciously – almost immediately, and if the initial exchange is not well handled it takes a lot more energy to recover the situation.

Michael Dell, head of Dell Computers, is the youngest CEO in history to head a Fortune 500 company. He realises the power of being open-minded to every step of the customer's experience, and talks about knowing your customers' 'pulse':

'We take our customers' pulse regularly – through more than 300,000 telephone, online, and face-to-face interactions every week – and we're constantly humbled by the experience. They've taught us things that have directly affected our success; they've kept us on course and prevented us from doing things that would have been disastrous.'[4]

Managing the perceptions of your customers is a critical part of delivering great service, and when the concept of Moments of Truth is explained to people, they realise its potential for tuning in to the customer more effectively.

[4] Michael Dell, *Direct from Dell*, HarperCollins Business, 1999, ISBN: 0002570696.

However:

- Customer service professionals often know the expression Moments of Truth – 62 per cent in a recent Service Legends survey – but a much smaller proportion (only 29 per cent) could describe what it meant clearly.
- A small proportion of line managers – around 18 per cent in our survey – know the concept. As they are the ones whose actions are most likely to affect the customer's experience, this seems like a dangerously low percentage. (We didn't attempt to get them to describe what a Moment of Truth was so as not to subject them to undue embarrassment!)
- Even when the concept is understood, it's rarely applied at the cutting edge where the customer experiences contact with the service organisation.

So let's consider how approaching your customers' Moments of Truth with an open or beginner's mind can put you more closely in tune with their needs and wants.

How to make Moments of Truth work for you

Mind the gap! Understand that the customer's Moments of Truth aren't yours!

Here is one of the great gaps that causes customers unhappiness – they feel you do not understand (a) their experience, and (b) how they interpret these experiences in their unique, emotional, subjective and idiosyncratic frames.

The gap is an intrinsic part of the human condition. Even in close personal relationships, *the number one human blind spot is the inability to perceive the world the way someone else does*.

Let's take the phenomenon of falling in love. Initially it's wonderful, in no small reason because at last I have found someone who is sensible, sensitive and perceptive just like the most sensible, sensitive and perceptive person I've ever met – myself. It's *selective perception*. I screen out the aspects of that other person that are completely different from or even at odds with my own character. I tune in to the characteristics that are familiar and comfortable to me.

And after six weeks . . . ? I start noting differences that could provide enough material to keep a therapist busy for the next 20 years. One of the main problems in relationships is the unrealistic expectation that all difficulties could be satisfied 'if only' the other person could be a little more like oneself, or could talk more about his experience of these differences in order to create better understanding.

Here I don't mean to be cynical about love. I'm merely pointing out that real love – based on an appreciation and valuing of differences – begins after 'falling in love' is over. After all, weren't you initially also attracted by the unique qualities of that other person? Now we are not usually called upon to fall in love with our customers but we can draw valuable lessons from our personal experience.

> **How you feel – not think – about your customers will help you to tune into their Moments of Truth more effectively**

Customers will quickly sense how you feel about them. Think honestly about whether you really value and appreciate your customers or whether you got into the habit of criticising them when they're not around.

The best customer relationships are like long-term personal partnerships, where the instinct is not to judge but to value and appreciate, even when the behaviour of the other seems curious. It's curious because it's maybe not what *you* would do, but will be consistent with the unique frame of experience of the other party. If you operate more from the heart and less from the brain you will tend to be more forgiving. And customers will sense how you feel about them. Try to seek the highest qualities in them or you may find yourself continually stressed.

In responding to your customer you need empathy at all times. Remember you're always dealing with an individual each and every time you're in contact, and each moment is a new beginning to the relationship for that customer.

Understand the power of expectations

Clearly a customer has a different set of Moments of Truth that need satisfying if he or she is eating in a roadside café or at a top restaurant. In general, the more a customer is paying, the more they will expect. It would be unreasonable to judge a Little Chef by the standards of the Ritz, and vice versa.

A phrase that has become common in customer service is 'exceeding expectations'. The problem with this is that expectations are often so low that exceeding them – though it may produce a transient moment of pleasure for the customer – isn't an exciting achievement. Sometimes we expect such a mediocre level of service that we become slightly suspicious when our low expectations are exceeded and it's extraordinarily good.

Le Manoir aux Quat' Saisons is one of England's finest restaurants, set in a lovely country house in Oxfordshire with its own walled vegetable garden. Walking from the drawing room to the restaurant I was rather taken aback by the experience of *seven* different staff members wishing me '*Bon appetit*' or 'Enjoy your meal'. Expectations had been built up to a grand level, and woe betide the organisation that fails to deliver after this kind of build-up. Fortunately, the meal certainly delivered the promise.

The message is that it takes more courage to consciously raise customers' expectations. If you can live up to this promise they will be more delighted than when you merely improve on mediocrity.

Ensure your internal talk is all positive

Those who are truly in love with their partners don't habitually speak ill of them behind their backs. In a road rescue organisation I worked with, staff had developed negative internal talk about their customers. They used the expression 'abuser' to describe people who called out the service several times a week, or who broke the rules by swapping one card between several members of a family. The problem was that this attitude tainted the company's perception of the 95 per cent of customers who were honest and merely expected delivery of what they had paid for. It's difficult to switch seamlessly from this negative mindset to presenting an all-helpful, positive approach to an honest but demanding customer.

This is a delicate balance. Customers are not perfect and, given a choice, your first instinct should be to support your own people. However, eradicating negative language about the customers will help to reduce negative encounters. Language is important. We know how hurtful a criticism or unfair label can be in personal relationships, but often forget this in the world of commerce where we're all meant to be so much thicker-skinned. Obviously, to speak well of others is an admirable principle in daily life and it applies equally to the profession of serving.

Embrace difference

Undoubtedly when you cross the threshold of your home in the evening you say something like: 'Darling, you're one in a million!' No? Well, even if you do, the intention is noble, but the statement inaccurate. According to some geneticists, your partner is one in 3,000,000,000,000,000,000,000,000,000, 000,000,000,000, unless he or she happens to be your identical twin, when the odds are slightly reduced.

In other words, individuals are more individual than we usually realise. So to serve each unique customer superbly in each unique encounter, it's vital to hold in our minds that this is never a routine, it's always a new moment that has never existed before and will never occur again.

This may sound idealistic or even spiritual. But that's how it is. Embracing difference means reaching out from one's own small isolated self to embrace a wider reality. If your consciousness – and your heart – is more expanded, then you can touch others with ease. If you are locked into thinking that your frame of experience *is* reality, you will be immersed in your own narrower sense of expertise, and find it more difficult to recognise and respond to the uniqueness of each of your customers.

But what are the signs that an organisation embraces the essential uniqueness and difference of each customer? First, they will take their experiences, however personal or even bizarre, absolutely seriously. Second, they won't use phrases like 'Well, no one else has complained!' or, 'Most of our customers prefer it this way.'

Also, you will experience that they give the most valuable of all currencies, *quality time*, to understanding your needs and wants. Almost nothing else can make you feel so valued – even loved – as time *given* willingly to sort out your request or problem. *Warning*: never use the word 'busy' within earshot of your customers. Of course you are, but if you do say it, your customers' Moment of Truth will be: 'Busy means too busy to attend to *me*.'

Beware the corporate radar – think wider, smaller and sooner

Corporate radar is often not sensitive enough to pick up the quirky and unique nature of some of the customers' real Moments of Truth. Because they exist outside your antenna's sensitivity they are too small to be picked up on your screen, or occur before your systems are fully alerted. Nevertheless they loom large on the customer's screen and may strongly influence his or her judgment of you.

This is where beginner's mind can be useful in understanding what's really important to the customer. One of Europe's leading motoring correspondents recently wrote that he was fed up with reviewing yet another lookalike 16-valve turbocharged machine, and would give anything for a proper glove compartment and two inches of extra leg room. Experts – the manufacturers – are in danger when they sneer at these apparently petty customer perceptions. They may talk grandly of ergonomics and customer-friendly design. They've just forgotten to ask customers, who naturally approach the whole experience with the naïvety of a beginner.

When I check into a hotel there are two trivial Moments of Truth for me that are apparently nowhere on the corporate radar screen. After paying £100 for a night I expect to be able to hang my suit on a proper hanger, not one of those unstealable but unusable devices that unceremoniously dumps it on the floor. Second, is there real milk for my tea, or do I have to put up with the UHT substitute, which I cannot stand? Trivial? Yes, but highly important to my experience as a humble customer. I've already rated the hotel as poor in quality just by these small omissions.

If you think that this applies only to the consumer experience, think again – because it's just as true for business-to-business. One of my clients provides some of the world's best lifting machinery. Technically it's excellent, delivery and maintenance are good and there are rarely complaints about product quality. However, customers are continually enraged by the almost incomprehensible nature of this company's invoices, claiming that even a qualified actuary would have trouble understanding them. Where is it on the corporate radar that you have to ensure clear paperwork, delivery schedules and invoices? Obviously, nowhere *inside* the supplier.

The message is simple – getting into the customer's frame means understanding that

- No Moments of Truth are too small for you to ignore – all must be taken seriously;
- What *you* think are their Moments of Truth almost certainly *aren't*;
- Customers make their judgments sooner and more quickly than you think, and
- They need almost no data to make these judgments.

Listening for Moments of Truth

What are your customers' most significant Moments of Truth? Remember the blind spot – they are almost certainly not what you think they are! How do you find out? There are two main ways:

- Ask your customers – open-endedly, naïvely and without judgment. This is *not* the same as looking at the results of customer surveys, which tend to ask the questions that are in your frame of experience, not the customer's.

Remember *not* to filter out the Moments of Truth that may seem insignificant or comparatively unimportant to you, but are vital to the customer. Specifically, focus on discovering which Moments of Truth occur outside, or on the fringes of your 'corporate radar', i.e. at the very first possible moment that the potential customer may hear about you, or first come into contact with you.

- Play-act having a beginner's mind about your own company, or even industry. What would you expect to be the critical encounters by which you would judge the service provider? What helps in this process is to have the innocence of a Forrest Gump. You know nothing, so you approach everything open-mindedly without judgment.

From these two avenues – deep listening and using your imagination to play-act innocently the customer's experience – you should be able to predict fairly accurately the key snapshots the customer takes of you and uses to form his or her overall impression. One warning – if the list of Moments of Truth you have come up with after this process is close to what you already knew, then you probably haven't done it right. 'Right' meaning with an open, beginner's mind.

One barrier can be your own personal head chatter. Head chatter is your frame of experience talking to itself and passing an almost unconscious expert's judgment on what you are hearing. Remember, this is as difficult as learning to love another, deeply understanding his or her needs and preferences. It's not going to be easy. Treat it as an ongoing process of discovery rather than as a skill to be mastered swiftly.

Naturally once you have identified (or re-identified) the customer's most critical Moments of Truth, mobilise yourself to address them and monitor improvements in the way the customer judges you. If, for instance, the customer is asking for a human sales assistant to speak to rather than an automated dialling system, how easy can you make this for him or her, and how clearly can you communicate that it is available? In the USA many customers pretend that they have an old-style rotary phone by not pressing any buttons when asked – they then achieve their aim of being able to speak to a real person. Finally, how can you demonstrate to the customer that this improvement in the service is genuinely the result of valuing his or her feedback?

Beyond staying in touch with your existing customers, listening to what they're saying with an open mind can also help your organisation to learn. Michael Dell understands this clearly when he says: 'Customer feedback also helps you benefit from the larger marketplace of ideas. There are hundreds, perhaps thousands, of companies in my business. If one company has a good idea, customers are quick to adopt it. They will say, "Gee, how come you can't do it like these guys?" Those are great learning opportunities.'

Most customers have had it 'up to here' with customer satisfaction questionnaires, which seem to disappear into some organisational black hole and have no impact on the perceived quality of service to them. There is no more powerful tool for bringing yourself into closer relationship with customers than *demonstrating* that their voices have been heard. In this way you can build a listening legend.

What happens when you don't listen to the customer?

What follows is an amusing example of how difficult it can be to listen in practice. Does this sound at all familiar?

> Here is some correspondence, circulated by e-mail, which actually occurred between a London hotel's staff and one of its guests. The London hotel involved submitted this to the *Sunday Times*.

> Dear Maid,
>
> Please do not leave any more of those little bars of soap in my bathroom
> since I have brought my own bath-sized Dial. Please remove the 6 unopened
> little bars from the shelf under the medicine chest and another 3 in the
> shower soap dish. They are in my way.
>
> Thank you, S. Stone

> Dear Room 635,
>
> I am not your regular maid. She will be back tomorrow, Thursday, from her day
> off. I took the 3 hotel soaps out of the shower soap dish as you requested.
> The 6 bars on your shelf I took out of your way and put on top of your
> Kleenex dispenser in case you should change your mind. This leaves only the
> 3 bars I left today. My instructions from the management is to leave 3 soaps
> daily. I hope this is satisfactory.
>
> Kathy, Relief Maid

> Dear Maid
>
> I hope you are my regular maid. Apparently Kathy did not tell you about my
> note to her concerning the little bars of soap. When I got back to my room
> this evening I found you had added 3 little Camays to the shelf under my
> medicine cabinet. I am going to be here in the hotel for two weeks and have
> brought my own bath-size Dial so I won't need those 6 little Camays which are
> on the shelf. They are in my way when shaving, brushing teeth, etc.
>
> Please remove them. S. Stone

> Dear Mr. Stone,
>
> My day off was last Wed so the relief maid left 3 hotel soaps which we are
> instructed by the management. I took the 6 soaps which were in your way on
> the shelf and put them in the soap dish where your Dial was. I put the Dial
> in the medicine cabinet for your convenience. I didn't remove the 3
> complimentary soaps which are always placed inside the medicine cabinet for
> all new check-ins and which you did not object to when you checked in last
> Monday. Please let me know if I can be of further assistance.
>
> Your regular maid, Dotty

> Dear Mr. Stone,
>
> The assistant manager, Mr. Franklin, informed me this a.m. that you called
> him last evening and said you were unhappy with your maid service. I have
> assigned a new girl to your room. I hope you will accept my apologies for any
> past inconvenience. If you have any future complaints please contact me so
> I can give it my personal attention. Call extension 1108 between 8am and 5pm.
>
> Thank you. Isabel Lopez, Housekeeper

> Dear Miss Lopez,
>
> It is impossible to contact you by phone since I leave the hotel for business
> at 7.45am and don't get back before 5.30 or 6pm. That's the reason I called
> Mr. Franklin last night. You were already off duty. I only asked
> Mr. Franklin if he could do anything about those little bars of soap. The
> new maid you assigned me must have thought I was a new check-in today, since
> she left another 3 bars of hotel soap in my medicine cabinet along with her
> regular delivery of 3 bars on the bathroom shelf. In just 5 days here I have
> accumulated 24 little bars of soap. Why are you doing this to me?
>
> S. Stone

> Dear Mr. Stone,
>
> Your maid, Kathy, has been instructed to stop delivering soap to your room and
> remove the extra soaps. If I can be of further assistance, please call
> extension 1108 between 8am and 5pm.
>
> Thank you,
> Isabel Lopez, Housekeeper

> Dear Mr. Franklin,
>
> My bath-size Dial is missing. Every bar of soap was taken from my room
> including my own bath-size Dial. I came in late last night and had to call
> the bellhop to bring me 4 little Cashmere Bouquets.
>
> S. Stone

> Dear Mr. Stone,
>
> I have informed our housekeeper, Isabel Lopez, of your soap problem.
> I cannot understand why there was no soap in your room since our maids
> are instructed to leave 3 bars of soap each time they service a room.
> The situation will be rectified immediately. Please accept my apologies
> for the inconvenience.
>
> Martin L. Franklin, Assistant Manager

> Dear Ms Lopez,
>
> Who left 54 little bars of Camay in my room?! I came in last night and
> found 54 little bars of soap. I don't want 54 little bars of Camay. I want
> my one bar of bath-size Dial! Do you realize I have 54 bars of soap in here.
> All I want is my bath-size Dial. Please give me back my bath-size Dial.
>
> S. Stone

> Dear Mr. Stone,
>
> You complained of too much soap in your room so I had them removed. Then
> you complained to Mr. Franklin that all your soap was missing so I personally
> returned them. The 24 Camays which had been taken and the 3 Camays you are
> supposed to receive daily. I don't know anything about the 4 Cashmere
> Bouquets.
>
> Obviously your maid, Kathy, did not know I had returned your soaps so she
> also brought 24 Camays plus the 3 daily Camays. I don't know where you got
> the idea this hotel issues bath-size Dial. I was able to locate some bath-
> size Ivory which I left in your room.
>
> Isabel Lopez, Housekeeper

> Dear Ms. Lopez,
>
> Just a short note to bring you up to date on my latest soap inventory. As of
> today I possess:
>
> — On shelf under medicine cabinet - 18 Camay in 4 stacks of 4 and 1 stack
> of 2.
> — On Kleenex dispenser - 11 Camay in 2 stacks of 4 and 1 stack of 3.
> — On bedroom dresser - 1 stack of 3 Cashmere Bouquet, 1 stack of 4 hotel-
> size Ivory, and 8 Camay in 2 stacks of 4.
> — Inside medicine cabinet - 14 Camay in 3 stacks of 4 and 1 stack of 2.
> — In shower soap dish - 6 Camay, very moist.
> — On northeast corner of tub - 1 Cashmere Bouquet, slightly used.
> — On northwest corner of tub - 6 Camays in 2 stacks of 3.
>
> Please ask Kathy when she services my room to make sure the stacks are
> neatly piled and dusted. Also, please advise her that stacks of more than
> 4 have a tendency to tip. May I suggest that my bedroom window sill is not
> in use and will make an excellent spot for future soap deliveries. One more
> item – I have purchased another bar of bath-sized Dial which I am keeping in
> hotel vault in order to avoid further misunderstandings.
>
> S. Stone

Mr Stone may have been a particularly demanding customer, but his experience, although extreme, reminds us that customers have unique Moments of Truth when it comes to experiencing service. The most powerful message to instil in your people almost ad nauseam is that *the only real market is the market of one. The individual.*

Keeping your frame open enough to understand your customers' Moments of Truth – their perceptions, their reality – is one major benefit of developing the outlook of a beginner. But it can also change the way you think about every aspect of your business with stunning benefits to your customers. The story of St Luke's advertising agency is a great tale of how approaching one industry with the mind of a beginner can successfully outflank the entrenched position of experts. It's followed by a checklist of mind-opening ideas you can use to challenge the accepted norms in your own business.

Beginner's mind equals an open mind

St Luke's is a London-based advertising agency that has successfully changed all the rules about how an agency should think and be. It was voted Agency of the Year by *Campaign* magazine in 1997, ahead of industry giants such as Abbot Mead Vickers and C & M Saatchi. It has been responsible for mould-breaking campaigns such as IKEA's full-frontal assault on the UK's taste for cluttered home furnishings, 'chuck out the chintz', and advertising the Boots No. 7 cosmetic brand without the use of glamorous models or even a photograph of the product.

In his inspiring book *Open Minds*, co-founder Andy Law[5] describes his company as one that has chosen to change the DNA of the business.

'St Luke's,' he writes, 'furiously seeks a new, better, more fulfilling and fairer role for business in the lives of its employees – who are all also its shareholders – and in the lives of the people it touches whether purposely or inadvertently.'

What is remarkable is that St Luke's doesn't even *sound* like an advertising agency. Its competitors are all called something like Bogelby, Bogart and Snark, a list of the founders' names. St Luke's is, in fact, the patron saint of creative individuals and doctors, expressing tersely the

[5] Orion Business Books, 1998, ISBN: 0752813889. St Luke's is the advertising industry's one and only co-owned venture.

agency's role of creatively acting as corporate doctors to their clients' sales or image problems.

But perhaps the most exciting feature of this business is its ownership structure, which to my mind is a real application of beginner's mind to what in many respects is a conservative industry. If you don't believe me, the other evening I watched nine TV adverts that used a 1960s or 1970s pop song as the backing score. Innovation factor: around 10 per cent; copying: 90 per cent.

Every employee, after completing a successful six-month apprenticeship, owns the company. 'Shares,' Law says, 'are distributed every year in equal proportion to everyone who has been in the company for the previous year.' This means receptionists, accounts clerks, *everybody*. Naturally there are two sides to this coin – if you're an owner you're more responsible to your colleagues as well as to yourself, but you will also be more loyal, committed and passionate about the business. Trust becomes the binding force rather than hierarchy. And there aren't many formal structures at St Luke's.

Law is perceptive when he says that ownership is better than empowerment. The word ownership is often used in major companies, usually in the form of a hopeful plea to the gods: 'Dear Lord, please let my people take more ownership and remove this weight from my back' is how the prayer runs. St Luke's has realised that only ownership brings true ownership.

This is not a business of crazy freaks uninterested in profits, however unconventional and zany their sense of fun may be. David Abraham, a co-founder with Andy Law, says: 'At the end of the day, are we still trying to sell more stuff? The answer is "yes".'

They certainly enjoy making money and have a great emotional investment in promoting the success of the business as well. It's just that they are tackling fundamentally the question of what a business could and should be like, above all creating an environment where people can be themselves and don't have to leave their personality and beliefs at the door.

Fortunately, their clients enjoy the offbeat yet professional style as well. In pitching to Virgin for the Eurostar contract, they threw out their fancy typed materials and turned up at Branson's house with just a sketch pad and a photograph of Eric Cantona, the unconventional French soccer star who later featured in the campaign when St Luke's won the contract.

A great example of orientating around the customer is St Luke's concept of Client Project Rooms. With a major client they will dedicate a room entirely to their project. The office space and mental resources of St Luke's are handed over to the client for a monthly fee, and the client contributes to how the space looks. This gesture of commitment to and collaboration with their clients became one of the most successful of their ideas. There are practical benefits for this as well. If a document relates, for instance, to Virgin, it will be found in the Virgin Room.

This way of organising your activities with the customer foremost rather than your own processes demonstrates powerful attention to a specific customer's issues and also greatly impresses him or her when visiting the business.

The reason I've chosen to focus on St Luke's is because it demonstrates wonderfully the power of approaching an industry and its customers with beginner's mind. All right, you may say, this is OK for a funky advertising agency, but what can I apply to my business?

Mind-opening ideas from St Luke's

- **Look at the DNA of your business.**
  What do people think they are there to do? What are their expectations of the work environment? Do they understand their importance in making the business tick? The extent to which you can tackle these fundamental questions will determine how the body of your department/function/company unfolds from its DNA.

- **Unlearn what you know about your industry.**
  Experience often creates limiting assumptions about how you should behave, dress, act and even what your physical environment should look like. Again, the problem with an assumption is that we don't know we're making it. Get those who don't know what's impossible to help you: articles, friends, people from other cultures and industries.

- **Create ownership.**
  I can sense a big and fair *Yes, but* coming here. If you are in a large organisation this may genuinely be outside your power, but bear in mind it's not a new idea. The John Lewis group, with 37,500 partners (employees) and sales of £3.5 billion, have had a form of staff ownership since 1928. In 1998 each partner received a bonus of 22 per cent of their annual earnings, roughly equivalent to 12 weeks' extra pay. So the moral is – lobby for ownership, it provides a direct route to winning people's commitment. The customer immediately feels the effect in a myriad of different and often subtle ways.

- **Organise around the customer.**
  What's your equivalent of St Luke's Client Project Rooms? You probably have more customers than they do, but apply beginner's mind to creating an environment where customers *see* that your focus is on them. Many companies claim to be customer-focused, but if you walked around the building you might see massive wall displays telling you how wonderful they are and barely a sign that the customer exists. Personal photographs, press clippings, issues that concern the client – all of these could be made into impressive and living displays that hit the customer in the face when he or she walks into your business. Forget 'employee of the month'. What about 'customer of the month'? Or of the week? Or even of the day?

- **Naming is important.**
  St Luke's broke the mould of the advertising world. Most people think it's a hospital when they first hear the name. You may not be able to rename your corporation, but you can apply an open mind to thinking what you call your department and your people. John Lewis has partners, Marriott has associates and so on. Of course, the naming is worthless if you don't back it up with commitment to the essence of what it means. And why not create *ad hoc* titles such as Chief Story-teller, Executive Vice-President for Mayhem and Amusement, or whatever reflects the real spirit of the job?

  Never underestimate the power of naming. If you have a Director of Customer Loyalty, or a Manager of Interactive Marketing it demonstrates your organisation's priorities. Always ensure that these people are never time-servers, but treat the role as a finite project rather than a self-perpetuating appointment. A vital benefit of these roles is to focus your whole business's attention on new priorities.

Shocking yourself into beginner's mind

A great deal of management literature today talks about the importance of continually reinventing your business. However, this can be particularly problematic when the existing ways of doing things have brought you success. If your tennis backhand is reasonable, it's more difficult to make the jump to being superb because it means letting go of what gets you by at present. Here are a number of ways to shock yourself into beginner's mind in order to unlearn what you think you know:

'Time for our weekly brain-stem-storming session.'[6]

Teach yourself ignorance

As adults we often act as if we know the answers. For instance, if somebody mentions a recent report or book on a topic you're meant to be knowledgeable about and you've never heard of it, how often do you find yourself saying something like 'Well, of course I don't remember all the details' while thinking to yourself, 'What the hell are they talking about? I'd better look that up later!'

To learn, we need to ask curious and even difficult questions. Next time you find yourself pretending to know the answer, particularly to a customer's query, try being bold enough to say either 'I don't know, but will find out and get back to you', or simply listen. We could call this the Columbo approach to learning, allowing oneself to ask incredibly naïve, even idiotic questions. By admitting his ignorance and not making any assumptions, the shambling TV detective elicits the information that enables him to solve the case. Try it!

[6] The Far Side by Gary Larson ©1992 FarWorks, Inc. Used with permission. All rights reserved.

Hang around more

Where do you get good ideas? Unlikely to be from sitting at a desk or in front of a PC screen. Try hanging around other parts of your business, or with suppliers and customers. Michael Dell, founder of Dell Computers, claims to spend 40 per cent of his time with his customers. When asked, 'Isn't that too much?' he responds, 'I thought that was my job.'

This goes against the grain of current industrial experience that says that every nanosecond of your time should be spent in concentrated, result-producing activity. But focused laziness, getting outside the usual routine box or physical environment, allows you to see the world with fresh eyes. Hanging around with customers can produce both very tangible results (remember the executives of Intuit software literally looking over the shoulders of users?), as well as greater empathy and understanding of how the customer feels and thinks.

Be a provocative customer

With mystery shopping – testing what it's like to be a customer of your own business – the best technique is to do your own. The one practical problem with this is it can make people tense and defensive if they feel you are checking up on them. The tip is to encourage everyone in the business to develop this same self-critical attitude, and to ask every day 'What would it be like to be a customer of this department/division/organisation?' Alex Camara, formerly head of Sainsbury's retail innovation team, likes to pose the question to his people: 'Would you pay for the service that you are giving to others?'

It means creating an environment where nobody walks past examples of poor service, irrespective of competence, experience in the business, or position in the hierarchy. Everyone needs to become a provocative customer.

Swap jobs for a week

A popular means of opening your mind to the customer is to swap jobs for a day. John Sculley of Apple Computers was well known for spending a day on the customer helpdesk, and even the chief executive of the RAC, the leading road recovery service, mans the telephones in periods of particularly bad weather.

But a single day simply isn't enough really to understand the pressures people are under in dealing with customers, or to experience a sufficiently wide range of issues to inspire positive change. And, most important, truly to feel what it's like to be continuously in direct contact with worried or aggrieved customers.

A popular TV series places chief executives in front-line roles in their own companies for a week. Why not make your own low-budget documentary to highlight his or her experiences? And why not take an even greater risk and ask front-line people, perhaps not to run the company for a week, but at least to shadow senior managers and to give them feedback on gaps between what they assume is happening with customers and the day-to-day reality.

Buy a new newspaper

It's comfortable to reinforce our existing frame of experience with ideas we consider to be sensible, for example like the ones that are already in our heads. A recent book industry campaign was entitled 'You are what you read'. And if what you read is the same political, social and economic view day after day, then to a large measure you will become that.

Reading broadens the mind only if you read broadly. So tomorrow go out and order publications and a daily newspaper that contain views perhaps the opposite of those you hold. I'm not suggesting that you buy *Pit Bull Terrier Weekly*, or *Pravda*, but that you keep your mind alive and awake by dipping into publications outside your usual field. I'm frequently amazed at how little the average manager knows of what is going on outside his or her own narrow concerns. The benefits of reading more widely may not be immediately tangible, but the longer-term result is usually a more open-minded view of the world. This helps to avoid hardening of the categories when new and untested solutions to customer issues are required.

Think like a child

We tend to remember the firsts in life – the first day we went to school, the first time we drove a car, fell in love, or went skiing. Life is a series of beginnings, but unfortunately, as people grow older there's a tendency to do more of the same and to create fewer new starts. No wonder an elderly person can't remember what he or she did yesterday, but can recall with crystal clarity the earlier events of life. This may be not attributable so much to neuronal decline as the fact that the earlier highlights were much more interesting and therefore more memorable.

I know of no better way to re-ignite the excitement of a fresh start, a new beginning, than to observe minds that are just being formed – children's minds. I'm convinced that the younger generation has developed genetic-ally modified hands to enable them effortlessly to use keyboards, control pads and computers. They don't seem to be at all threatened by the tech-nological revolution. How old is the worried character who makes the 'Over the Hill?' quote in *Microserfs*? 35? 45? No, 23!

> ### Over the hill?
>
> 'I wonder if I've missed the boat on CD-ROM interactive – if
> I'm too old. The big companies are zeroing in on the
> 10-year-olds. I think you only ever truly feel comfortable
> with the level of digitisation that was normal for you from
> the age of 5 to 15.
>
> Microserfs, *Douglas Coupland*[8]

We all know about getting the young to help us load software, but the innocence of their beginner's minds can also be invaluable in rethinking our lives. A couple of years ago, my son, then 10, was complaining about not seeing enough of me. I said to him: 'Jamie, I know that you think that I work too hard.' He looked at me thoughtfully and replied, 'No, Dad, you don't work too hard, you work *too much*!' This simple perception is one of the most revealing pieces of personal coaching I've had, and I have tried to respond to the common sense in it.

This doesn't mean that we should necessarily be asking 10-year-olds to run our companies, but rather that we should be aware how much the groove of experience can fetter our imagination. And though customers are, of course, not necessarily children, they, too, are not weighed down by too much knowledge of the inner workings of our industry. They don't want to know what's in the computer, they just want it to make their life easier. They often have no idea of the technicalities of their pension policy, but they want to know how this helps provide the security they need for their own unique, never-to-be-repeated situation. Adopting a child-like, open and curious attitude towards the perceptions of others, particularly your customers, will expand the range of possibilities for you.

For some penetrating questions, activities, and ideas relating to this chapter turn to page 248.

---

[8] HarperCollins, 1996, ISBN: 0060987049.

Chapter Six

Think *Both/And*

'The test of a first-rate intelligence is the ability to hold two opposed ideas in the mind at the same time, and still retain the ability to function.'

F. Scott Fitzgerald (1896–1940), novelist[1]

'It is only with the heart that one can see rightly; what is essential is invisible to the eye.'

Antoine de Saint-Exupéry (1900–44)[2]

Thinking *Both/And* helps you to:

- Understand that customers want efficiency *and* a relationship
- Develop your customers' positive feelings for you
- Remember that women are customers, too.

IF we've had some education we've probably been taught to think in adversarial terms – that *either* something is true *or* untrue. Unfortunately, this doesn't equip us too well for real life, which is much messier and abounds in paradoxes. What our education should have encouraged us to do is to think *both/and*, because this duality more accurately mirrors the complexity of real life. Let's explore how this approach to seeing the world and making choices can help us to understand the needs of our customers better.

Were you brought up with the idea that the Japanese are not creative, but simply copy? Most westerners born between 1950 and 1970 seem to have been infected by this misconception, in business terms an incredibly costly mistake for the West.

[1] *The Crack-Up*, ed: Wilson, New Directions, 1993, ISBN: 0811212475.

[2] *Le Petit Prince*, Harcourt Brace, 1943, ISBN: 0152438181. French author, commercial-airline and wartime reconnaissance pilot lost in action in World War II.

As a result, we failed to notice that the Japanese had a strategic weapon in the form of *both/and* thinking, and were applying it imaginatively to their commercial activities. Think back to the heyday of Japan's economic miracle. Initially, the European and American view was that surely the Japanese couldn't be producing great quality *and* providing highly competitive pricing. And how could they both copy *and* create anew? To take a famous example, how could they produce high-quality large motorbikes *and* the small bikes they first launched on an unsuspecting Europe?

The fact that the Japanese managed to do both successfully is a triumph over our conventional western *either/or* thinking. Even as they swamped the lower end of the market with motorbikes, they were already testing large machines on European roads.

Though it's now better understood that you can have good quality *and* a good price, reliability *and* speed of service, innovation *and* continuous improvement, an *either/or* perspective still colours much of our thinking because it's almost subliminally familiar. Most of us have been taught to split, dissect and analyse rather than to link, integrate and synthesise.

Either/or thinking has similarly hampered the ability of many businesses to relate to the customer's need for *both* an efficient service or product *and* the desire for their emotional needs to be satisfied. They have assumed that customers are primarily interested in price, quality and fitness for purpose. They have believed that as long as they were efficient, they would continue to thrive.

However, as customers we tend to be *both/and* thinkers, wanting a good price *and* great performance, speed *and* quality, efficiency *and* friendliness. Most significantly we want our rational minds to be satisfied *and* to feel there's an emotional connection. *This is the most important both/and for the future of customer service.* The rest of this chapter explores how to balance fulfilling the customer's emotional, or relationship needs together with their practical requirements.

The death of *either/or*

Both/and thinking forms a key part of any leader's work. How to keep the business performing, meeting its short-term quarterly targets while at the same time sowing the seeds of future long-term growth. How to increase both volume *and* margins. How to provide strong leadership while giving others their head. This need to think at both ends of the scale was well expressed to me by a managing director who said that taking his business through a major restructuring was like performing open-heart surgery while keeping the patient tap-dancing at the same time. In other words, to manage major changes with longer-term benefits together with keeping the eye on short-term financial targets.

Even the time-honoured notion that we should listen to our customers takes on a different light when we subject it to thinking *both/and*. Over-reliance on listening to the customer will drag you into a continual round of fixing yesterday's problems. Anticipating what customers might want in the future, but don't yet know that's what they want, is just as worthy of your full attention. The paradox is therefore: *listen/don't listen*. Or we could even say listen to customers with 100 per cent focus and ignore them in equal measure. You have to stretch your mind to both ends of this continuum to create success.

Another striking example of *both/and* is the need, increasingly recog-nised, for large organisations to be small in their thinking. Large because they want global reach, market share and widespread recognition of their brand, small because they also need to be innovative, fleet of foot and highly responsive. They want to have the attributes of a battle-cruiser and those of a small speedboat. No one has expressed this paradox better than Jack Welch of General Electric, who says:

'What we are trying relentlessly to do is to get that small-company soul – and small-company speed – inside our big-company body.'

Confusing? Yes! And yet the notion of *both/and* should be familiar to us because much of everyday life is taken up with balancing apparent opposites – career ambitions with family life, enjoying the present while building for the future, working hard and taking time to relax.

It's also familiar because, as customers, we buy with our feelings *and* our minds. Often we make a major purchase, like a house, a car, or a new set of clothes because we *feel* good about:

- How we will look in them;
- The individual selling to us, and
- The company we are buying from.

Whenever I am faced by a financial adviser selling me life insurance or pensions the logical side of my brain tries to pay attention, but inevitably goes missing for quite long periods. I recognise by the end of the conversation that I have little hope of being able to evaluate the validity of the proposal logically, but I *do* have a strong feeling as to whether I trust the adviser. I buy on the basis of trust. This doesn't mean my intellect doesn't come into play but, if I'm honest, a gut feeling that this is the right thing to do comes first.

Then the rationalising follows. Often we've bought something that we think we can't afford (logically) and so this side of ourselves needs convincing. I may read the papers more intently just *after* my purchase to convince myself that, yes, I did get a good deal on my car and yes, house prices are moving up so it was good to buy when I did.

Both mind and heart need satisfying. However, over the past century, business has been dominated by the rational approach, ever since F. W. Taylor's influential 1911 work *Principles of Scientific Management* launched us out on the path of analysing, measuring and calculating everything to death.

It's not that this approach was entirely wrong – it brought efficiency and predictability to business endeavour. It's simply that it's only one side of the picture. As customers we are even more fired by our emotional drives than by our rational needs. *We have served the mind. Now we need to feed the customer's emotions, too.*

Efficiency *and* relationship

What does *both/and* thinking really mean for customer service? Taking the example of running an airline, we can look at a basic model that explores the comparative importance of operational efficiency and quality of relationship to the customer. Among the operational factors are:

- Punctuality
- Safety record
- Efficiency
- Baggage retrieval
- Pricing
- Choice of routing
- Food and drink
- In-flight entertainment/information
- Seating
- Cleanliness.

We won't choose to travel with an airline where flights are always late and aircraft regularly develop faults, no matter how many smiling faces greet us. But getting the operational stuff right – an essential prerequisite for competing internationally – is not enough to impress and win our custom in the future. Aeroflot jokes still abound, but for most of us the operational factors are at best a dissatisfier. But I do love the comment by a US air traffic expert that operational quality could be defined as:

NUMBER OF TAKE-OFFS = NUMBER OF LANDINGS

The equally important *relational* side of the equation for an airline includes:

- Spontaneity
- Enthusiasm
- Added extras
- Interest and concern
- Recovery from operational glitches
- Good humour
- Being treated as an individual.

It's much more than people saying 'Have a nice day' interminably. It's a demonstration that at last three of the 'I's that customers want – Individuality, Imagination, and Intimacy – have been taken seriously and acted upon.

The customer's experience – 1

Great   Legendary
                                                                         Service

| THE HARD OPERATIONAL PREFORMANCE | • TAX AUTHORITIES
• BANKS
• FINANCIAL SERVICES PROVIDERS
• SUPERMARKETS | |
| | • GOVERNMENT UTILITIES
• RAILWAYS | • CORNER SHOP
• SMALL BUSINESS GENERALY
• HEALTH SERVICES |

Average

Poor   Average   Great

THE SOFT, RELATIONAL EXPERIENCE

Chart 1

Let's look at these dimensions of service – the hard and the soft – visually. Chart 1 is the result of 10 years of asking business groups how they would rate organisations they are familiar with. There's no science to this, but rather an intuitive response from their perception as customers. It's interesting that most groups I've worked with:

- Find it easier to choose inadequate suppliers than great ones;
- Rarely volunteer many examples for the top right-hand box, and
- If they do offer top-right box answers, usually come up with the same names – Virgin Atlantic, First Direct and so on.

Many successful organisations are put in the top left-hand box. Efficient, good value for money, but dull. Until recently this was no barrier to success, but competition in most sectors is now so intense that to become a legend it's necessary to go for the *both/and* of stunningly reliable products *and* a memorable relationship.

Think where you would rank your department or organisation. You can probably do this intuitively, but if you want to be more rational, use your own list of key operational and relational factors that your customers judge you by. These may indeed be their critical Moments of Truth. I suggest putting a limit on around seven factors in each list.

Of course, this is still intensely subjective and so a valuable next step is to get colleagues also to describe where you think you are on this chart, and *why*. My experience is that people invariably have different perceptions and the debate that explores the thinking behind the perceptions is invaluable. Prepare to be surprised.

While it's interesting and fun to rank other organisations, the real benefit of looking at service in this way is to rate your own business. Why not try evaluating where you think your company/unit/department appears on this chart. Put an 'x' where you think you are now, an 'x' where you think you need to be over the next year or so, and join the two with a line.

For instance, you may feel that you have sacrificed flexibility and relationship-building for rational measures of performance and therefore are too far over to the left-hand side of the model. Or perhaps you have recently over-focused on building a sense of empowered customer care with your people while neglecting to build the operational systems – IT, delivery, distribution – to enable you to fulfil promises to your customer. Here you might place yourself in the bottom right-hand box.

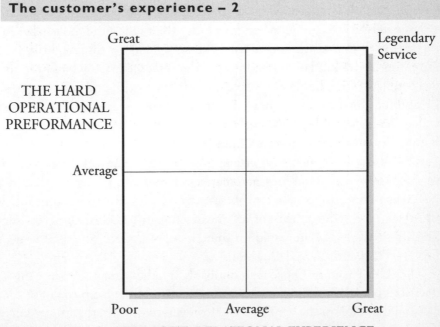

The customer's experience – 2

THE HARD OPERATIONAL PREFORMANCE

Great — Legendary Service

Average

Poor — Average — Great

THE SOFT, RELATIONAL EXPERIENCE

Chart 2

Then get a colleague or your team to rate the business. And finally, your customers.

If you want to make this more empirical, you can try articulating the key operational and relationship factors that make up the two scales, similar to the list of operational and relational factors on previous pages. These may indeed be the customers' critical Moments of Truth. I suggest putting a limit on around seven factors that make up the two scales, horizontal and vertical.

The most powerful check is, of course, the perception of your customers, whose views will rarely be the same as your perceptions from inside the business. Naturally, a judgment on one of the scales will influence a customer's rating of the other. For example, you may regard yourself as highly friendly, responsive and easy to do business with (relationally strong), but the customer may score you more poorly on this if you're having problems with product reliability and delivery (operational).

In filling out this chart the majority of us have a blinding glimpse of the obvious – we probably have a truckload of figures for the operational side of the scale and far less data on the soft stuff, the quality of relationship. This demonstrates again the potential gap between supplier's and customer's differing sense of priorities. Some organisations have been tempted to remedy this by applying operational thinking to the relationship of the equation. Beware of this!

One example is a fast-food chain where staff are trained to give customers two seconds of eye contact when they order their chips and milkshake. My suggestion to you, as an act of consumer assertiveness, is that next time you are eating at this kind of restaurant, give the server *four seconds* of intensive eye contact back. They are probably not trained for this and will need to go behind the chip machine to have therapy from the supervisor with all those badges on his shoulder. Customers want to be served by people, or robots, but not one masquerading as another.

One of the least successful attempts to operationalise the relational is illustrated by the ubiquitous automated telephone answering services. I have yet to find someone who can say a good word for them, other than those who are selling them, or are mean enough to count the costs supposedly saved. Many are based on the concept of addressing a customer's FAQs – Frequently Asked Questions.

The UK Passport Office can probably predict that 80 per cent of questions put to it will be about renewing a passport, replacing a lost one, or chasing the status of the application. However, aside from the frustration of waiting and punching a lot of buttons, 100 per cent of us will probably have, at some time or other, a question that does not fit the 80 per cent covered by the automatic system. That means that 100 per cent of us will be intensely irritated at our inability to speak to a human, even though we ask the same questions the machine was designed to address.

This technology gives the illusion of an efficient operation, but misses entirely an opportunity to build a personal relationship with customers. From an expense-saving perspective it may work, but has anyone evaluated the cost of the lack of human contact? While this may not be important to public bodies that are monopolies, it can certainly damage anyone operating in a competitive arena.

So where should you choose to focus your energy to provide an all-round great experience for the customer? To a great extent this will depend on how you rated yourself – and how your customers rated you – on Chart 2. But the blind spot for most organisations is that they over-focus on the operational side of the equation. In other words, resources, time, money and effort are put into areas that make relatively little difference to the customer's perception. People will forgive you a great deal, even occasional major product defects, if the relationship is right.

'The customer relationship itself is the asset . . . a company that has established a relationship based on trust with its customers possesses a priceless asset.'

Leif Edvinsson and John Richardson [3]

If you forget this you may waste energy improving what the customer doesn't value at all. Take, for instance, electronics giant Motorola's obsessive focus on hard, measurable product quality, often called the pursuit of six-sigma quality – 99.9999 per cent product reliability. Meanwhile the market in mobile phones was being stolen from it by people who focused *both* on product *and* back-up and service quality. Telecom companies such as Nokia and Ericsson also used a weapon I would place in the relational camp, customer-loved DESIGN.

As a customer, it's hard for me to comprehend what total quality means to me – but I can buy beauty. I can relate to it. That's why I would add it to the list of key relational items you have to get right if you want to attract customers. It's not surprising that in 1998 Nokia's Christmas advertisements for its mobile phones featured not one technical detail or a single price, but focused on a variety of attractively coloured covers that you could slip onto

[3] *Strategic Trends in Services: An Inquiry Into the Global Service Economy*. Edvinsson was formerly vice-president and corporate director of Intellectual Capital at Skandia, Stockholm.

your elegant handset. Swatch thinking (a different coloured strap for different occasions) – rather than McThinking (the same process everywhere) had come to the world of high technology.

> **As a customer**
> **I can't really judge total quality – whatever that is –**
> **but I can buy beauty.**

Relationship makes the difference

Perhaps business shies away from focusing on elements that create relationships because they are less tangible, less easy to measure and necessarily more subjective. It runs counter to the scientific principles of management that still drive so much decision-making. This is true even though a great deal has been written on the predominance of the emotional connection in bonding customers to a particular supplier.

Hard-nosed entrepreneur Charles Dunstone, founder of the successful Carphone Warehouse mobile phone company, believes the emotional side of customer relationships is important enough to articulate in his brand values:

Rational mission	Emotional proposition
Recognisable brand	Innovative
Impartiality	Young
Meaningful guarantees	Friendly
Wide range	Unconventional
Knowledge	Customers' champion

Dunstone clearly understands the importance of relating to the whole brain of the customer and to that of his own people, even though for me his emotional list is still too rational. But he's made a valiant attempt to be up front about the softer aspects that most businesses find so difficult to focus on.

Robin Reid, a former managing director of Mobil's giant refinery in Essex, said to me: 'The soft stuff is hard! But it's what really drives the business. Attitudes, commitment, teamwork, innovation, passion for the customer – that's what's going to make you stand apart, rarely the products, delivery and price. With the hard stuff you have to be in the same range as your competitors. Better if you can be. With the soft stuff, there is no limit to what you can achieve.'

Our love affair with technology can endanger our closeness to the customer in soft emotional terms. It doesn't need to, as the earlier section on the Internet in Chapter 1 demonstrates. However, the wizardry of the system can be seductive and blind us to the need to reach out more to our customers. A recent article in *Business Week* headed 'E-Retailers Aren't Reaching Out Enough'[4] describes how Internet retailers are ignoring many of the opportunities for relationship-building that the new technology should give them.

To demonstrate this, the marketing software firm Rubric Inc., based in San Mateo, California, got 50 people to buy 50 dollars' worth of products at one of 50 top websites. The results were as shown in the 'Missed Opportunities' box below:

Missed Opportunities		
	Yes	No
Did the site ask you if you wanted information on related products?	53%	47%
Did the site send a follow-up marketing offer?	16%	84%
Were marketing communications personalised?	4%	96%
Did the site recognise you as a repeat buyer?	25%	75%
Did the site respond to your e-mailed questions?	60%	40%
	Data: Rubric Inc.	

Analysing these figures provides some interesting findings. Staying in touch with customers and clear, timely communications are surely the basics of building a strong relationship, but with only 16 per cent being sent a follow-up offer, and only four per cent of communications personalised, it seems these simple principles have been ignored. Again, any good relationship is two-way and only a 60 per cent response to e-mailed questions demonstrates a fundamental lack of awareness of the power of dialogue in building loyalty. Note that nowhere does the research say that the technology failed, so the retailers may have a misguidedly positive view of how well they are doing.

[4] 2 August 1999.

Again, remember the *both/and*. There's a strong interplay between the two aspects as reliable products make a relationship easier, while friendlier staff make operational hiccups more acceptable.

But to remedy the imbalance in most organisations, let's plunge into the business of managing the customer's feelings. Or as I call it, Finding Your Service Heart.

Finding your service heart

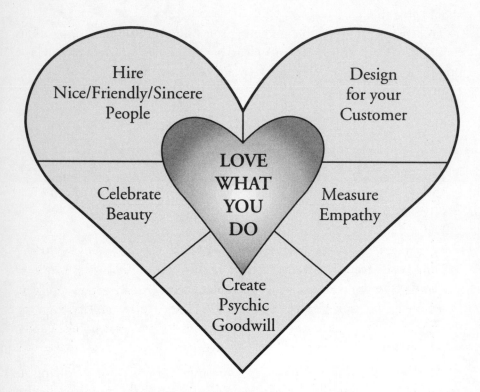

There are five chambers in the service heart:

- Hire nice/friendly/sincere people
- Design for your customer
- Measure empathy
- Create psychic goodwill
- Celebrate beauty

And finally, in the centre: love what you do. I've ranked these from the most to the least tangible. Let's explore their impact in building closer relationships with your customers.

Friendliness, niceness and sincerity

Ken McCulloch, founder of the superb One, Devonshire Gardens Hotel in Glasgow and more recently the Malmaison chain, says the secret of his hotel's reputation for service is to hire nice, friendly people. And for his customers the great service experience isn't an add-on – it's a natural spilling over of the personality of his people into a job they (mostly) love.

The simple observation that nice people tend to deliver good service is *so* obvious that it's seen as beneath most managers, especially in a world where we still talk of humans as resources. Niceness and friendliness do not fit most complex models of competencies and, as they often elude precise psychological definition, are excluded from most recruitment processes. But it's clear that *there are many people in service roles who shouldn't be*. They don't have either the temperament *or* the skills and, of these two, a service temperament is the real gem.

McCulloch puts four penetrating questions to would-be recruits:

1. Do you understand what we're trying to do here?
2. Can you deliver it?
3. How?
4. When?

He is a sincere but canny man who is actually looking for a lot more than mere niceness. He says to his people: 'Welcome to the greatest industry in the world – you may start washing dishes, but you can get to the top anywhere in the world.' This is inspiration *plus* niceness, and no wonder Malmaison hotels have won the Tatler award for the best hotels in the world under £100. Let's add to niceness and friendliness the word enthusiastic – McCulloch says that he employs only enthusiasts and observes that if you build a great place to work you'll attract great people. And here's the passion: 'We hate mediocrity,' he says.

But like most great enthusiasts – and Ken McCulloch is the kind of man you really believe when he says, 'I *love* this business' – high aspirations are backed up by fanatical attention to detail. Every employee carries a pocket card that sets out the grand plan in everyday language and behaviour:

* Take responsibility;
* Know your subject;
* Be enthusiastic;
* Look immaculate;
* Be positive;

❋ Prepare for service;
❋ Communicate with each other;
❋ Be yourself, and
❋ Enjoy yourself.

Do your people have an authentic and meaningful list to refer to? It goes without saying that the management of Malmaison hotels live by these authentic messages and that a plastic card of second-hand values won't work. Much thought needs to go into creating the friendliness and sincerity that most businesses find so hard to demonstrate to their customers.

When Newcastle United's manager Ruud Gullit resigned from his job, his short thank-you speech included a dedication to the staff who had been looking after him at the Malmaison hotel. As he has a reputation for being hard to please, this was a great accolade.

Why is being likeable so important to customers? In his new book *Why Customers Like You*,[5] customer service expert Dr David Freemantle describes how business has over-relied on IQ and under-invested in developing EQ, or the emotional intelligence of its employees. As most service work involves a strong emotional element this is an extraordinary omission.

Freemantle says: 'Emotional connectivity is at the centre of all relationships, and is thus at the centre of excellent customer service (as opposed to automated, mechanical service).' The conclusion is so simple that many organisations may think it simplistic. If people like you they'll be more drawn to repeating the experience of doing business with you. A likeable organisation means an aggregation of likeable people who are providing the millions of Moments of Truth per year that their customers experience.

This is part of Service with a big 'S' because people are not merely buying your product or service, but the values that you stand for. They are buying the intangibles of sincerity, trust and likeability that are embodied in the likeable, sincere individuals who serve them. As Ben Cohen and Jerry Greenfield, founders Ben & Jerry's Ice Cream, say: 'Our customers don't simply like our ice cream – they like what our company stands for. They like how doing business with us makes them feel.'[6]

[5] Nicholas Brealey, 1998, ISBN: 1857882016.

[6] *Ben & Jerry's Double Dip*, Simon & Schuster, 1997, ISBN: 0684834995. The story of Ben and Jerry setting up shop after taking a five-dollar-correspondence course in ice cream-making is just about in the realms of folklore, but why not have some fun and check out their website at www.benjerry.com to explore their mission statement, the Ben & Jerry's Foundation and their library? And you can have a virtual drool over the latest flavour, now packed in eco-friendly, unbleached paper cartons.

It's the same when people buy from The Body Shop (environmental values), Virgin (youthfulness, innovation and what Branson himself describes as 'cheeky'), and L. L. Bean (integrity and fairness).

However, I think it's naïve to connect likeability alone with profitability. I wish it were true that the most likeable organisations were the most successful, but it certainly isn't so, yet. Think of the world's top organisations as measured in purely commercial terms. Like them? Not necessarily, but I share with David Freemantle an act of faith that the future need not be like the present.

Design for your customers

Great design is something we buy with the right side of our brain – the curves of a Nokia 'banana' mobile phone, the minimalist lines of a Bang & Olufsen television set, the reassuring solidity of a Grolsch spring-topped lager bottle. A well-known writer on science recently wrote how captivated and 'in lust' he was with the design of his new mobile phone. The 'feel' of design can penetrate the logical brain of the most hardened consumer.

But design is not just about product. It's also about the customer's experience of service. For instance, how good it is to go to a website that's really been designed with the customer in mind.

Hotels can learn from this, too. I'm already favourably disposed to those where you can fill in the details of your registration card when you get to your room and bring it down in your own time, instead of fumbling for your passport number in a reception desk queue.

Many systems seem to be designed, at least in the UK, as anti-customer arrangements. Oxford railway station is a prime example. For my mother to cross the station to the far platform is an irksome trek and trolleys are usually tidied away so you reach them only *after* you have towed heavy bags almost the whole way to the taxi rank. British trains are also designed to be as tricky as possible for people to load their baggage on to. A great deal of planning must have gone into this.

Here's my Top Ten and Bottom Ten of products or processes designed with the customer in mind, or not. The most important point to recognise is that the Top Ten were all created *by design*, with the exception of laid-back Dutch taxi drivers: design that is sensitive to the customer's experience. The Bottom Ten is created, or allowed to happen, by focusing inwardly on your own operation rather than outwardly on the customer's experience. Note that the distinction between product and service dissolves here in my perception – as it does for all of us when we are customers.

Customer Design – My Bottom Ten

1. The queuing system in the tunnel before boarding a plane.
2. Stainless-steel teapots that pour everywhere but into the cup.
3. Price stickers on perfume that ruin the packaging when you try to pull them off.
4. Hotel check-in procedures.
5. Water-saving taps in motorway service stations that deliver such an uncontrollably powerful jet of water that you can have a shower without taking your clothes off.
6. Paying systems at self-service restaurants – the food is usually cold by the time you've paid and found a clean table.
7. The siting of petrol pump numbers at self-service stations – they are always invisible from where you pay.
8. Milk cartons in the UK – advanced psycho-motor skills are needed to open one.
9. Automated telephone answering systems that provide no clue of which option to press – you listen to a whole Phil Collins album before you get to speak to a human being who might know.
10. Hangers in hotel rooms that cannot be detached – unstealable, but unusable.

Customer Design – My Top Ten

1. The book-ordering system on amazon.com, especially how it keeps you in touch with the progress of your order.
2. Hotels where I don't have to fill in a registration card.
3. Most products from Sony – they feel good *and* work well.
4. Copenhagen airport – how relaxing to walk on wooden floors when you're changing flights.
5. Staedtler coloured felt pens – German-made, and the ink actually flows.
6. The way Dutch taxi drivers swipe your credit card just before you arrive – no waiting.
7. The solid feel of a Mont Blanc pen.
8. Restaurants where the staff play with customers' children.
9. The hour-glass timer you tip up while queuing at some US car hire firms – if it runs down before you are served, you get big discounts.
10. The eye contact Asda supermarket staff make with you – and the impression they convey of never being too busy to respond.

Customer-led design should not be sidelined as mere product design. It needs to be applied to every process the customer goes through. This is a wonderful opportunity for creating synergy between customer service professionals and great designers. *Where is your service process designer?* If the job doesn't exist, it's necessary to invent it. The prime focus will be to look at everything that touches the customer in the light of design that will improve, quicken, simplify and charm them. We need to put the art back into service, as a healthy counterpoint to the pseudo-science it's threatening to become.

What about:

- The ergonomics of the queue (physical and telephone)?
- The beauty of the ordering system?
- The aesthetics of the delivery?
  or even
- The chemistry of the check-in?

Finally, we can learn something about design from the creative act of making music. Bob Dylan once remarked that he liked to keep the structure and format of his songs as tight and narrow as possible in order to allow a clear channel for emotion to flow through. This is a great metaphor for customer-centred design – the more simple, clear and beautiful your systems are, the easier it is for your people to have the time and energy to relate emotionally to your customers.

They can manage the relationship, not the system.

Measure empathy

Outside a Georgian building in Abingdon, near Oxford, a plaque describes the business of its occupants as Empathy Architects. Though a few visitors have dropped by to ask whether they could have a new conservatory or bathroom designed for them, Harding & Yorke's business is measuring the empathy rating of its major blue-chip clients.

They do this by analysing scores of customer contacts over the telephone, in writing and face-to-face, based on the conviction that this Empathy Rating™ is an accurate assessment of how it feels to be a customer as well as a profound analysis of the underlying culture creating those feelings.

Founder John Pearson says: 'In the long term, empathy may well become as fundamental to every company as quality or profit.' He points out that even exceeding expectations on operational matters can create problems. Giving customers more than they expect – such as doing it cheaper, faster, better, and giving away freebies – actually resets their expectations and becomes the new norm.

Since this usually costs more and you end up little further on than when you started, it's a bit like chasing your tail. As a result it is rarely, if ever, that you find a company's success is based solely on this approach. If you merely shower customers with extras they'll say: 'Thank you very much,' but this won't in itself achieve long-term loyalty.

Loyalty is more likely to be achieved by focusing on the *way* you do it, as much as *what* you do. Many attempts at relational improvements are based around *avoiding upsetting customers* rather than putting effort into making them feel good. This usually means being pleasant to them, but it's not enough. Everyday experience tells us that when we as customers get what we ask for, and it's done in a pleasant enough manner, we don't suddenly say how brilliant it was and start to sing the praises of the supplier. *We hardly even notice.* To be served pleasantly with what we asked for has simply become our expectation and doesn't move us one way or the other.

Empathy, however, is far beyond just being nice to one's customers. We could describe this as being right at the top of the relational scale in our earlier model. It encompasses relationship and rapport building, making the customer feel important and valued in his or her individuality. The dictionary definition describes empathy as having the ability to identify one's self mentally with a person and so understand his or her feelings.

Empathy means using your imagination to understand what the customer feels. It is not about being lovey-dovey or using 'Have a nice day' slogans. It's about making customers feel good by giving them individual service. And it necessarily implies being flexible to the different styles of your customers. Some people feel good when they have a short, efficient and courteous transaction. Some like a more personal approach. There is no single formula for getting this right – it requires ability and flexibility to recognise the other's needs, to put yourself in his or her shoes and relate appropriately to that person.

The hotel industry has defined its guests as falling into the categories of 'relators' or 'isolators'. Relators love the staff to know their names and to develop a relationship with the porter, the receptionists and even the chef.

Isolators, on the other hand, like to close the door and see hotel staff only when they need something, such as a fax or a room service meal.

I recognise that in a hotel situation I'm often an isolator. The staff think they are being empathetic when they continually knock at my door asking me if they can turn down my bed, check my minibar, or give me a free invitation to cocktails. It has the opposite effect on me because I experience no great feeling of empathy to find my bedcovers turned down and a chocolate awaiting me. Next to 'room service', to me the finest words in the English language are 'do not disturb'.

It takes sensitive staff to respond appropriately to each individual guest's need for a certain style of service rather than following a 'one size suits all' philosophy. It takes empathy.

Of course, to be able to respond empathetically to customers is based on first feeling at ease with yourself. Many people in service roles are stressed and unable to screen out the interference of their own anxiety and to tune in to the signals that the customer is sending. If you're stressed, you can't be empathetic.

If organisations are serious about the wellbeing of their people, they will help them not just to learn how to do, but also how to be. There is a great wave of interest in relaxation techniques, but most are faddish and short-lived in their results. In fact, I would call it the relaxation scam. If a consultant turns up at your door offering to play relaxation tapes or to guide your people through progressive muscle relaxation it should make you, paradoxically, rather stressed because it isn't going to be effective.

But in many companies I work with I notice that the people who give the best service tend to be those who have some method of experiencing the still point of their turning world and to regenerate themselves from within. Something more profound than mere relaxation.

The one I have direct experience of sounds weird, but it works. It's a technique called Transcendental Meditation (TM), which I've practised for more than 20 years. It's a simple mental practice performed twice daily for 15 to 20 minutes sitting quietly with the eyes closed. It has the advantage that it's free from any religious belief system and doesn't require a change in lifestyle. During TM, people naturally achieve a state of restful alertness, that produces profound mental and physical benefits. Research has shown that high blood pressure is reduced, together with heart rate, and most measures of stress and anxiety. The positive effects of this profound state of rest continue into the working day.

Giving good service depends on being relaxed, but also highly focused and not thrown by the inevitable high demands of your customers. My experience of TM is that it helps you to feel this way. It is not simply a nice idea, like the purely intellectual nature of most customer service training, but actually changes your physiology so that you can stay calm and focus on what's important even in a highly pressured situation.

There's also considerable research on TM in organisations. In a five-month study by the Japanese Institute of Health it was found that over 400 workers who learned TM showed significant decreases in anxiety, emotional instability, neurosis and sleeping problems. And in America a long-term study showed notably lower health insurance utilisation among 2000 subjects practising TM compared with 600 controls who were clients of the same health insurance carrier. Organisations seriously concerned with rising health costs might also look at the study of TM practitioners in Canada, which found a significant reduction in health care costs – on average 10 per cent per annum.

To relate better to customers the first essential relationship to create is the one with yourself. This is a more precise way of understanding the obvious truth that empathy comes from within.

Create psychic goodwill

Psychic Added Value is an expression coined by management writer James J. Lynch.[7] He defines it as: 'The boost a customer experiences when using a product or service.'

Lynch argues that there are six major sources of psychic added value:

Enhanced self-esteem   – customer made to feel important in the eyes of the service provider.

Reduced anxiety   – fears and concerns, identified, articulated, and assuaged by behaviour of service provider.

Increased self-confidence   – customer made to feel proficient in use of equipment, knowledgeable in understanding of advice or service offered by service provider.

Comfort   – customer made to feel physically and mentally at ease by caring ambience and behaviour of service provider.

Social status   – customer made to believe that product/service will enhance social status.

[7] *The Psychology of Customer Care*, Macmillan, 1992, ISBN: 0333557697.

Reassurance   – customer convinced that decision to buy
                                   goods or service is the right one.

Here's the core of every relational customer service improvement. Build training of your people around these issues rather than vague exhortations to treat the customer well and they will begin to tune in to some of the real needs of your customers as human beings. I'm not suggesting we turn everyone into therapists – a nightmarish prospect – but to build a legend the foundations need to be solid and they are made so by your people really 'getting' the *why* of great service.

This knowledge can be drawn out of – the real meaning of educate – good people by remembering how as customers themselves, their own self-esteem and confidence has been battered by unhappy service encounters. It's also a great list for use *internally*. The same factors should drive the manager or supervisor of service people to create a culture where people boost each other's self-esteem inside the organisation.

An objection I've heard to this line of thinking is: 'Wait a minute, my people are *only* answering the telephone (or driving trucks, or managing reception). Why do they need to know all of this?'

My problem is with the word 'only'. Any role can be turned into an art form, as you will discover in the section ahead on how to celebrate beauty. But the real reason is that the customer has a radar that can detect insincerity when someone has been trained in the *what* rather than the *why* and *how*.

A few years ago I checked into a five-star hotel in the south of England. Some receptionists, such as the one at this hotel, compete to see how quickly they can slap a registration card in front of you without eye contact – little psychic added-value here. As I walked to my room, heavy bags in hand, she called me back. 'Excuse me, sir,' she intoned listlessly, 'but I forgot to give you your welcome card.' She then off-handedly pushed a small pre-printed card towards me. She knew *what* to do – forgetfully in this case – but gave me, the customer, the impression that she had no idea *why*.

As I run a conference business and book many hotels, I can be rather harsh as a customer. I haven't used that hotel again. I wouldn't say my self-esteem was damaged, but the encounter didn't reduce anxiety or increase my feeling of comfort.

Of course, humour is a great way to reach out to others and give them a boost. Naturally, this can't be prescribed, but in Virgin Atlantic the flair of its cabin crew expresses itself in easy humour. One cabin crew member, Chris Marley, who was asked by a passenger the name of an island they were flying past, replied: 'I don't know, dear, we usually don't get this far!'

Celebrate beauty

What's a word like beauty doing in a business book? Because it's behind any endeavour to create something great, to bring something better into the world. Tom Peters describes this wonderfully when he talks about the Michelangelos of Housekeeping at Ritz-Carlton hotels. Customer service writer Chris Daffy reinforces it when he recounts a Nile cruise holiday where the high point for his friends was returning to their cabins each night to see the beautiful configurations the housekeepers had shaped the towels into – swans, boats and palaces. The floor attendants at the Oriental Hotel, Bangkok, display this in every graceful and elegant movement they make just in bringing fresh orange juice.

> 'Have nothing in your houses that you do not know to be useful, or believe to be beautiful.'
>
> *William Morris (1834–96) craftsman and poet*

Beauty is often *simplicity*. Mathematicians talk about a beautiful solution that is often the most simple. What did we do before Post-it notes?

Behind this is a belief system that customers deserve (and even crave) a little beauty in their lives. I've observed that the best sales representatives in New York stores seem to be engaged in a kind of ritual dance, as if they're in the movies. Even the way they count your change or close the till has a certain energetic dance to it.

Dancing in customer service – why not? A relationship is rather like an intimate dance. Dance also has more religious connotations – dervishes whirl, gospel church congregation members rock, people in many spiritual traditions shake easily with bliss and laughter. Hindus believe that the universe was created through the cosmic dance of the god Shiva.

Why shouldn't hotel receptionists, retail staff and even telemarketers dance for their customers? Or, to push the idea even further, why not use the metaphor of religion to talk about blessing each service encounter? In a Greek monastery shop on the island of Corfu, I picked up a small icon and asked the priest how much it was. He gently took it from my hand, kissed and blessed it, and handed it back to me. Needless to say, I bought it. Sharp sales technique or real beauty in service? No contest – I loved the process and still recall it 15 years later.

It started me thinking of service exchanges as potentially carrying a curse or a blessing. If we feel blessed, we've been touched by a little beauty.

Experiencing Beauty in Service

- Was I enriched by it?
- Did it amaze me?
- Did I learn something?
- Did I want to repeat it?
- Will I encourage others to experience it?

If your customers can say yes to most of the questions in the box above, you have taken service to the level of an art form. Yes to all and you have created a masterpiece – and as a by-product won yourself some devoted customers.

I have not tried to define beauty. As we all know, it's in the eye of the beholder, just like a customer's judgment of your service. But I believe that intuitively we know it when we see it.

Not being able to find the words to describe a phenomenon shouldn't lessen the significance of our emotional and intuitive responses. Rolling Stones guitarist Ron Wood describes this feeling for 'something right' when he says: 'There's a basic rule that runs through all kinds of music, a kind of unwritten rule. I don't know what it is. But I've got it.'

Similarly, great service organisations seem to have got it and may be the last ones to be able to articulate *how* they got it! Beauty may be intangible and elusive to define, but real enough to the individual who experiences it.

> 'When I am working on a problem I never think about beauty. I think only about how to solve the problem. But when I have finished, if the solution is not beautiful, I know it is wrong.'
>
> *Buckminster Fuller (1885–1993) inventor, designer and philosopher famous for creating the geodesic dome*

Love what you do

Ivor Spencer heads an internationally renowned school for butlers. It is based in Dulwich, south London, and numbers many celebrities and royals among his clients. 'In this profession,' he told me, 'you have to love what you do. How can you give service otherwise? I love it every day, and have done so the past 50 years. If you don't, the client will know. They can sense it.'

Ken McCulloch, founder of Malmaison hotels, hires only enthusiasts. Like Ivor Spencer, he has realised that this touches the right side of the brain of every customer who comes into contact with his people. What these two have in common, like other champions of superb service, is the insight to raise service from the level of servility and servitude to that of a noble profession.

In Britain, service is still tainted with the memory of being 'in service', meaning inferior. In the days of a more stratified society we used to talk about the upstairs-downstairs divisions. The downstairs psychology of many people giving service still persists, hence the ritual dance so often encountered as the server proves in various subtle ways that he is just as important as you, and it's only bad luck – a temporary situation – that's keeping him in this lousy job. He wants you to be sure of that. In short, he doesn't love what he does, and this is all too soon shared with you.

People who love what they do are also less likely to suffer from serious stress. Surveys repeatedly find that hating your job is near the top of the list of stresses. It's not surprising that the majority of heart attacks therefore still occur between 4pm and 6pm on Mondays and Fridays. But if the job appears to be lousy, what can you do about it? Here are three strategies.

Find an enthusiast

In any field you can choose to listen to the moaners or be inspired by an enthusiast. There are people who bring energy and enthusiasm to the most mundane of roles. Janitorial firm *ServiceMASTER*® has raised this to an art form, giving people real pride in what others see as a dead-end job.

When I was studying for my Bar exams I remember suffering from near-terminal ennui with many of the topics. One night I was sitting at Gray's Inn in London having dinner when I overheard a conversation from further down the table. An American was enthusing about how fascinating she found Land Law. She raved about how much insight it had given her into the whole English system of land ownership, the demographics of its society and English attitudes to property today.

Feeling rather negative about the subject – I never realised a piece of legislation could have so many sections as the Law of Property Act 1925 – my first impression was that she was somewhat disturbed. However, as I listened, some of her enthusiasm touched me despite my cynicism. I can't say that studying Law became my favourite leisure activity, but I did experience a noticeable difference when I got down to the law books and thought more deeply about the relevance of what I was studying to our contemporary lives. I never met this lady to thank her, but that one injection of enthusiasm went a long way . . .

If you can encourage enthusiasts to describe what they love about their work it will have a similar effect. Most people, especially in Europe, are more ready for a gripe session and may even feel embarrassed about displaying undue positivity. But stories that come from the heart tend to touch the enthusiast that is hidden in most of us.

Act 'as if'

When I began teaching management many years ago, I was given an invaluable piece of advice: 'Just act *as if* you're a great teacher and really know how to communicate this material,' said my mentor. To my amazement, it worked. Naturally there's a boundary over which you cross when you're faking it and should be admitting your incompetence, but this advice was an enormous boost to my self-confidence and helped me greatly to communicate what I did know.

Why not inaugurate a day where you act as if there's no place you'd rather be than performing your work role? When this works, try introducing the idea to those who work around you. Some may consider it phoney, but I can almost guarantee that the overall effect will be to reawaken sleeping positivity. Time will pass more quickly, and people will be surprised at the warmer response they receive from everyone else they deal with.

This advice to act 'as if' is used by sports coaches and even in the arts. Donald Fagen, lead singer of Steely Dan, the jazz-rock phenomenon of the '70s and early '80s, claimed that he was not a genuine singer and was merely acting like one to do demos of his songs until the group found a real one. They never did. You can go a long way acting 'as if'.

Have fun

Many years ago, Avis executive Robert Townsend wrote a provocative book called *Up the Organisation*. Most people remember this for his saying that if you're not in business for profits *and* fun, then you should get out. Today, many organisations have become very dull, serious, fear-driven places. It's not surprising that this translates into uninteresting encounters for their customers.

When people love what they do, it can't be anything but fun. If you're having fun, so will your customers. Herb Kelleher, charismatic CEO of SouthWest Airlines, spells out six guidelines for the 'SouthWest Way to a Sense of Humor'. They are:

- Think funny;
- Adopt a playful attitude;
- Be the first to laugh;
- Laugh with, not at;
- Laugh at yourself, and
- Take work seriously, but not yourself.

This attitude is also expressed at the corporate level. SouthWest Airlines found that a rival was claiming to have come first in an important customer satisfaction measure, and was using the information in its publicity material. Most CEOs would have reached for a lawyer but instead, SouthWest placed a full-page advertisement that said:

'After lengthy deliberation at the highest executive level and extensive consultation with our legal department, we have arrived at an official response to Northwest Airlines' claim to be the number one in customer satisfaction:

"Liar, liar – pants on fire!"'

Virgin Atlantic has almost enshrined fun as a corporate value and practises it wonderfully. My favourite advertisement is the one that featured a picture of Saddam Hussein shortly before the Gulf War. It read: 'Visit the USA before the USA visits you. Only £220.'

But you expect some businesses to be fun. For instance, when you reach the Dilbert Zone website you're not surprised to read the introduction: 'Congratulations. You've found the DILBERT HOME PAGE. This is a sure indication that you're a little bit smarter and a little bit sexier than the people who are looking at the Smithsonian website.'

Or the introduction to the Web-based fantasy role-playing game, Ultima Online, which describes the problems you will face if you don't keep up with your playing: 'Lag can be not only annoying , but deadly in UO. There is nothing worse than freezing up in the middle of a battle only to return to a grey screen and learning that you have been killed.'

The challenge, however, is to make working in, say, a manufacturing site or a call centre as much fun as those who are obviously marketing fun for a living. Encouraging people who work together to play together is not an optional add-on. It feeds the quality of relationships in a business to break down the barriers between work and play.

Perhaps prescribing how people should have fun is an oxymoron. When fun activities are designed by people working in the business themselves rather than imposed by management, it becomes a more natural part of the culture.

Rotating people through teams that are responsible for putting on imaginative and fun events is one route. Management has to set the climate that allows you to enjoy yourself and you don't have to leave your sense of play at the door. What you can do as a leader is give permission. Andy Law, co-founder of the mould-breaking St Luke's advertising agency in London describes "*Ten Ways To Create A Revolution In Your Company.*"[8]

1. Ask yourself what you want out of life.
2. Ask yourself what really matters to you.
3. Give all your work clothes to Oxfam and wear what you feel is really you.
4. Talk to people (even those you don't like) about 1 and 2.
    (*You should be feeling very uncomfortable now. You may even be sick. This is normal.*)
5. Give up something you most need at work (desk, company car).
6. Trust everyone you meet. Keep every agreement you make.
    (*You should be feeling a little better now.*)
7. Undergo a group experience. (Anything goes, parachuting, holidaying.)
8. Rewrite your business plan to align all of the above with your customers.
9. Draw a line on the office floor and invite everyone to a brave new world.
10. Share everything you do and own fairly with everyone who crosses the line. (*You should be feeling liberated. Soon you will have, in this order, the following: grateful customers, inspired employees, friendly communities, money.*)

Sounds like fun? It certainly wouldn't suit everybody, but it sets the tone for

---

[8] Andy Law, *Open Minds*, Orion Business Books, 1998, ISBN: 0752813889.

what kind of business this is. It's interesting that St Luke's has organised a parents' evening to break down the work/play divide, introducing mothers and fathers to the business family. In many companies I have worked with, this would be unheard of. Why these artificial barriers? How do you communicate to the people you work with that you love what you do and it's all right for them to love it too? If the leader's not having fun, nor will anyone else.

Are women customers from Venus?

You can't think *both/and* without realising that half the world is different from the other half. Obvious? I'm quite convinced business hasn't woken up to this. John Gray's successful book, *Men Are from Mars, Women Are from Venus* seems to have tapped into a raw nerve in our society – do men understand women and vice-versa? Perceptive as it is, the book is based on a shockingly obvious concept. Men and women are . . . er . . . wait for it . . . different! And in business terms, believe it or not, women are customers, too.

This comprehension has barely dawned in the field of customer service. Yes, some car manufacturers are now attempting to design vehicles, at least on the inside, with women in mind. This is a positive step forward from Ford's giant blooper, advertising the Mondeo as Man and Machine in Perfect Harmony. It's fascinating to compare this 10 years later with the legendary Saturn advertisements that make a point of treating women respectfully and intelligently. And, yes, some hotel chains are designing rooms with their female customers' tastes in mind.

However, the notion of serving men *and* women in the different ways they value is in its infancy. It shouldn't be. Tom Peters, in *The Circle Of Innovation*,[9] quotes Australian research which shows that women either make or decisively influence an average of 90 per cent of product-buying choices.

So what? In hard marketing terms you could say there's a golden opportunity here, as if we had suddenly discovered nearly three billion new customers worldwide. There *are* already products designed for women. There need to be a lot more if the Australian research is typical, which I believe it is. But the real opportunity is to learn about the feminine attitude (note, I don't just say women's attitude) to service.

Faith Popcorn,[10] author of *Clicking*, summarises a fundamental difference

[9] Hodder & Stoughton, 1997, ISBN: 0 3340 71720 3.

[10] Author and founder of BrainReserve, a futurist marketing consultancy she established in 1974. *Clicking*, Harper Business, 1998, ISBN: 0 88730 857 0.

between the sexes when she says: 'Men and women . . . don't buy for the same reasons. He simply wants the transaction to take place. She's interested in creating a relationship.'

This agrees very much with Gray's thinking on Mars and Venus. Men, he explains, favour giving advice and problem-solving, whereas women primarily want an empathetic ear to share their problems with. It's all a question of emphasis – many men today also want a listening ear (they must do – there are four therapists in my street) and women obviously solve problems and take decisions. Of course, these are *tendencies* we are talking about. It's hard to imagine Margaret Thatcher sharing her emotional problems with others, except perhaps over a cup of tea with that nice General Pinochet.

But it does give us some strong clues as to how to build closer relationships, which women seem to be better at than men. What we can *all* learn from the female perspective and apply to *all* customers is to:

- Focus on connection, care, and understanding *first, then* move to *problem-solving*;
- Make customers feel included – emphasise inclusion over separation;
- Spend more time on building empathy and trust than *you* think is necessary (especially if you're a man);
- Explore shared values;
- Develop trust – women are usually more concerned about business ethics than men, and
- Listen for the feelings behind the words.

Can a man understand this? No and yes. No, because there are fundamentally different ways in which men and women see the world, the female view having been discounted or denigrated in most societies at least until recently. Yes, because we are also describing here the feminine side of us all. Men appreciate empathy and a good relationship, too. It's simply that it tends not to be our first reflex.

The dangers for men who don't see the far-reaching effects of the rise and rise of women in society are immense. I say 'rise and rise' looking to the near future because, of course, in large organisations it's still a man's world. Particularly, it seems, in the USA, where more than 97 per cent of senior corporate managers are men. But what this hides is the entrepreneurial drive of so many women who, when faced with what has been called the glass ceiling in the old-fashioned corporate world, have either started their own businesses or shot to the top of fast-growing small and medium enterprises where more of a meritocracy apparently exists.

In the USA, women are already more educated than their male counterparts. In Britain, girls are beating boys hands-down in the educational system. Single black women, as a group, are the best-educated sector of English society. Recent reports even indicate that women make better managers.

There are two main conclusions to this discussion. First, that women themselves, their needs and preferences, are vastly undervalued by business in the way that it serves them. Women may be from Venus, but they're also your biggest customers.

Second, that we should look to understand how to bring more feminine values to customer service. More empathy, more sensitivity, more emotional connectivity.

For some penetrating questions, activities, and ideas relating to this chapter, turn to page 250.

Chapter Seven

The Power of Attention

'Your defect is lack of attention . . . and you're not alone. It's every player's greatest defect.'

Paolo Maurensig, Italian author[1]

'What you put your attention on grows.'

Traditional saying

Focusing the power of attention on your people will:

- Create great relationships inside your business;

- Inspire self-belief, and

- Make your customers feel your attention is fully on them.

HOW many times did you write last year's date on cheques and notes at the start of this year? You weren't paying attention to what you were doing, and so both habit and the past took over, quite literally. To change anything in our personal or work lives we have to bring our full attention to bear. *Are you paying attention?* That question re-creates a shock from the past, doesn't it? It may even project you back into your schooldays when you often *weren't*!

The same question is just as pertinent to how we lead our lives today. Most of us have our attention divided and fragmented by a myriad competing demands. At home children, the telephone, TV, radio and Web-surfing might simultaneously compete for our attention. And in the office 'attention deficit disorder' is created by telephone, e-mails, constant interruptions and the routine crises that come with running a business.

So numerous are the claims on our attention and focus that the average American gives a TV programme less than two minutes of semi-attention before channel-hopping. In this climate it's not surprising that many

[1] *The Luneburg Variation: A Novel*, Owl Books, 1998, ISBN: 0805060286.

customers feel they're experiencing lack of care especially when the quality of attention bestowed on them wavers constantly.

More or less anything is possible *when* you put your attention on it. This was true for Ray Kroc, originator of McDonald's, who famously said that the secret of his success was that he took perfecting the hamburger more seriously than anyone else. It's also true for Sir Richard Branson, whose 80-page faxes to his staff in Virgin Atlantic are legendary both for their creativity and attention to detail.

It's true for entrepreneur Julian Richer, who enthusiastically encourages and fanatically follows through *every* employee suggestion, claiming that he runs his business on the high-octane fuel of these ideas from the front line. He spends his weekly train trip from his home in York to the London head-quarters of Richer Sounds poring over the latest influx of ideas, and has a full-time assistant whose job is to communicate and implement them.

Above all, it's clear to your customers whether or not your attention is fully focused on them because organisations are increasingly transparent. This is not simply in a financial sense. I believe the quality of service that

Transparency and the customer

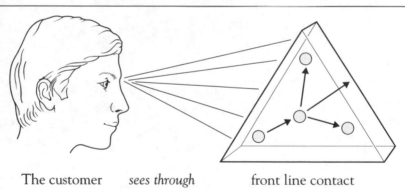

The customer   *sees through*   front line contact

you or I as customers receive from the persons serving us is an accurate mirror of the quality of the relationship they have with their supervisor. Think of your own contact with a delivery person, a waitress, a call-centre operative. It's easy to sense the quality of management behind each individual, and the culture they represent. Do they have the desire, the energy, the information and the power to do a great job of serving you? Each individual representative of a company contains the DNA of that organisation. This is when customers play God, creating the whole physiology of the corporate body that is serving them from a small fragment that they determine must be its DNA.

This concept should make you sweat a little if you really get it. *It means that from one or two service encounters customers can see through the whole inner workings of your organisation.* These are transparent to them. They will see through the inner workings of your organisation from their experience of each Moment of Truth. And, like paparazzi, they will have mentally photographed you, developed the picture and publicised it to others without your even knowing that you are in the frame.

Technology has magnified this effect. We talk about the death of distance in terms of telecommunications, but it's just as relevant to customer relations. Our customers are within a hair's-breadth and less than a nanosecond away from us. And what they see can be a fascinating lesson to us. I have often brought major customers in front of a supplier and been fascinated to see how transparent the inner workings of a business are to someone who is supposedly an outsider. Frequently the outsider has a greater clarity of insight about the culture, management style and internal communications than the people inside the box. *If you want to learn from your customers, listen harder to their insights about the inner workings of your business than to their service complaints.* The latter certainly need attending to, but the ideas you gain from the former will help you to make more fundamental changes.

As a customer you decide a business either has its attention on you and your experience, or it doesn't. And that the person serving you has 'batteries included', or doesn't. It's as simple as that. Reflect on the parallel in intimate personal friendships – giving full attention to another person is one of the greatest gifts we can bestow. Long-term couples often have to remind themselves of this to keep their relationship vibrant. 'You're not listening to me', or 'You're not paying attention' are two of the most familiar criticisms levelled at the other party.

We experience this as customers if our reasonable – to us – request is discounted or met with mere compliance rather than enthusiasm. Or if we're standing in a queue and the salesperson gives us no sign that we exist until he or she says, 'Next!' We feel unattended to most of all when a phone call isn't returned. Woody Allen once remarked that the Hollywood scene was worse than dog eats dog, it's where one dog doesn't return another dog's phone call!

Fred Smith, charismatic founder of worldwide parcels delivery company FedEx, built his business around this principle of attention, with the clear rule that the sun was not to set on a customer query without him or her receiving a call back, even if it was to say: 'We can't find the parcel, but we're working on it.' Today, of course, many of these customers track their parcels through customer-oriented software, allowing them to put their own attention on the progress of their goods. In this way, technology is providing a sophisticated form of DIY.

Attention may not make the queue move faster or the parcel arrive more swiftly, but it makes us as customers feel that something is happening, someone knows that we and our requests have not been forgotten. What do you do to make your customers feel fully 'attended to' in each phase of their contact with you?

What is attention?

Attention can be broken down into four elements:

Intention: An unswerving and clearly visualised picture of the future you want to create for your business, totally irrespective of external circumstances. As George Bernard Shaw[2] once remarked: 'The people who get on in this world are the people who get up and look for the circumstances they want, and if they can't find them, make them.'

One of the characteristics of legendary service providers is that however busy they are they don't lose sight of the intention to do a great job for you. It is clear in every contact, pronouncement and action. They don't allow circumstances to get in the way.

Time: If you say you value a particular goal – for instance, becoming famous for service – how much of your *quality time* do you give to attaining this goal? What percentage of your *diary* time do you deliberately book to be with customers, and with your own service deliverers in their work setting? And what high-level *briefing* time do you spend ensuring reinforcement and follow-through of your service mission?

YOU ARE YOUR DIARY!

Remember Michael Dell's 40 per cent of diary time spent with customers? Dell also once remarked that the most important thing to figure out was what not to do, allowing you to give the most precious gift of all to your customers: time.

---

[2] Irish dramatist, essayist, popular speaker and pamphleteer (1856–1950).

Energy: If you're passionate about service, it's obvious that your enthusiasm and commitment will be infused into others if you demonstrate untiring energy in achieving your aims. A great miscalculation many leaders make is to overestimate the power of what they say and underestimate the power of what they do. Out of sight stays out of mind for most people.

> ### The Leader's Blind Spot
>
> Most leaders *overestimate* the power of what they say and *underestimate* the power of what they do.

What's less obvious is that if you put energy into what you whole-heartedly believe in, it actually *gives you back* greater energy. Friends of the late musician Yehudi Menuhin were always encouraging him to slow down and not give such a high proportion of his energy to the various spiritual and philanthropic causes he put so much into in the latter years of his life. His experience was that he received back much more life energy because he was doing what he valued most highly. Energy creates energy!

Resources: A famous trade union leader from the USA once remarked that it was easy to see what an organisation values just by looking at where it spends its money. One complaint of service providers is that they feel insufficiently supported by the organisation to give the great service being blithely promised to its customers. If your attention on service is to be effective, it needs supporting by all available resources. When you consider how transparent your inner workings are to customers, be aware that they will know when cost-cutting affects the service to them. An example from my own experience is claiming air miles. I needed a great deal of patience in dealing with the British Airways scheme. It appears to me as a humble customer that these people are under-resourced, judging by some of the lengthiest telephone queues I've experienced, and that BA's attention is far more on the upfront marketing of these offers than in providing a hassle-free service when I claim air miles.

Of course, resources mean more than money, but don't underestimate the financial element. If people are seen as an overhead, they will be treated as an expensive cost, not as a valuable resource. They will feel this, and so will your customers.

Attention is most powerful when it is focused on creating possibilities rather than reacting to problems. There's an ancient puzzle that illustrates this. Suppose you have an indelible line:

———————

How do you remove it? The very lateral answer is that you draw a much larger line to put your attention on, thereby rendering the indelible one insignificant:

———————

This is a useful metaphor to remind us that though it's necessary to try to reduce service problems – lengthy queuing lines, promises not met, discourteous staff – the *way* in which you do this is continually to put your attention on creating something greater.

To remind us how precious a tool attention is, this is one chess master talking to his pupil:

> 'Your defect is lack of attention . . . and you're not alone. It's every player's greatest defect. And when I say attention, I mean something far greater than is commonly thought. In their holy festival the Mayan priests competed in a game similar to the modern jai alai, but as they grasped and hurled the ball they believed that the slightest error would cause the sun to fall from the sky. *That's the kind of attention I'm talking about, as if your own life were at stake.*' [my italics.]
>
> *Paolo Maurensig* [3]

What to put your attention on

There are three main areas to focus the power of your attention to create a service legend. These are:

- Creating great in-company relationships
- Inspiring self-belief
- Putting the human touch into customer relationships.

[3] *The Luneburg Variation: A Novel*, Owl Books, 1998, ISBN: 0805060286.

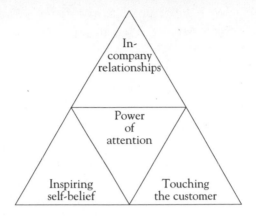

Creating great in-company relationships

We have said that your inner relationships are transparent to the customer. In particular, he or she will see clearly whether you have more of a tribal or a partnership orientation within. A tribal climate is characterised by gaps between functions or in the chain of events that delivers the service experience to the customer. The main characteristics are described in the box below.

Tribal orientation

- It's us versus them (e.g. the field vs. head office, manufacturing vs. sales)
- Rigid Digits – They/It/the 'System' are to blame
- Information, experience and even customer knowledge is retained for the benefit of the functional 'tribe'.

The themes here are *powerlessness* and *isolation*. There's an inability to stretch out beyond the perceived boundaries of a functional box. Customers may find themselves caught in the cross-fire between service and sales, head office and the field. But wait a minute – they don't really care which gap they're caught in as they are looking for a *whole solution* and do not wish to be sucked into the gaps between the inner tribes. They quickly become aware whether your attention is focused inwardly, or orientated outwards towards fulfilling their needs.

Many organisations have responded to this problem by invoking the notion of the internal customer. That means that everyone in the inner chain serves his or her colleagues with the same quality as if they were an end user. It sounds seductive and has been a useful stepping-stone idea to move away from the worst vicissitudes of tribal warfare.

However, problems come with the idea. In several clients I have observed that one tribe has used the idea as a stick to beat other functions with, safely hiding behind the rationale: 'We are your customers – please just do it.' A certain recipe for a rapid return to internecine strife. Clarifying who your customers are is a vital debate for any business, particularly when you are supplying raw materials or working through distributors or agents. The ultimate customer must always be the person who uses the product or service, but in reality you may be several steps removed from him or her in the chain.

It's misleading to think of the next link in the chain as the customer – far more useful to remove the barriers and work more intimately together to provide excellence for the final user. This is not always as easy as it sounds, because some distributors may even have opposing aims to their suppliers, leading to a reduction in the quality of service the real customer receives. I've observed this particularly in the building and automotive components trades. Tribal behaviour is bad news for the customer, but organisations that work on the notion of internal customers also lag behind those who strive to blur the distinction between themselves and the next link in the chain, their *partners* in service.

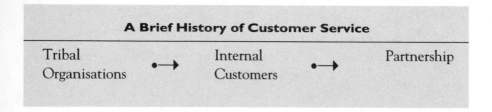

A Brief History of Customer Service

Tribal Organisations ●→ Internal Customers ●→ Partnership

The characteristics of a partnership orientation are described in the box opposite.

Partnership Orientations:

- There's (almost) no 'us and them';
  – our colleagues are our partners;
  – we share responsibility for the customer's experience, and
  – we share successes and failures.
- We invent our own future and deserve our triumphs – if the system gets in the way, we change it.
- Sharing of customer information, knowledge and contacts is hardwired into our thinking.

How do you shift from a tribal to a partnership orientation? In the same way that you put your attention on a market of one with your customers, the secret is to start with a market of one internally. The individual.

The quality of your in-company relationships and consequently the creation of a partnership culture can be dramatically enhanced by focusing your attention on the following areas.

Creating Great In-company Relationships

* Appreciate! Appreciate! Appreciate!
* TLC, not TVC
* What's your project?
* Life-long learning.

Appreciate! Appreciate! Appreciate!

We all crave appreciation. It's a fundamental way of demonstrating that we exist. Think how appallingly children behave merely to receive attention, so that someone appreciates that they *exist*! As adults we may have developed a mask of nonchalance towards the opinions of others, although nearly all of us are deeply affected when another human reaches out and shows appreciation in a way that we value. Financial rewards and appraisals don't touch us in the same way that sincere appreciation does. And, of course, people who feel valued themselves will transmit this feeling to those whom they are serving.

The great idea in Ken Blanchard's famous book *The One Minute Manager*[4] is to *catch people out doing something right*. The book was a bestseller, but I see little evidence of the application of this idea. I have heard people who have worked for a company for 30 years claim that they have *never* received genuine and meaningful appreciation for what they have contributed. The shadow of Theory X thinking – assuming that people are intrinsically lazy and unmotivated and therefore only respond to strong control and even coercion – is still with us. *To make this more personal – can you think of someone who works with you to whom you are overdue in giving deserved praise?* When you get around to it, you'll probably discover it's a month too late. I know of no organisation that has erred too much on the side of praising its staff. Forget employee of the month schemes. It's the employee of *now* who needs appreciation.

Customers will *know* almost immediately whether or not your people are downtrodden or appreciated. They see through into your personal style of management and the quality of attention you give to relationships within the business.

A client was dismayed to have his presentation rated as 1 out of 10 by an employee at a recent conference. However, the delegate did remark that the year before he had given it 0 out of 10 and therefore felt that this year's was much better. It's possibly an unfair jump in logic, but it does seem that this person's experience of life is 1 out of 10, and therefore you couldn't have expected him to judge others any differently. *Unappreciated people won't appreciate their customers.*

TLC, not TVC

TLC, as we all know, stands for Tender Loving Care. We may not recognise TVC, but many of us have unknowingly practised it – Thinly Veiled Contempt. What do you really feel inside when you look at your people, or your customers? People can sense at a visceral level the quality of feeling behind your words. Our feelings are more transparent to others than we would usually believe.

In relationships, what we expect is often what we get. Sports coaches who expect only the best of their people tend to trigger performances of this kind by investing the individual with an unstoppable self-belief. Those who are over-critical, undermine.

[4] D. Kenneth Blanchard, S. Johnson, K. H. Blanchard, William Morrow & Company, 1982, ISBN: 0688014291.

Don't fool yourself that your inner views are hidden from your employees or your customers. Find positive qualities in them that you can focus on and develop. We can only radiate to customers *what we are*. Beware the fake notion of objectivity here. Modern physics has revealed that even in experiments that appear to be the summit of objective measurement the observer affects the observed. Or, to use the more dramatic words of biologist Darryl Reanney:[5] 'The world we see is the world we make.'

A kind of alchemy is created by the quality of attention you put on your people – they are changed by your perceptions, by your support or lack of it, and so in turn are you. Seeking for the highest potential in another is an act of co-creation. Judgment should whenever possible be withheld as a last resort. As in the Greek myth of Pygmalion, in coaching others we have a certain power to mould them.

The role of TLC in this process is profound. And there's nothing soft and fluffy about it, because raised expectations mean that your people develop a correspondingly greater sense of responsibility. Even military leaders talk about love for their soldiers, exemplifying the notion of the Servant Leader who demonstrates his or her TLC through respect. It's the most direct path to creating the only glue that can bind a leader and his or her followers – *trust*. As management writer Jim O'Toole[6] puts it:

'What creates trust, in the end, is the leader's manifest respect for the followers.'

What's your project?

The concept of continuous improvement that most medium- and large-sized companies are committed to can be misleading. All improvements are the result of discrete pushes, jumps or leaps, which occur only because attention has been focused on something that needs to change. Promises not kept, queuing times, speed of response to customer requests and accuracy of quotations are typical examples. The improvements are discontinuities, positive peaks in the flat line that is 'business as usual'. It appears to be continuous only when you join up the peaks on the graph at the end of the year.

[5] *Music of the Mind*, Souvenir Press, 1997, ISBN: 0285632884.

[6] *Leading Change*, Ballantine Books, 1996, ISBN: 0345402545.

To exhort people to become part of a philosophy of continuous improvement has little effect unless they have their own mini-projects that help them to direct their attention to creating these discontinuities. I call them mini-projects because change can be created by a thousand small steps of improvement that are within the power of individuals to implement. Examples might include:

- Getting to know my internal partners better;
- Improving my personal knowledge of the company's structure and products;
- Developing a way of categorising the common customer problems or complaints that I experience, and
- Educating myself about other organisations that are famous for service.

My experience of helping to make these projects successful is that:

- The individual should choose his or her own projects – commitment is then built in;
- They should be projects that are not merely inwardly focused, but that will make a real difference – however small – to the quality of service;
- Projects need to be consistent with your overall customer mission, vision and values;
- Successful completion deserves rewarding and celebrating;
- Everyone in the organisation, from customer to chairman, should have their own customer improvement project, and
- It's a non-stop process – you haven't got there when one project is completed. Choose a new one.

Naturally you will also have larger initiatives focused on improvements for your customers that need co-ordination across different business areas. It's not possible to have everyone trying to create, for example, his or her own version of the customer database. However, the benefit of individually selected and owned projects is that everyone takes an active part in improving service. The individual is the basic unit of the organisation, and the result of this individualised attention is a greater likelihood that the customer will feel your attention is fully on them.

Projects also bring benefits in removing the barriers set up by tribal thinking. There's a need to emphasise cross-functional projects above all others. If necessary, invent one simply to bring people more closely into partnership. Complete 'projectising' of your business will help to blow up the walls that exist between functions. The ideal is to create a climate that has completely porous boundaries between units. Functions? What functions?

Life-long learning

Much has been written about the Learning Organisation. It's a great concept, and one that looks set to make the transition from management theory to reality as Web-based technology allows instantaneous transfer of information about almost everything from any location on the globe. However, I can honestly say I've never yet seen a fully conscious learning *organisation*, but I have witnessed cultures where *individuals* learn.

The kind of improvement projects just described are one means of life-long learning. Learning is essential to survival. Without adaptation to change, a species may be threatened with extinction. In this case the species means organisations. But for the first time we live in an era where an individual is likely to live longer than the organisation for which he or she works. Ex-Shell planner Arie de Geus suggests in his fascinating book *The Living Company*[7] that the average lifespan of a company is 40 years, around half the time we expect to live as individuals. Today, it may be even shorter.

It's therefore clear that you should put your energy into educating the asset that has the most long-term value to you – the individual. Also, it's necessary for the individual's own career survival to keep upgrading his or her knowledge and skills, as the old lifelong contract with an organisation has been replaced by a new contract to oneself to keep learning (adapting) to survive and flourish in the job market.

Tom Peters talks passionately about this notion being acted on in the unlikely setting of Wisconsin-based Johnsonville Foods, where hourly-paid sausage workers can sign up for any education or training they like, *job-related or not*, and the company will pay. This is not philanthropy – it's based on the commonsense idea that if people's minds are stimulated and inspired by learning that is perceived as valuable to them as individuals, they will bring this into play in their daily work.

Experience has made me a great believer in the value of non-job-related training. Service Legends recently helped to pay for a loyal administrative assistant to study something apparently totally irrelevant to the office, a year-

7 Arie de Geus, Harvard Business School Press, 1997, ISBN: 087584782X.

long course in the History of Drawing. This assistant can take all the office skills and PC training she likes, but none creates quite such a buzz as learning something you're really interested in. *If you want to be interesting as a business, help your people to be interested in what means most to them.* It may seem like an unwarranted act of faith, but it's just common sense.

Far-sighted organisations tackle this broadening of the mind at source, at the level of the individual, encouraging him or her to be a co-creator in the process of lifelong-learning. It's not necessarily an easy option because with more knowledge tends to come more responsibility. Also more *self-responsibility.* Jack Welch, chairman of General Electric, observed that the organisation needs to help people through learning to become more valuable in the marketplace for when they are no longer needed by GE! Harsh? Perhaps, but also a more honest portrayal of the new realism and understanding that exists in the relationship between individuals and organisations in the 21st century.

Compare how different this is from the world of the old cradle-to-grave employment scenario. The individual was in many ways 'owned' by the employer. This is illustrated in the apocryphal story of an employee of a leading corporation in the '60s who had gone to a company-funded school, lived in a company-owned house, and worked for the company for his whole career. He arranged for his ashes to be sent in an urn after his death to the chairman of the company saying, 'Now you've got the damn lot!'

These days he probably wouldn't know whom to write to because the company would almost certainly have predeceased him. Life-long learning is the individual's responsibility, but wise employers will provide active and generous support.

Inspiring self-belief

If recognition of individuality is what customers seek most, this can be achieved only when the individuals serving them believe that they themselves are valued as individuals. Those who believe themselves to be insignificant cogs in a large machine will transmit this message in subtle ways to their customers. They would agree with Douglas Adams in *The Hitchhiker's Guide to the Galaxy:*[8] 'We no more know our own destiny than a tea leaf knows the destiny of the East India Company.'

---

[8] Ballantine Books, 1995, ISBN: 0345391802.

Self-belief about what, you might ask? *In the context of providing legendary service, it's having the attitude, energy, information and power to serve the customer as an equal.* The belief will usually manifest itself as a flexible, can-do attitude, rarely as 'I'll have to ask my supervisor if that's OK' and *never* as 'It's not our policy', or 'That's not my responsibility'. As Henry Ford[9] observed, 'If you think you can, or think you can't, you're usually right.'

Walking dead, spectators, cynics and players

A friend of mine lost all his hair after his first divorce. He would arrive home tired from work and settle down to read the newspaper. His five-year-old daughter would knock several times on his skull and, on receiving no response would announce loudly, 'Mummy, Mummy! Daddy's not in!'

Similarly, many service people are simply not 'in'. There's no human resonance, merely a muttered script such as the formulated repetition of 'Are you enjoying your meal, sir?' in a restaurant. It appears that waiters throughout the world are trained to time this question *precisely* at the moment when I am digesting the first mouthful. My inevitable response is therefore a grunt. Have you ever tried saying 'No!' at that moment? More often than not the waiter will retire to the kitchen to sulk, as his training does not extend to dealing with this.

It's not that this service is bad, it's merely lacklustre. Let's explore how you can help your customers to experience more positive and vital energy from the person serving them.

---

[9] American industrialist and pioneer automobile manufacturer (1863–1947).

Service Styles

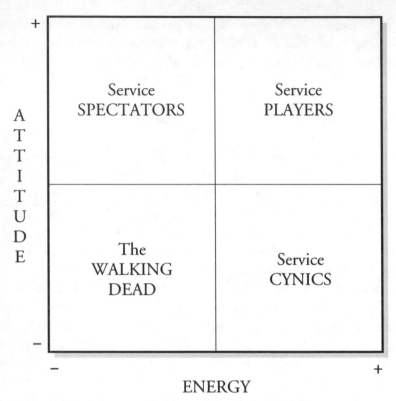

© *Deva Partnership Ltd 2000*

The Service Styles chart enables you to think about what part your people are playing in your own service performance. There's no hard-and-fast categorisation, but a useful language to talk about the quality of attitude and energy displayed, which will naturally be transmitted to the customer. Here's a description of the four styles.

The **Walking Dead** are listless or negative in their attitude and don't have enough energy to make significant changes to their day-to-day lives. It wasn't a core competence you hired them for – the ability to walk while apparently being dead – but the unremitting torpor of organisational life allows many to slip into this pattern of behaviour. As a customer you experience it when you ask for a carrier bag at most small UK retail outlets.

Lo and behold, they will give you . . . a bag! The thought that you might also want them to put your goods into the bag has not occurred to them. *Their attention is not on your experience*.

How often have you been served by the walking dead? Comedian and author Ben Elton captures their disposition excellently when he writes:

> Jack's coffee arrived, about half of it still in the cup, the rest in the saucer lapping around the grimy thumb of Jack's server.
>
> 'One coffee,' the server said. 'Enjoy your meal.'
>
> The fact that Jack was clearly not having a meal was of no concern to this boy, whose instructions were to say 'enjoy the meal' on delivery of every order, and that was what he did.
>
> Jack reflected on the problems of imposing a corporate culture. There was simply no point in attempting to make English kids into Americans. You could put the silly hat on the British teenager, but you still had a British teenager under the hat. You could make them say, 'Enjoy your meal', 'Have a nice day', and 'Hi, my name is Cindy – how may I help you right now?' as much as you liked, but it still always came out sounding like 'F*** off'.[10]

Spectators are rather more insidious in their effect on others in the culture, because though they have a positive attitude and seem to make all the right noises, they rarely have the energy to put their shorts on, get out there and play. Spectating is a wonderful role we all love to play. As Spectator Manager of the English football team, I have comfortably won every World Cup Final since 1966.

Similarly, spectators provide a constant commentary on how the business could be run better if only they were given their head. Nothing, of course, would frighten them more. My experience is that they quite often hold senior positions in companies and deep down are relieved when they are eventually 'found out', perhaps by a dynamic new leader who isn't prepared to have so many potential players voicing well-intentioned but essentially useless advice from the touchline. In short, spectators are dangerous because they are not 'in play', while giving the impression through their pronouncements that they are, or would like to be, 'if only'. Spectators are unlikely to take full ownership for resolving the customer's problem because they are high on opinion, low on action.

[10] © Ben Elton 1998. Extracted from *Blast From The Past*, published by Bantam Press, a division of Transworld Publishers. All rights reserved.

Cynics are to be cherished. Why? Because they have a great deal of energy, and may often be extremely loyal to the organisation's deepest values, but see a great deal of management activity as compromising their ability to do a good job for the customer. The downside of being served by a cynic often means listening to a monologue on how they would love to serve us better, but the company has (a) halved the workforce, (b) under-invested in new technology, or (c) been badly managed.

In their positive incarnation they are merely sceptics, a valuable foil to poorly thought-out strategies. But the blind spot we all have is that while we believe we are merely being sceptical, others feel the negativity we project as depressingly cynical. 'It's flavour of the month' is the enthusiasm-flattening response when you try to introduce a new customer service initiative to a group of cynics.

In one major company I have worked with I discovered a 'Survivors' Club' of cynics. They had been through 20 years of every form of Change Management the company had thrown at them – throwing being the correct verb because so little of it stuck. They had survived Management by Objectives, Matrix Management, TQM, Business Process Re-Engineering and still emerged essentially unchanged. It's not surprising that the business is now going through a period of desperate restructuring which even the survivors may not survive!

But the great thing about cynics is that they have energy and, in my experience, can be brought more easily into play than spectators, if only you give them something meaningful to play with. This is a challenge in a world where so many managers are content to let their people act as if they are only performing a McJob.

Players have the energy and self-belief to test their ideas in practice. They believe that what they do can and does make a difference, and are prepared to take the risks necessary to prove this. They act, therefore, on the assumption that their actions *do* help to shape the future. They may only be a small percentage of the workforce. For example, when I was running a company-wide business improvement initiative for a UK firm, I found only about 30 to 40 real players out of 1,200 who were really prepared to take part, partly because of a strong spectator element among senior management. Happily, this was enough to create significant change in the culture, most notably in getting newly functionalised 'tribes' to co-operate more effectively.

Players serving a customer won't create false barriers such as 'It's against company policy', 'I don't have the authority' or 'Not my department'. They will treat the customer's request as *their* ball to run with, staying in touch until the job is finished or satisfactorily handed over to someone who can complete it.

In fact, these styles are all aspects of one's self. There are issues on which I become the walking dead, a spectator or cynic. Beware of the trap that makes you think, 'I'm a player, and it's the rest of you who aren't pulling your weight.' Canvas the opinions of others and you may find you still have some way to go to be predominantly a player – in this context, a player for your customers. And if you've been served by a player, you are left with the positive impression that nothing is too much trouble to satisfy your needs.

One player makes a difference

Yvonne Stroud worked on reception at a major oil company's head office in London in the early '90s. She was not an employee – a sub-contractor

working for a security firm – but her reinvention of the security role (who has secrets worth stealing these days anyway?) became one of the most discussed topics in the firm.

Yvonne would remember the names and much of the personal background of literally hundreds of people who came in and out of the building. Visitors badges would be ready *before* they arrived and, if lacksadaisical secretaries kept people, among them major customers, waiting in reception she would harry them relentlessly.

Always smiling, with a quip or concerned question about a spouse's illness, she inspired the chairman to comment that if a small fraction of the managers had Yvonne's dedication and love of the job, the business could move mountains. A company-wide change programme used her unceasing energy and unfailing positivity as a role model.

> **'If only we had an army of Yvonnes!'**
>
> *UK company chairman*

Can you recognise your own players – or even a single player – from this description? Bear in mind that this story, like those of many lone players, did not finish completely happily. Old-style managers took offence at Yvonne's friendliness and some old-style secretaries were outraged that not only was she doing her job superbly, but was prodding them out of their own 'good enough is OK' torpor. She now works for a London law firm, where hopefully her energy and magic are appreciated.

The corporate immune system may quickly kill off players if they are not championed and supported. The message for all of us is that *our* behaviour creates the walking dead, spectators, cynics and players around us. We all own the responsibility for creating players.

Championing players

Do you find yourself surrounded by the walking dead and cynics? The humbling truth for all of us as leaders is that it's the attention – or lack of it – we pay our people that creates or allows these tendencies to exist. Therefore, if you really want to transform attitudes, the first step is to think about your own leadership, and the second how you can lessen the negative effects of what is perceived by your people to be absurd work.

How, then, do you bring people into play? The first and most obvious factor is to *give them something to play with*. This means involvement, a more honest word than empowerment. Empowerment implies that we had the power to give away in the first place, increasingly unlikely when many of our people are knowledge workers who possess more information about the job than we do. Like motivation, empowerment is intrinsic; that is, it comes from within and can't be foisted on an unwilling party. What you can do, however, is create the climate where a person's innate desire to play – to whatever capacity he or she possesses – is brought out. One way to achieve this is by involving people in the customer-focused improvement projects described in the earlier section on developing inner relationships.

The Legacy of McJobs

'. . . idleness, indifference, and irresponsibility are healthy responses to absurd work.'

Herzberg[11]

The benefits of involvement are well expressed by Chris Jackson, head of strategy development at telecoms giant Nokia, when he says: 'By engaging more people, the ability to implement strategy becomes more viable. We won a high level of commitment by the process and we ended up with lots of options we hadn't looked at in the past.'

Inspiring players doesn't mean abdicating leadership. One paradox of leadership is that a strong and purposeful hand is necessary to create involved, committed players. It's *both/and* again, not *either/or*. It's necessary both to challenge and support people to bring them fully into play.

Champions won't walk past poor quality or inferior performance. It's not an easy option to work with a champion who hates mediocrity. Change is inevitable. The walking dead may leave, the spectators may have to get more involved and the cynics become inspired to play once the champion involves them in the process of creating something truly great. Helping the cynics to understand the 'why' that underpins your actions and to include them in owning the problem are the secrets behind unleashing their energy in a more positive direction.

---

[11] Frederick Herzberg, pioneer in the field of motivation.

Benjamin Zander[12] of the Boston Philharmonic Orchestra talks about being a 'ruthless architect' of the possibilities of the people who play with him. As a champion of your people you may think that ruthless is too extreme. However, great champions set as much store by challenging their people as by supporting them. They realise that before you can ask someone to do something, you have to help them to be something, an essential part of the philosophy of *ServiceMASTER®*, who believe this applies to cleaners as much as to managers.

Putting the human touch into customer relationships

A theme that runs through *Batteries Included!* is the need to touch your customers in a human and emotional way. However, the pressures of organisational life all too often blunt this natural response of one human being to empathise with and reach out to another. *Put simply, there's too much emphasis on serving the system and not enough on serving the customer.*

Again, it's all a question of where you concentrate your *attention*. If you're having a conversation with someone at a party you feel somehow diminished if his or her attention keeps drifting to the food tray or someone else's conversation. *Attention is a gift* and we can all sense whether it's being bestowed or withheld. Whatever his faults, people who have met Bill Clinton have observed an extraordinary ability to make the person he is with feel that he or she is the recipient of his complete attention, that nothing and no one else in the world is more important at that moment.

This is the way we want to feel as a customer. We want the experience that whoever is serving us has a laser-like focus on us, and that our concerns and needs are all that matter. It's an irrational, perhaps even a totally unrealistic need, but then so are many of the emotional needs that drive us. And when we've been touched by a warm exchange it feels as real to us as the more tangible benefit we derive from the goods or service we have purchased.

We are emotional beings. All of us who experienced, or witnessed,

---

[12] Conductor of the Boston Philharmonic – the only orchestra in which students, professionals and amateurs are able to play side-by-side – and lecturer on leadership, creativity, coaching and teamwork.

depending on your point of view, the flood of feeling after the tragic death of Princess Diana became keenly aware that even the so-called British reserve is a thin patina covering deep wells of emotion.

Earlier, I called the human face of service 'relational' and proposed that you focus on hiring friendly people, designing with the customer's experience in mind, boosting his or her psychic sense of self-worth, empathising with the customer and celebrating beauty. The effect of paying attention to these areas is likely to be customers who feel better about your organisation. Now it's time to address the question of 'touching' the customer even more directly by looking at the human laws of legendary service, timeless principles of good personal relationships that can dramatically improve the bond between you and your customers.

The human laws of legendary service

A great deal of research in recent years has focused on why customers migrate from their suppliers and choose fresh ones. The Swedish Post Office research in the chart below is typical. It reinforces the view that although we are dealing with the 'soft stuff' here, it does have a very direct impact on the harder measures of customer retention and loyalty. Lack of attention – or interest – is felt so strongly by customers that they will take their business elsewhere. Sixty-eight per cent of them!

Why Companies Lose Customers

	%
Lack of interest on part of supplier	68
Unsatisfactory handling of complaints	14
Lower prices	9
Competitor wins over customer	5
Customer moves away	3
Customer dies	1

Source: Swedish Post Office, 1990
Satsa pa kunden (Focus on the Customer), Stockholm

Applying the four human principles of legendary service will have a magical effect on your customers' perception that you are interested and fully attending to them. The principles are:

- Contact, contact, contact;
- Understanding;
- Appreciating and valuing, and
- The little touches count.

Contact, Contact, Contact

Customers know you have
your attention on them only if you're in *contact*

How do we know another person is thinking about us if we experience no contact from them? Without it, how do we know, as a consumer, that our order is being processed or, in a business-to-business setting, that our components are being produced to schedule?

Technology helps, but there is no substitute for human contact. This is because we're wary of new technology. When fax machines were first in use people would often telephone to check that the pages had been transmitted. I see the same process at work with users new to e-mail. Human contact gives us the reassurance we need – *we trust human contact more than we trust technology*. Technology writer Kevin Kelly's observation that the network economy 'starts with chips and ends with trust' is spot-on. This is why several research studies have concluded that if all you do is contact customers shortly after their purchase was made or delivery received to ask 'Was everything all right?' their rating of your service soars.

Alienation is a common feature of our information age – we are swimming in information, starved of enough meaningful human contact. But why should a simple call impress us? Think of it this way. One of the most effective ways of breaking down resistance in a prisoner is to put him or her in solitary confinement. The need for human contact is so strong that very often the prisoner will subsequently open up to the questioners because he or she craves a connection. This may also be why there's a tendency for some kidnap victims to bond with their captors.

Do you put your customers into solitary confinement? Do you starve them of contact until the next time they want to make a purchase?

Dialogue, interactivity and contact is what makes a relationship. And this doesn't mean bombarding people with mailshots. It means finding channels to stay in touch, preferably in a one-to-one way. Customers value this contact, especially when there's no short-term sales motivation from your end. I have purchased major products such as houses and cars, and never heard a word from the agent or car retailer. If they had made a simple call to stay in touch they would have begun to build a relationship rather than merely sell a product. It's the long-term relationship that's the priceless asset, not just the one-off transaction.

Consider these key questions:

- What can we do continually to stay in contact with our customers?

- How can we do this in a way that is genuinely building a long-term relationship, not just a short-term sales focus?

- How can we ensure the customer feels that we have our full attention on him or her in these contact moments?

Understanding

Customers feel close to you only when you demonstrate *understanding* of their situation

One of the characteristics of a close relationship is that you feel the other person understands you. Of course, this may turn out to be one of life's great self-delusions – in all of us there's considerable mystery that can never be known. However, we feel warmer towards another who *appears* to know our situation, and who demonstrates verbally or non-verbally that he or she cares.

Customer care is one of the great euphemisms of our age. The Great British Builder doesn't know what it means. He seems not to have heard of Alexander Graham Bell's marvellous discovery, or at least doesn't use it sufficiently to stay in contact with his customers. After going through four different firms, I have finally hired the only one that understands the importance of communication and reliably lets me know when a date has to be changed or broken. I have not assessed these builders on their building skills and, provided the house doesn't collapse after their ministrations, I don't care – I have hired them on the basis of this most elementary of communication skills. There's a huge opportunity for firms of adequate builders to make a fortune simply by understanding this basic requirement.

Try Harry Ramsden's fish and chip franchise at Heathrow Airport's Terminal 1. Not because of the food, which is OK, but because the first question the waiter asks you is, 'When does your flight leave?' He will then rush your order, if necessary, to reduce potential anxiety. While this may be blindingly obvious, it's not a form of understanding practised by many others serving at airports, or railway or bus stations, who are so engrossed in their world that they are only dimly aware why you are there and why you might be in a hurry.

How can you make understanding of the customer's situation clear to service providers? Not just intellectually, but emotionally? Playing the customer in role plays helps, but there's no substitute for coaching your people in the use of:

- Imagination – stretching the mind and heart to empathise and sense 'How would I want to be treated in this situation?'
- Innocent listening – how to detect in the tone of voice and body language feelings behind the words, and
- Full attention – being fully mindful of customers' experiences, allowing suitable time and space for them to express themselves, especially if they are unhappy for some reason.

Appreciating and valuing

> Customers appreciate *you* more
> when they feel *appreciated and valued*

When we're appreciated it's positive reinforcement of that most fragile of human needs, the recognition that we exist and matter. However, we need to find new ways of saying this because there's nothing more annoying than being kept waiting on the phone for 10 minutes – it's probably only three minutes but, as a customer, it *feels* like 10 – while hearing a prerecorded message saying, 'We value your call'. Or to fly to a remote location where there's zero choice of airlines only to be told: 'Thank you for choosing Mongolian Airways'.

The appreciation of the customer has become formalised in these ways and carries no feeling tone. I think I'd even warm to a telephone message that says, 'We're as pissed off as you are to keep you waiting – do hang on and you'll get a big apology.' This is similar to our need to be understood, except that it entails more reaching out to demonstrate that you appreciate and value both the business customers bring and, more fundamentally, that you appreciate *them and what they're putting up with*.

In the corporate world, doesn't the Harrods hamper at Christmas or the expenses-paid convention in Thailand achieve this? Not really. Few believe that you're bestowing these gifts for a purely altruistic reason. 'We're paying, so now we can sell to you' is the implicit message. It's significant that when Gary Unsworth of Nichols Foods took his vending business clients to observe Colombia coffee growers at work, he specifically designed it not to be a selling trip, and yet a decade later five of the six clients are still with him. Real appreciation entails giving, either of an educational experience such as the Colombian trip, or in the more personal sense of giving of yourself.

In some firms this has become formalised – several now put on their employees' payslips that the salary is courtesy of the customer who really pays them. I think this is window-dressing. Really appreciating and valuing the customer is meaningless if the customers themselves don't feel valued. I recall a phenomenally successful salesman in the car trade who would always make a point of warmly thanking each customer for their interest even if they didn't make a purchase. It's not surprising that many of them remembered this the next time they were trading in their vehicles. Serve the customers, not the transaction, and they will naturally be drawn to you.

So how can you get a whole workforce genuinely to convey this appreciation to customers? First of all, they have really to 'get it' on the level of feeling – understanding that customers have choice and will tend to exercise that choice, all other factors being equal (which they often are) in favour of suppliers who welcome and appreciate their business. Second, they have to be encouraged to come up with their own way of conveying this appreciation, not just as a standardised formula on a letter or e-mail.

And finally, much imagination has to be exercised to demonstrate this appreciation by *action*. It could take the form of systematically calling customers to thank them, or inviting them not just to the ritual golf day, but to some experience you know from thoughtful use of your database that they will value. This could be sending flowers on anniversaries, birthday cards, or tickets to events – sports, opera, or theatre – that you know will mean a lot to them.

The little touches count

The *little touches* – thank-yous, apologies, reaching out – go a long way to pleasing the customer.

'Thank you is the most underused phrase in the business vocabulary,' says Julian Stainton, the service-obsessed chief of Western Provident Association, a health insurer transformed by this common-sense application of human principles to a highly systematised industry.

The little touches do count and are remembered because it's a sign of genuine care when the server reaches out to provide more than the expected. Whenever I have asked groups to recount their experiences of superb service, the stories have this one recurring theme – that the individual serving them put him or herself out to fulfil their needs even if it was 'outside the box' of their own job. Stories such as:

- The life insurance company clerk who took important papers to be signed by a customer in hospital in her own free time;
- The sales assistant who found her firm was out of stock of a birthday gift requested by a young girl. She bought the present with her own money from a rival store, then personally delivered it in time for the birthday party, and
- The carpet layers who insist on cleaning and dusting the room – and even cleaning the windows – to a much higher standard than before they arrived.

We all have similar stories, but what's sad is that we regard them as exceptional. They have to be turned into an everyday reflex for any organisation that seeks to achieve legendary status. There's no better way of encouraging this to become part of your culture than by regular story-telling sessions. In some companies there is a 'Wow' board where positive letters are posted. This is admirable, but it doesn't have the same emotional effect as hearing these same 'wows' from your peer group, told as a story.

Often shyness or fear of blowing one's own trumpet needs to be overcome, but the more people can be encouraged to tell these tales of everyday heroism, the more they become part of what's expected. And the more likely it is that you will create experiences that the customer will talk about. Again, these individual tales build the legend. Create your own fund of great stories rather than investing time hearing about Sally Bloggs in X Ltd who achieved these miracles.

But what about the phenomenon of people who have received good service, for example, from a hotel, restaurant or dressmaker, who deliberately keep this a secret because they don't want others to know about this provider? My experience is that this quickly becomes an open secret because people tend to whisper about their positive experience, with the proviso 'But don't tell anybody else'. Pretty quickly the secret is out, even if it's kept within a narrow affinity group of like-minded customers. A most striking example of this is when newspaper correspondents write in glowing terms about their favourite secret holiday location, while simultaneously bemoaning the fact that now everyone will know about it.

It's vital to handle the little touches well when the customer is close enough to touch. Much of the good intention that goes into focusing on the customer can be lost when this intimate, close-up contact is mishandled. Think, for example, of shopping for clothes. Nine times out of 10 the routine question, 'Can I help you?' triggers the reflex, 'No, thank you. Just looking'. If you're going to ask this question in the first place, at least ask the open-ended version, '*What* can I help you with?'

Julian Richer comments that his staff are dissuaded from using the ritualised 'How may I help you?' question. Instead they make eye contact and just say 'Hello'. They know that if the customer wants help, he or she will now find it easier to ask, but will do so in his or her own way. *This is so basic that it leaves me to conclude that most organisations have invested almost zero time in coaching people about intimate contact with the customer.* The vicious circle is that if you assume people are just passing through – annual attrition rates in some call centres, for example, are around 150 per cent – then you will not think it's worth giving them this attention. It becomes a negative self-fulfilling prophesy. Contrast this with the attitude of Richer Sounds, which believes that the most humble job is the first rung on a serious career ladder. New employees have to read and understand about the service principles of the company *before* they join, even if they're only applying for a summer job.

Have you noticed the body language of refreshment trolley staff on many British trains? They will peer reluctantly into your carriage, asking 'Coffee? Tea?' in such an unenthusiastic manner that you don't even look up from the paper. It probably takes them a week to sell a small trolley's worth, partly because their whole demeanour says, 'You don't want any of this, do you?

I'm not really bothered either.' It's not that they're unpleasant, but rather that you have to make a conscious effort to buy from them.

When I was travelling to London recently I noticed the contrast with someone who had mastered the essentials of close-up service. He pushed the refreshment cart boldly into the middle of the carriage, looked straight at all of us and announced, 'Good morning, ladies and gentlemen. Beautiful day. Now what would you like from my lovely trolley? I have fresh sandwiches, tea, coffee, muffins . . .' He cleaned up. Nearly everyone bought an item or two from him. The sandwiches may not have been the best in the world, but the atmosphere in the carriage had changed noticeably for the better. There was no sales push involved, just a fresh and open attitude to service. And he said a big 'thank you' to the whole carriage when he left.

There's a new quasi-science that describes the need for these more intimate skills. Naturally, it's called '*proxemics*' and it covers what you need to do when you're in close proximity to the customer. I extend this to mean psychological as well as physical proximity, as in telephone conversations.

Again, Richer Sounds has thought about these proxemics very carefully. Staff will make eye contact with people in the queue behind the one they are serving and always ask the customer if it's all right to take a phone call. They are also aware of how annoying it can be to be approached on two or three separate occasions by a different member of staff with the same offer of help. To counter this they have developed an internal shorthand, using expressions like 'Has that window been cleaned yet?' as a discreet way of asking whether a particular customer has already been approached.

This might all seem like small beer, but when you add up the dozens – no, hundreds and thousands – of Moments of Truth well handled in this way, it makes a positive impression. There's a subtlety of attention that makes any interchange more graceful, more elegant, more self-affirming. As customers we may make poor experts on product quality, except in cases of extreme horror or delight, but we sense in a visceral way the effect of charm, care, and even a certain amount of beauty in these encounters.

You can introduce the skill of proxemics to the most apparently humble of roles. Check-out staff in Asda and their baggers have it. Those in Sainsbury's seem not to. Sales assistants in Richer Sounds have it. My experience is that it's more rare in Dixons. Cabin staff in Virgin Atlantic possess it. Again, my recent experience is that those on United don't. The difference is like day and night. Training in the skills is not enough in itself; it needs backing up by appropriate systems and management coaching. But there's no excuse for every organisation not to consider carefully how customers can almost 'smell' whether you have put your attention on improving their experience. Or not.

Finally, use your imagination to ensure that the little touches are really what the customers want and not merely what you think they want. A supposedly helpful question I'm asked when I check out of hotels is not something like 'Do you have a long journey?', or 'I hope you enjoyed your stay – when will we be seeing you again?' but is inevitably 'Would you like your credit card slip stapled to your bill, sir?'

My irrational but heartfelt response to this well-intentioned offer is to think that staff have been on a two-day seminar on advanced origami and paper folding, but have not received even five minutes' instruction in showing their guests a little touch of thoughtfulness.

What are the small rituals your people go through in front of customers that make sense to you, but irritate the hell out of them? Your customers will surely be able to let you know.

For some penetrating questions, activities and ideas relating to this chapter turn to page 252.

Chapter Eight

What If? Why Not?

'Some people see things and say "why?" But I dream things that never were – and I say ' "why not?" '[1]

John F. Kennedy (1917–63), US president

'We all agree that your theory is crazy, but is it crazy enough?'

Niels Bohr (1885–1962),
Danish physicist and Nobel Prize-winner

Thinking *What If? Why Not?* helps you to:

- Be more creative about your service offering;

- Open your mind to new possibilities, and

- Ask provocative questions to unlock your imagination.

WERE you ever told off for daydreaming? It's a shame, really, because that's often when we have our best ideas. In adult life we tend to adopt the stance of serious, focused, rational thinkers. We easily forget that it's as important to dream as it is to do. The poet Robert Bly captures this beautifully when he says that whatever separates a man from the tiger and the waterfall, kills him. He is describing the riches of the natural and imaginative world, without which our lives become arid and brittle. Thinking *what if?* opens a door to the imagination; thinking *why not?* is having the conviction to make the idea work.

One of my favourite architects is Gaudí, whose extraordinary vision transformed the Spanish city of Barcelona. His cathedral, La Sagrada Família, was completely 'outside the box' of any other architect's thinking

---

[1] Address before the Irish Parliament, Dublin, 28 June 1963, quoting George Bernard Shaw, *Back to Methuselah*, 1921.

earlier this century. It appears to be lighter than air and captures the essence of a spiritual building – that it should be really uplifting. Unlike many architects, Gaudí did not use flying buttresses – which he compared to the crutches of a cripple – but concentrated the weight on the supporting columns, and used different materials depending on the weight they had to bear. Unfortunately, he was killed by a tram in 1926 before the project was completed – it's *still* unfinished – and his body was discovered in a pauper's hospital only several days after his death.

However, Gaudí's vision lives on. It seems that every fresh generation of architects continues the dream and it's hard to imagine either that it ever will be finished or that the people of Barcelona even *want* to complete it. This illustrates the lasting power of what I call *what if? why not?* thinking to transform a familiar landscape. While designing a new type of cathedral is highly unlikely to be your prime concern, Gaudí's masterpiece demonstrates that great innovations often come from thinking the unthinkable.

What do we mean, then, when we talk about applying creativity to customer service? It means that great imagination (*what if?* thinking) courageously acted upon can create long-lasting structures that are a source of inspiration to others. Passion is also necessary for making the idea work in practice. Gaudí lived for his vision.

What if? means being open to possibilities that seem *im*possible or even crazy from the standpoint of conventional thinking. *Why not?* comes from the passion needed to push through all obstacles and make the idea come alive.

What if? Why not? thinking is the customer's friend. What if we were to provide free customer access on the Internet, thought an employee of Dixons, the UK high street electronics retailer, only a short year ago. Freeserve was worth £1.7 billion in a few months. Why not provide natural cosmetics to customers in the simplest, most functional containers to cut costs and make a statement about our environmental values? The Body Shop legend was born.

Of course, it's still true that necessity is the mother of invention, because in the early days Anita Roddick couldn't *afford* fancy packaging. She started her whole empire with a loan of only £4,000. So, if we're already successful, how do we engineer our own *creative imperative*? Paradoxically, great success can sow the seeds of eventual failure because there's too much conventional, or ancestral, thinking that goes into perpetuating the existing structure rather than giving birth to the new. We could call this the failure of success. IBM, Sears, General Motors and other megalithic companies have experienced the problems created when you don't continue to think *what if?* or *why not?*

Let's explore how to focus this imaginative thinking on your own customer service. The diagram *What If? Why Not? Thinking in Practice* introduces a model[2] that makes the nice idea of creative thinking more practical. The model uses colour as shorthand for essential stages in the thinking process. Blue comes first meaning 'blue sky' or open-minded thinking where all possibilities – from the mundane to the bizarre – are considered without judgment. This is really the home of *what if? why not?* thinking.

Red thinking means 'stop', as with traffic lights: analyse, check and, if necessary, temper the blue-sky idea with a dose of reality.

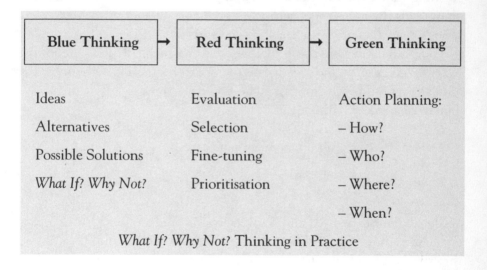

Blue Thinking	→	Red Thinking	→	Green Thinking
Ideas		Evaluation		Action Planning:
Alternatives		Selection		– How?
Possible Solutions		Fine-tuning		– Who?
What If? Why Not?		Prioritisation		– Where?
				– When?

What If? Why Not? Thinking in Practice

Green naturally means 'go'. Once we've had the idea (blue), evaluated its chances of success in solving a problem or seizing an opportunity (red), then we can apply well-known action-planning skills to make sure the idea lives.

The problem is that we muddle up the colours. I've frequently been at meetings where some people are in blue (busy generating novel solutions), others majoring on red thinking (deeply analysing, checking and judging any ideas they hear), while others spark on green (pointing

[2] Originated by Mark Brown, author of *The Dinosaur Strain*, Element Books, 2000, ISBN: 1852300485.

out anxiously that time is passing and there's an urgent need to implement the idea, even before it's been conceived). All of this is happening simultaneously.

The value of the model in helping you to think *what if? why not?* – primarily blue thinking – is to create greater awareness of which colour you're in. All stages are necessary to turn a creative idea into practice. This is one reason why brainstorming often doesn't work. It's usually practised as a partially misunderstood version of blue thinking and the ideas stay on the whiteboard because they haven't been tested rigorously enough in the red phase, or received sufficient thought on how they will be implemented at the green stage.

Because the pressures of working life so often colour our thinking red and green, it's not so easy to stand back and really open our minds in the blue phase. This chapter is about getting into the blue sufficiently to create ideas about service that are fresh, leading-edge and new.

The main obstacle to this is that we confuse which colour we are in. For example, going green too soon means that we rush to action without having fully thought through an idea. The credo of those of us who have a preference for green thinking is:

- Ready!   or, in more extreme cases   • Fire!
- Fire!   • Ready!
- Aim!   • Aim!

But the worst enemy of blue thinking is going red too soon, which means strangling a novel idea before it's had time to take its first full breath. Red thinking is valuable when you're in the phase of selecting the most viable solutions, but if you do it too early in the blue while you're still trying to think *what if? why not?* it will express itself as the ultimate assassin of your ideas, *yes, but* thinking.

The menace of Yes, but thinking

There are two main ways of *yes, butting*. First, *yes, butting* ideas from other people. It's one of the reasons why organisations *don't* learn from other organisations. Before the potential of the idea is fully explored, the frame of experience shuts down like a portcullis on the new notion, attacking any apparent weakness and effectively assassinating it. No further exploration or adaptation can occur.

The kind of expressions most of us use to say *yes*, *but* to something new, something outside our own frame, include:

- With respect . . .
- With the greatest respect!
- I hear what you say, *but* . . .
- I see your point, *but* . . .
- I don't have a problem with that
- It's all right in theory, *but* . . .
- I'll think about it – I'm very open-minded.

For your information, the only people who are really open-minded are village idiots and the dead. What these words actually mean is:

• With respect	– I don't like it!
• With the greatest respect	– I don't like it one little bit!
• I hear what you say	– But it's just not very good
• I see your point	– Yeah, but mine's better!
• I don't have a problem	– Except . . .
• It's all right in theory	– It won't work
• I'll think about it	– In the next life, maybe!

One of my clients would inadvertently deflate people who came to him with a new idea by saying cheerfully, 'Leave it with me!' The suggestion usually ended up in another colour of thinking – black, and not much comes out of a black hole. It took him some time to wonder why people stopped coming to him with their fresh, blue ideas.

There are many famous *yes*, *buts* in the history of business. For instance, a certain Mr Rees, head of the Post Office in England, said that the Americans required the telephone for geographical reasons. We in England did not because we had plenty of messenger boys. *Plus ça change*, a cynic might add.

Then in 1962 there was the Decca record executive who auditioned the Beatles, but concluded that there was no future in guitar groups. And in 1979 the famous pronouncement by Ken Olsen, founder of Digital Equipment, who ventured: 'There was is no reason why anyone should want a computer in their home.' How ironic, then, to see DEC swallowed by PC giant Compaq.

Yes, *butting* has even been practised by that most prescient of the current crop of great entrepreneurs, his Nerdship himself, William Gates III, who initially was not as impressed by the business potential of the Internet as some of his rivals. To his credit, he accomplished one of the swiftest U-turns in modern business when he announced his Internet strategy in December 1995.

It may be an entertaining spectator sport to mock other people's yes, buts, but it's far more difficult to develop an awareness of when we are limiting our own potential by indulging in yes, butting *ourselves.*

The second and arguably more dangerous form of *yes, butting* is when we reject our own dreams and courageous ideas. This self-limitation may take the form of apathy. The idea is potentially good, but would take too much energy and time to implement. Or it could be fear – dare I say it? Or even self-denigration – a tape that plays inside our minds saying 'It's no good', 'It's not original', 'How do I know if it will work?' The tragedy is that many potentially great ideas never see the light of day. They've been *yes-butted* to death by their originators.

In some businesses *yes, but* thinking is so rife that I've introduced a fine box into which people put money – say £1 – every time they *yes, but* a new idea. Interestingly, the most common *yes, but*, which stops people putting money in the box, is that mysteriously they don't have any cash on them! Naturally it's not so much the precise words as the attitude that we all display in doubting the new. The *yes, but* box is a humorous and memorable way of helping a group to stick with the blue phase of thinking in everyday work, as well as in formal sessions devoted to generating ideas.

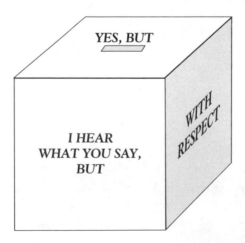

The following sections address how to think *what if?* or *why not?* They will help you to consider more deeply the service you offer to your customers and to break down the barriers erected by *yes, but* thinking.

Where do great ideas come from?

Most people say they get their inspiration when they are more settled in their mind, resting, on holiday, driving in a relaxed way, walking the dog, or in the shower. Anywhere except when they are analysing at their desks, standing in front of a flipchart, or gazing at a PC screen. Suddenly the idea is there, fully formed, often surprising the individual who has become a channel for it.

Songwriter and former Beatle Paul McCartney says that a new tune is in his head when he wakes up, and Bach remarked that when he got up in the morning he had trouble not treading on all the ideas that filled his room.

Einstein talked about going to a quiet place inside himself where the solution was self-evident. Kekulé, the great chemist, 'saw' his discovery of the benzene ring in a dream image of a snake chasing its own tale. Pilkington realised the concept of manufacturing glass in a float tank while observing dishes floating in the sink while he was washing up. And Barnes Wallis crystallised the idea of the bouncing dam-buster bomb from seeing children skimming stones on Hampstead Pond. These are all striking examples of how the creative process works.

We may not have realised it, but the same process is active in our daily problem-solving – we analyse the problem and leave it to incubate in our minds, much like putting down a crossword puzzle, picking it up an hour later and suddenly finding solutions to clues that baffled us a short while before. Rarely are we conscious of this process – we've unconsciously tapped into another *level* of our mind.

Illumination, or 'Eureka' emerges. 'Yes, that's how to write that proposal.' 'Now I know what to say to the boss.' These are typical experiences we are all familiar with. It may not be a ground-breaking scientific discovery that emerges, but it's the same mechanics of effortless problem-solving at work. The most profound ideas come to us when we're most relaxed – the hard work is then taking them through the red phase to reach green, or action.

Accessing deeper levels of thought is therefore familiar to us all. It's also evident that just as finer levels of physical creation are more dynamic – splitting an atom is more powerful than splitting an apple – finer levels of thought are also more far-reaching in their effect. Ideas have given birth to nations and created world religions that have outlasted any of our business structures.

Unless your business is also an ideas factory, you're unlikely to be able to change or adapt fast enough to survive. This realisation has led many businesses to focus on topics such as knowledge management and organisational learning, and to produce some of the most extraordinary job titles, such as – wait for it – Director of Intellectual Capital! Perhaps the first person in the world to have this trend-setting title was Leif Edvinsson of Skandia AB, the successful Swedish insurance business. And you think you have a problem describing to your family what you do for a living at the end of a working day . . . !

But there is good reasoning behind this focus on the intellectual assets of an organisation. As a recent business magazine headline shouted:

Microsoft's Only Factory Asset Is The Human Imagination!

If you're just beginning to consider this, again remember the old saying that 'It is later than you think'. Your competitors may already be investing heavily in developing their people's imagination. As a nation the Japanese have been doing this for years. According to the Spring 1991 issue of *Sloan Management Review*, Japanese companies received nearly 48 million improvement proposals from employees in 1986. In the same period their counterparts in the United States received only about one million. Toyota alone recorded 2.65 million employee proposals in that year.

Furthermore, more than 70 per cent of the Japanese ideas found their way to the green stage (were implemented), compared with only 20 per cent of American ideas. Another fascinating revelation to emerge from this report was that the Japanese record these figures religiously. It would seem that to do so is in itself a way of putting the power of attention on what you want to grow.

There's a shocking conclusion to this discussion of the role of imagination in business. You can't grow without it and yet most organisational climates seem to have the effect of killing it. What follows are seven provocative *what if? why not?* questions designed to stimulate the creativity to transform your service. In answering them, don't merely rely on a logical approach to these questions – they are designed deliberately to stimulate your intuition, to tap into the right side of your brain. And remember that good ideas will probably come to you when you least expect them to do so.

Seven provocative questions

The inquisitive mind has always been enriched in its search for new ideas by being engaging with challenging questions. You can take the seven provocations listed on the next page, in any order, but try to create the right state of mind for allowing blue thinking to flow. Go for a walk, sit by the river and wait for Eureka to happen.

What if . . .

1. We all became better customers?

2. You were married to your customers?

3. Service was like music?

4. Business was like theatre?

5. Customers were fundamentally disloyal?

6. You forgot to measure customer satisfaction?

7. Service was spiritual?

Before starting, there are a couple of helpful techniques for gaining the most inspiration from the seven provocations and similar ones you might dream up for yourself. The first is to stay in the blue long enough to allow the birth of a new idea. Only in this way can you escape the gravitational pull of conventional and existing thought patterns and enter the fertile ground of beginner's mind where all possibilities exist in a latent state. Here are a number of tips to help you stay blue:

- Generate ideas, don't judge;
- 'And' and 'build', no *yes, buts*;
- Don't even *think* a *yes, but*;
- Build and explore;
- Find the right physical environment for creativity, and
- Have fun!

The principles described above can either be used individually or in a team setting. In a team situation staying in the blue means fully opening your mind to another's thinking rather than rehearsing an internal dialogue that you trot out in a gap in the conversation.

Second, the creative seed of *what if!* thinking is more likely to flower if you can entertain even a wildly outrageous idea and suspend the tendency to *yes, but* by thinking of *two good things to say about it* before allowing any judgment. This has a surprisingly powerful effect in opening the mind to the possibilities rather than the absurdities in the potential of the new thought. For instance, suppose you were to be told that tomorrow your job was relocated to Iceland? Immediately a host of *yes, buts* about the difficulties of adjustment, language, education or weather might crowd into your mind. Thinking of two good things to say about the idea can subtly transform your thinking. Iceland has a beautiful landscape, a small and highly sophisticated population, relative freedom from pollution and the incomparable beauty of the northern lights.

I'm not suggesting for a minute that you welcome every wild idea with open arms – a certain path to early insanity. What I'm saying is that when you consciously allow yourself to think 'blue', it's necessary to shock, provoke and even trick your existing mindset into positive new avenues of thought.

Here are the provocations. They are each different entry points for opening your mind to a specific aspect of service, and you can start with any of them as they are not sequential.

1. What If . . . we all became better customers?

In the past we have all been used to a certain degree of ritual humiliation, at least in Europe, in our role as customers. Perhaps now the pendulum has swung too far in the other direction. A dangerous trend I see today is that of customer as bully. Thousands of assaults – verbal and physical – are recorded on service representatives annually. One airline has found that on average every 35th passenger is abusive to some degree to the staff member who welcomes him or her on to a flight. How then, does that person act warmly to the 36th and subsequent passengers? He or she would be inhuman if some degree of resentment weren't conveyed.

Perhaps it's time we remedied the balance to think about how we could be better service providers *and* better customers. In our daily life most of us are customers and suppliers of a service. And, let's face it, we are more critical as customers than as service deliverers. When you walk into someone else's business – a hotel, restaurant, bank, or even another part of your own organisation – how quickly do you make judgments as to how it could be run better? Most groups to whom I have posed this question respond, 'straight away' or 'almost immediately'.

From the outside we are experts, whereas from the inside we can easily become wrapped up in the thousand and one distractions that prevent us from giving the service we ourselves would expect and demand as customers. It's one of life's great blind spots that we don't see ourselves as our customers do.

What if we were all to become better customers? This could create a revolution in the quality of service we receive because a relationship takes two and overbearing, angry customers tend to produce a negative response in even the most patient of service representatives.

Bad customers – yes, they do exist – are so demanding that they always expect to be let down. Miraculously, they are usually right. I used to run seminars on service with a consultant for whom the glass was always half empty. In fact, I'd put her in the category of someone who would complain, 'There isn't even a glass.' She would arrive at the session with tales of service woes she had experienced on the lengthy journey to the venue. If you or I had seen this aggressive person coming towards us, only on our best behaviour would we have wanted to give her good service.

This sort of individual is rather like the character in Douglas Adams's novel, *So Long and Thanks for All the Fish.* He is a truck driver and everywhere he goes, rain follows him. Finally he realises that is because he *is* the God of Rain! Many who consistently experience bad service are bad service gods or goddesses.

Of course, this doesn't mean to say that bad service doesn't exist. Who hasn't experienced a sunny demeanour crumble when faced with surly and unhelpful so-called service representatives? But the second type of person, the one who expects others to be friendly and helpful, loads the dice in favour of more positive outcomes.

A colleague woke up one morning, feeling happy and contented before a long business trip across the USA. His daughter had just got into college, the sun was shining, and he felt good. He smiled at everyone, was polite and charming and arrived at his destination after what could have been tortuous travel with tales of how positively helpful everyone – cab drivers, airline check-in staff, restaurant waiters – had been to him. Powerful testimony for the idea that 'the world is as we are' and that great service is a two-way relationship.

I have a fantasy that I would like to see realised. Suppose all the thousands of people who are put through customer service training were also to go through an intensive session entitled *'How to Be a Better Customer'*? Though even in my fantasy I don't expect this to eradicate poor service from the world, just imagine the positive effects. Not only would they tend, on average, to receive better service, but also, as people become became more consciously positive in their role as customers, it would have the knock-on effect of improving their empathy when they were on the other side of the desk or the other end of the telephone.

Service is not subservience. It's a dance that takes two, at its best when both parties see themselves as equals. Perhaps not equals in status terms, but equal in the sense of both contributing to achieving the same end. If service representatives see themselves as subservient, this will breed resentment in our increasingly meritocratic society. And we all know the effect of the other extreme when they see themselves as superior and display arrogance to the ignorant customer. Even the gods of the medical profession have begun to learn this lesson.

So what does it take to be a better customer?

- *Expect a positive outcome*. If you want results rather than a good gripe, try a little attitude adjustment before you deal with your supplier.
- *Use the same highest level of skills you employ when you are serving others*. Good eye contact, patience, respect for the individual.
- *Balance your complaints with appreciation, if possible*.

This last point needs explaining. If ever I'm sending a letter or e-mail of complaint, I find that I get a better response and some real behaviour change if I'm also able to pinpoint what was good in the transaction without deflecting from my anger about what was dreadful. If all your feedback is negative, however justified you feel this to be, something in the listener is bound to go into defensive mode. A simple law of physics is also a law of human exchanges – action and reaction are opposite and equal.

One barrier to implementing this thinking successfully is that we often have a preference for being right over being happy. I first caught myself falling into this trap when travelling on British Rail, as it then was. A series of ubiquitous advertisements displayed statistics showing that the vast majority of trains actually arrived on time. A pattern of dots in one colour denoting trains that arrived on time filled more than 90 per cent of the advertisement. This was *not* my perception or that of my fellow passengers. For the next month I kept records of how late was each train I travelled on. I worked out that each was something like 28 minutes late, bringing me as close to becoming a train-spotter as I've ever wanted. However, I then experienced a run of three journeys where all the trains arrived on the dot. Was I pleased? Absolutely not – it upset my findings! I gave up this apprenticeship in train-spotting immediately because I realised I was more concerned about being right in my complaints than in having a good experience as a customer.

The message is to remember the positive experiences you have had from the supplier as well as the negative. If we expect those giving us service to be compassionate and empathetic, then the more we display this ourselves, the more we are likely to receive it.

2. What if . . . you were married to your customers?

Marriage is a fertile metaphor to refresh your thinking. Forget about service for a minute and let's think about marriage. There's usually a period of courtship, getting to know the other's likes and dislikes, intense excitement at the beginning, the exchange of tokens (gifts and rings), the wedding, honeymoon and then the accommodation needed to maintain the relationship long-term throughout life's vicissitudes. Perhaps other rivals for affection come along. Children may replace the other partner as the principal object of love. Attempts may be needed to revitalise the relationship, since partners will need continually to make themselves attractive to their mates, and so on.

Thinking *what if? why not?* means using these concepts as a creative trigger. For example, the idea of attractiveness could be linked back to service, getting you to think of the way your people look and dress, the appeal or otherwise of the physical environment and even the tone of voice used on the telephone. You can then build this idea even further by repeatedly asking, 'How should we be on the telephone to be more attractive and give better attention?' or 'What can we do about our appearance to make us more sexy to the customer?' And so on.

The chart overleaf gives examples of the way in which you can use this *what if?* to spark creative ideas about service. By moving further away from the familiar field – here into the world of marriage – and then linking back, new possibilities open up, many of them also sound and practical.

OUR SERVICE: Key questions and potential answers	LINKING BACK	WHAT IF? You were married to your customers? There would be:

How do we make our offerings
more appealing to potential
customers?
• Dress better – ourselves and
  our environment
• Demonstrate we are in love
  with them
• Explore likes and dislikes
	←————	A courtship

How do we make our commitment
clear?
• Publicise that we're
  interested only in a long-
  term relationship
• Give amazing terms and
  conditions that really draw
  the customer in
• Give a valuable token that
  demonstrates we would like
  a long-lasting relationship
	←————	An engagement ring

How do we demonstrate our sense
of commitment to our customers?
• Ensure positive excitement
  in the first few months
• Make new customers feel truly
  pampered
• Give surprises
	←————	A honeymoon

How do we ensure the post-
honeymoon slump doesn't happen?
• Constant contact
• Adjusting to changing needs
• Paying attention to individuality
• Celebrating important dates – a
  a card, or present on the anni-
  versary of you becoming a customer
	←————	Not taking the
		partner for granted

3. What if . . . service was like music?

A superficial understanding of this *what if?* is that all aspects of your organisation need to be working in concert to play great music for your customers. But let's explore the image more profoundly to generate some original insights.

What made the legendary violinist, Yehudi Menuhin, touch the lives of so many? Certainly, he had the most superb *technique*, but so have many others. What marked him out as such an extraordinary person was both his sublime *expression* as a violinist and his service for humanitarian causes.

Let's take the step back to customer service using these special attributes of Menuhin's. Firstly, service is not mere technique – procedures, systems, scripts, accuracy correlate with playing the notes correctly and in the right order. Like the Lane Group example at the start of this book, you can get the technology and the technique right, but the customer still feels a void, in this case a *lack of expression* that made them boring to The Body Shop!

So how can you encourage your people, even in a tightly scripted environment, to express more of themselves in every note they play with the customer? Do you need to coach them in expressiveness, body language, eye contact and the subtle skills of relating? How can you create such simple systems that these they free your people to give maximum expression to their emotions?

Secondly, Menuhin's persona was always bigger than that of a mere musician. He saw himself as a channel for a highly individual and spiritual view of all people on earth as essentially connected and united in their difficulties, needs and aspirations. But how do you connect this notion to the apparently mundane task of answering the telephone in a call centre or installing a piece of engineering plant for a customer? A cynic will say: 'Not at all.' The creative mind will stay with *what if? why not?* thinking and see this as part of the intangible but infectious enthusiasm your people can convey if they feel connected to a vision of service that transcends the perceived limitations of their own specific role.

This inspires a much wider understanding of their role than the narrow, technical nature of the job. It invokes a deeper sense of service to the community and even the world, and is a modern-day example of the time-honoured story of the stonemason who believes he is not just cutting stone, but is building a cathedral. *How can you help your people to realise the wider sense of purpose behind their specific task?*

It's a justifiable objection to say that this is all right for a chief executive, but what about our hourly paid workers? I experienced how this notion can apply at all levels when I asked a girl serving at the Häagen-Dazs ice-cream emporium in Leicester Square, London, what she thought she was really there to do. Without referring to a plastic laminated card, she replied with a genuine smile that she was there to help customers enjoy their day better. Was this an individual view, or the results of intensive brainwashing from the training department? As a customer, I don't care, but I was impressed and have continued to frequent the restaurant.

So – one last dive into the world of music, this time at the other end of the spectrum from virtuoso classical violin playing. Compare and contrast the guitar playing of Jeff Beck and Eric Clapton. Beck, a former member of the Yardbirds, is a guitar phenomenon – his 1999 album is described as sounding like a match thrown into a box of fireworks. His critics would say it's virtuosity for its own sake, the profusion of notes with which he showers the listener barely holding a melody together. Clapton, on the other hand, has been dubbed 'legendary', perhaps because his avowed intent is always to produce the most beautiful sound, often sublimating his own virtuosity to the overall impact of the song's essential harmonies or vocal message. The opening bars of his massive hit, 'Layla', are a notable exception.

How do we relate this to serving your customers? Here are some examples. Do you shower your customers with a bewildering proliferation of 'notes' or offers? One business that, to my mind, does this, is the mail-order office goods supplier Viking Direct – it produces too many catalogues and too many specials that make me feel overwhelmed and even frustrated. So, how can you make your 'notes' cleaner and simpler – like Clapton's guitar – easier to pick out and understand, more clearly in line with the overall harmony or relationship you are trying to build with your customers? How can you create systems that are breathtaking in their simplicity and even beauty?

4. What if . . . Business was like theatre?

Theatre is a rich, creative metaphor for re-imagining your service. Which play best characterises your efforts for the customer? Is it a tragedy – for instance, *Macbeth* – and if so, who are the three witches among your customers prophesying doom, and how can you listen to these portents more effectively?

And if it's a comedy, is everyone laughing with you or at you? Is it a *Comedy of Errors*?

Do all your 'players' know their scripts, and where exactly in your dealings with customers is there scope for improvisation? As many actors will tell you, the best *ad libs* are thoroughly rehearsed. Do you therefore spend enough time rehearsing critical interactions with the customer?

What about the audience? Are they at a distance, huddling in the back rows, and if so, how can you bring them closer? What can you do to ensure more audience/customer participation and how can you encourage your players to mingle more with the audience? One theatre director I know insists that during rehearsals those actors not taking part in a specific scene sit in the audience's seats to get a clearer perception of how it all looks and feels. In other words, to understand the customer's experience. What would it mean for your business to sit in the customer's seat?

Let's consider the stage itself. Theatre in the round is becoming fashionable again, reviving Shakespearean times when the audience sat on all sides of the stage. How can you bring your customers into more intimate contact with you so that they can experience your organisation from every perspective? And, paradoxically, how can you keep the off-stage apparatus – scenery, costume changes, ropes and lighting – hidden from the audience so that you always present your most immaculate face to them?

Do the programme notes clearly explain – in jargon-free language – what the play is about? Or, extending the metaphor slightly to that of opera, do you need clear lucid programme notes that translate the complexities of your performance to them? What would surtitles – the words clearly displayed above the stage at an opera – be, applied to the world of customer service? How can you make what you do more simple and accessible to your customers?

Disney is, of course, a strong example of an organisation using the image of theatre in practice. In the language of theatre the employees in its theme parks are cast members, they audition for their jobs and are either on stage or off stage. Some hotels obviously use this image of theatre. Ken McCulloch's Malmaison staff are expected to be immaculate in their appearance because they are giving a performance. The uniform of the Geek Squad – a computer installation and repair firm in Minneapolis – includes white shirts, thin black ties, pocket protectors and badges, and they drive to their appointments in old cars. They make their service calls a memorable encounter.[4]

---

[4] *The Experience Economy*, ibid.

5. What if . . . customers were fundamentally disloyal?

Wake up – they are! As customers, most of us are having several relationships on the side, keeping our options open and prepared to go for a new one if it seems more attractive, simple to understand and cheaper. And we can hardly be blamed for this because dozens of sexy offers land on our doormats every week hoping to entice us away from our long-standing primary relationships. Most of these are good for a quick fling – a cheap flight or inexpensive international phone calls – but it's unlikely to be a long-lasting love affair if we don't also experience an emotional connection with the offerer.

If we hold in our mind this idea of fundamental disloyalty it could inspire us to think how extraordinary we have to make the relationship with the customer for them to stay for the long-term. Consider the following ideas:

Show loyalty to the customer.

One problem with many financially-based loyalty schemes is that they don't last long enough for a busy and overwhelmed customer to take advantage of them. By the time I've read my offers on cheap flights to the Seychelles or Cuba, the window of opportunity is gone. Flights next month leaving on Tuesdays only from Gatwick are unlikely to fit my diary. Not surprisingly, one of the most successful customer loyalty schemes has been oil company Mobil's Premier Points, simply because it has maintained the scheme long enough for us to become used to it and to accumulate enough points for it to be worthwhile. The offer has even outlasted the major disruption of a merger with BP and the disappearance of Mobil forecourts in the UK. Loyalty is rewarded by loyalty.

Give more than cheap prices.

There is an old adage in business that says: 'Customers who choose you on price will also leave you on price.' To continue the metaphor of a personal relationship, you will experience a great number of one-night stands if *all* you're offering is cheaper prices. And of course you may find yourself in a downward spiral of bloody price wars and be faced by the frightening spectre of commodity hell!

American Express card magazines are full of offers that go far beyond mere cost savings – open days, sporting and cultural events, lectures and meetings are included. *Anything that can make your customers more interesting is what they will be interested in.* It's the philosophy of a club, trying to discover common interests that bind your customers beyond the basic business service you are selling. People will pay a premium to *belong* to such a club.

Perhaps the most effective price offer in the UK also goes beyond price – it's the John Lewis department store's philosophy of being 'never knowingly undersold'. This not only allows customers to receive money back if a competitor is selling the same product more cheaply, but represents a solid commitment to giving value because the company has loyally continued the scheme for so long. By this simple phrase you also understand you are buying the intangibles of reliability, reputation and trust.

Serve the customer, not the transaction.

I recently terminated my road rescue service with one supplier. Not that I was unhappy with the service, but I'd discovered that I was also covered by my car manufacturer's service. What impressed me was how helpful and friendly the representative was in guiding me through the steps to cancel my standing order, which can be a difficult manacle to break in the UK. Even more important, he told me that my membership number would be held for me and if at any time I wanted to restart the service there would be no paperwork, merely a simple phone call.

In this encounter the supplier was losing my custom, but leaving the door wide open for future business. It had served me, not the immediate transaction, and if I change vehicles and need cover again it will be my first choice.

Customer loyalty is hailed as the most important area to focus on in the world of service. It isn't – it's the *outcome* of everything you do for and with your customers. Yes, you can help to 'lock in' customers by building smart relationships where they have invested time and effort into educating you, or by the offer of money-saving loyalty cards, but in the end they will stay with you because they *like* you. And if they migrate to another supplier it may not be because you're doing anything wrong, but merely that they're in search of newness. If you can keep providing that newness in the relationship, while paradoxically keeping the familiarity and consistency of your offer – for example, 'never knowingly undersold' – in their minds, they are more likely to stay. If they go, make it easy for them and leave the door open *clearly and happily.* Customers have long memories . . .

6. What if . . . you forgot to measure customer satisfaction?

There's a piece of received wisdom in business that says, 'What gets measured gets done!' What nonsense! Many measurement systems take on a life of their own and what gets done is more measurement. It may not even be measurement of the right things, for example, the factors that *really* influence the customer to stay or go. If you forget to measure customer satisfaction for a while the benefits might be:

- Greater focus on getting things done rather than spending time measuring what happens. More time scoring, less time recording the score, and

- Greater sensitivity to the customers' real needs rather than what you *assume* are their needs. They're measuring you on their own scorecard, which is almost certainly not the one you are using to track their experience.

But if you have to measure, how do you do so in a way that brings you closer to understanding the customer's reality? There's much talk today about the 'balanced scorecard' in business, a more comprehensive way of measuring how well you are doing that goes far wider than the usual obsession with financials. What about a balanced customer scorecard that allows you to tune in more closely to the customer's real opinion of you?

These are the essential ingredients to consider in creating this customer-sensitive scorecard.

Use the customer's own language to come up with meaningful categories.

Customers don't use language like 'satisfaction', 'exceeding expectations' and so on. Try measuring whether you are:

- Super helpful
- *Demonstrating* that you care
- Amazingly responsive.

. . . and use your creativity to work out ways of measuring or monitoring.

Finally, don't over-categorise – frequently this 'blands out' the impact of the customers' real stories told in their own words. How can a questionnaire capture the powerful emotional content of comments such as: 'Why do your people never smile?' or 'It took me 10 minutes to extract an apology?'

Focus on the soft stuff more than the hard.

All right, the hard stuff – product failure, rates, queuing times, delivering 'on time in full' is vital, but you're probably on top of, or wrestling with it, every day already. See if you can find a way of measuring – or at least putting your attention on – the human factors such as:

- Delight
- Wow
- Joy
- Surprise

Include the small stuff.

Remember that what's small to you may loom large in the customer's consciousness. Invaluable points such as:

- Was it easy to find our phone number?
- Did the person who answered know to whom to put you through?
- Did they check back with you when you were kept waiting?
- Did we make it an enjoyable experience?
- Did we say 'thank you'?

Get 'front-line' input.

Companies still give too much credence to measuring what consultants or researchers advise them to, rather than what their own people can tell them from their daily experience. An accurate analysis of what customers really think is usually held in the minds of your sharpest service people. They listen, they experience, they live it, they fix it. Ask them first. Usually they're smart enough to 'mystery shop' their own service. If not, they shouldn't be on the job.

Understand (by asking) how well your people are supported to do a great job.

Prepare for some groans as stale chestnuts are re-roasted – new equipment, more pairs of hands, clearer priorities. *And*, more important, see beyond the gripes to the real gems that glisten beneath. Like the receptionist in a mail order company who observed at a meeting that nearly 30 per cent of callers – potential customers among them – put the phone down when they were put on hold. Her manager was furious when he discovered she had known this for about two years, but her defence was cast-iron: 'Nobody asked me'. No use invoking the false god of empowerment. If no one asked her, *her* perception is that no one valued her opinion. If your people aren't valued, how are they going to value your customers?

Monitor response – and response time – to customer feedback.

Legendary service providers listen *and* act on customer feedback. Swiftly. So why not include your rate of response to feedback as a measure on the scorecard itself? This stops it becoming *re*search – yesterday's news – and becomes more like *pro*search – a proactive style of learning from the data.

Record praise.

Too often attempts to evaluate the customer's experience focus on what's wrong rather than what's right. One way of tracking your success in building a legend is to measure how much praise you receive against the number of complaints. Traditional wisdom says that you're 10 to 20 times more likely to hear the bad news, but *this doesn't have to be so*. SouthWest Airlines receives five times as much positive feedback as it does negative comments.

7. What if . . . service was spiritual?

Present approaches to customer service are dominated by psychological and behavioural models. Behavioural strategies assume that if we *act* in the right way towards our customers, we can make them happy. A psychological perspective assumes that if we use our powers of analysis – and our databases

– to define the style, demographic background, needs and wants of our customers then we can move into a closer relationship with them. While there is nothing wrong with this, there is also a more profound level of understanding – the spiritual – that is at the basis of these more tangible and observable levels of psychology and behaviour.

By spiritual, I mean wholeness. It's an experience that transcends even the emotional level. Some form of this experience is familiar to nearly all of us. It's an inner sensation that we are essentially connected to and at one with others and the environment. It may be a few fleeting moments sitting by the sea or walking out in the dawn air, or we may be lucky enough to enjoy it for longer periods.

We can distinguish the spiritual from the religious, which for many means following a particular set of tenets, beliefs and rituals. In fact, business has already begun to use more spiritual language. We hear about 'service with soul', and even down-to-earth commentator Faith Popcorn makes pronouncements such as: 'Companies must wrap their products in their soul and ethics.'

But what does this mean in practice? In a famous parable from the Bible, Christ talks about building your house on shifting sands or on an immovable rock. This is a description of either aligning yourself with the more superficial changing levels of life, or being in tune with the underlying changeless level which we can call the spiritual.

LEVELS OF SERVICE

Behavioural

↑

Psychological/Emotional

↑

Spiritual

If you base your thinking about service on the outer levels of thought and action you will discover that your service 'house' doesn't have the same power or resilience to survive as the demands of your customers change. A further problem with over-focusing on the behavioural level of service is that learned techniques and skills are not flexible enough to deal with the customer's whole experience. Over-reliance on ritualised expressions of customer care, such as 'How may I help you?' or 'Are you enjoying your meal, sir?' are empty if not backed up by a deeper level of understanding; *Why* are we behaving this way in front of the customer? Such scripts, unsupported by real depth of thought or intention are like a badly fitting toupee – it's easy to see the joins.

Tapping the psychological level is a hollow pursuit if not based on deeper values such as understanding that 'I am fundamentally connected, or at one with the people I am serving.' The customer's response to psychological approaches tends to be short-lived pleasure followed by a growing suspicion that you are using these measures only to get a firmer armlock on him or her.

Let's think about the spiritual level, which is already part of the philosophy of a number of innovative businesses around the world. To quote Ben Cohen of ice-cream company, Ben & Jerry's: 'There is a spiritual aspect to our lives – when we give, we receive – when a business does something good for somebody, that somebody feels good about them.'

There are five characteristics of the spiritual experience that are relevant to customer service. These seem to be common to writers, researchers, students and practitioners of spiritual techniques and deep prayer in many of the world's great traditions. Their impact on how the customer feels is described in the chart 'Deeper levels of service'. For the sake of simplicity, I have included the emotional level with the psychological.

The aim of introducing these characteristics – *resonating, unifying, giving, nourishing, reaching out* – is to stimulate your own search for your company's most fundamental values and their practical application to your business goals.

Resonating is described as the experience of feeling in tune with yourself and your environment, spontaneously knowing that you are doing the right thing. Sports stars are familiar with this experience – they talk about being 'in the zone', where their body intuitively works out the best options with a precision that their more superficial rational self could never compute as quickly or as effectively. Resonating translates into the ability to tune in to the needs of others, to make them feel that you are on their wavelength. It's as close to telepathy as most of us are likely to get.

Unifying is the experience, however fleeting, of feeling complete, self-sufficient and fully at ease with one's self. It's at-one-ment, being whole and self-contained no matter what turbulence is going on in the environment.

A natural outcome of experiencing unity is the ability to see the world the way others see it, and therefore to find it more easy to empathise with their needs and wants. In this state I reach beyond the narrow limitations of myself – which has been called the 'skin-encapsulated ego' – and recognise all aspects of this self in what was previously perceived as 'other'. Treating

Deeper Levels of Service

THE CUSTOMER FEELS	Tuned into ⇐	Supported ⇐	Given to ⇐	Appreciated ⇐	Understood ⇐
BEHAVIOURAL Level of service	Reflecting back: language, voice tone and physical. Active listening	Sympathetic words and body language, expressing the desire to treat the customer as you would want to be treated yourself	Doing more than the expected, expressing 'yes'; offering, giving alternatives, demonstrating willingness to help	Showing appreciation and warmth for individual, giving positive and reassuring information and feedback	Exhibiting knowledge of the individual's situation and own willingness to reach out and help; use of humour
PSYCHOLOGICAL Level of service	Mirroring, tuning in, cultural and personal sensitivity	Bridging, linking, empathising	Relating generously, and positively to needs and wants of other party	Affirming identity and personal perceptions of another	Understanding, stretching of self. Anticipating needs
SPIRITUAL PRINCIPLES	Resonating	Unifying	Giving	Nourishing	Reaching out
	UNDERLYING FIELD OF SERVICE CONSCIOUSNESS				

the customer in the same way I would like to be treated myself becomes second nature.

Giving stems from an inner feeling of completeness, of abundance. Successful, fulfilled people spontaneously act on the urge that comes from deep inside to give to others, 'to put something back'. This is not confined to high-flyers and the wealthy. Anyone who has some degree of inner fulfilment experiences giving as a natural reflex. If one characteristic is at the heart of service with soul, it's giving. We've all experienced the positive influence of someone who gives of him- or herself when serving and sadly know what it's like when this is withheld. Service *is* giving.

Nourishing means being enriched in a way that food, clothes and the outer trappings of success can never do for us. Christ's image of drinking water and yet finding ourselves thirsty again describes the limited ability of sensory experience to fulfil us. He compares this with drinking from the deeper level of our inner self. This kind of nourishment stays with us and we feel more secure and stronger in our own sense of self. In service terms, insecure people have short fuses and are liable to crack under pressure from demanding customers. If you feel nourished from within you naturally transmit this to the people you are serving.

When we experience great service we can say we are nourished by it. We feel appreciated and psychologically fed by it.

Reaching out to others stems from a feeling of not being separate or disconnected from others. We all feel the difference it makes when someone reaches out and touches us through eye contact, or through attempts to solve our problem, or even through humour. In our high-tech world, high touch is all the more keenly needed. Intuitively we can sense if the person serving us has really reached out and made a connection with us, or is merely going through the motions.

I believe it's possible to discuss and understand these spiritual characteristics with the people in your organisation without offending their own personal religious or humanistic belief systems. This kind of discussion, properly managed, can be valuable in helping people to live out their cherished beliefs in a work setting, rather than feeling they have to leave them at the door for the eight hours they work with you. You might create your own version of the chart 'Deeper Levels of Service' to help you clarify what service with soul really means to you.

It's vital to recall other characteristics of the spiritual experience – joy, bliss, contentment. Your people will radiate who and how they are to your customers. There's no getting away from this; the inner fashions the outer. Unhappiness begets unhappiness, joy begets joy. To have delighted customers you need delighted people serving them. Joseph Campbell captures this beautifully when he says: 'When you follow your bliss ... doors will open where you would not have thought there would be doors, and where there wouldn't be a door for anyone else.'[5]

Further questions to recharge your batteries

By now I'm sure you've got the idea of thinking *what if? why not?* What follows is a list of further provocations to stretch your thinking and to help you recharge your mental batteries. Naturally, I hope you'll also create your own.

- What if . . . service was a feminine experience?
- What if . . . you could anticipate the customer's unspoken needs?
- What if . . . the customer *is* wrong?
- What if . . . you were in love with your customers?
- What if . . . your company was buried, and the corporate gravestone was inscribed: 'We did OK'?
- What if . . . everybody – backroom people too – *adopted* a customer?
- What if . . . your job could be replaced by a machine?
- What if . . . a customer had been looking over your shoulder all of last week?
- What if . . . you thought of service as a form of religion?

Finally, remember that these questions are just the starting point, and the ideas they inspire will probably come to you at odd moments. Carry a *what if?* notebook with you, and capture your intuitions and flashes of insight. Otherwise, it's like trying to recall dreams – we always tell ourselves we'll remember them in the morning and rarely do.

What If? Why Not? and you

Thinking *what if? why not?* will certainly help you to become more open to entertaining and applying new ideas. However, it shouldn't be mistaken for a form of mindless positive thinking, but as a way of loading the dice in favour of a better outcome even when you seem to be experiencing a run of failures, whether in your personal relationships or your career.

[5] *The Hero With A Thousand Faces*, Princeton University Press, 1990, ISBN: 0691017840.

Let's see how this orientation can help you succeed. We can describe two different ways of interpreting your life experiences, a mindset of success or of failure. If you expect success, but experience failure in the outer world – for instance, you gave a presentation that bombed completely – your response will tend to be, 'Try again, obviously I haven't yet invested enough time or skill in this.' The key word here is obviously 'yet'.

But if you adopt a failure mindset you may either reflect on this experience by concluding that, 'I am no good at presentations', and consequently tend to avoid giving them in future, or you may go into blame mode and start muttering about the lack of receptiveness of your audience. The failure frame of experience has now probably closed down the number of possibilities available to you.

Let's suppose you experience success. The person with a success mindset will interpret this as the natural reward for effort and skill put in. Someone with the expectation of failure may rationalise this by thinking, 'I was lucky', or 'I got away with it this time'. Strangely, the person who expects failure usually describes luck as something that happens to others, not to him or herself. 'The other queue always moves faster' becomes a conviction.

I'm not suggesting for a minute that we all become Pollyannas. But we do have more choice than we think to adopt an attitude that assumes success from our creative endeavours. If we expect defeat, we'll probably be right. *What if?* thinking means giving your dream the gifts of time and attention *Why not?* means having the persistence to believe that even if you've failed so far, it's simply a question of time before you eventually succeed.

Observe, if you can, the mental tapes that play in your mind. If you are frequently *yes, butting* your own budding ideas, you're likely to have a tendency also to judge harshly the ideas of others. To bring this home to you in a setting we all recognise, be more conscious of yourself in your next discussion with your partner, family, or colleagues at work. Every time you feel a *yes, but* coming on suspend your 'red' thinking – the tendency to judge – and stay open to the idea which you initially disliked, perhaps out of habit or mere rigidity, and imagine what's potentially useful in it. Even, or especially, if it means adjustment to your own frame of experience.

There is an old saying that we don't grow old, but when we stop growing we *are* old. The two most nimble-minded people I know are well into their seventies, and I've met some very senile apprentices. *What if?* we were all to stay more open to the possibilities rather than the *impossibilities* of life?

For some penetrating questions, activities and ideas relating to this chapter turn to page 254.

Chapter Nine

Recharging Your Batteries

ON the following pages you will find lists of penetrating questions, activities and suggestions. These will enable you to turn your inspiration into implementation at three levels: the individual, team and organisation. Each set of lists corresponds with the chapters entitled:

- New Millennium, New Trends
- What is Legendary Service?
- Change the Box
- Learn From the Future
- Develop Beginner's Mind;
- Think *Both/And*
- The Power of Attention
- *What If? Why Not?*

In some cases you may have to refer back to the chapter to revisit some of the concepts and examples as the Recharging Your Batteries ideas appear on the following pages in a condensed format. Remember not to shy away from tackling the challenging ideas if you want to create a real legend.

New millennium, New trends

Individual reflection
- Which of the 'I's are we strong in delivering to our customers?
- Where are we weak?
- How up-to-date is my knowledge of the service implications of the Internet?

Individual action
- Focus on one of the 'I's your business needs to improve on, working with a customer to understand how, in an ideal world, they would like to experience it.
- Take these findings and discuss with a cross-section of people who can influence the outcome.
- Spend a morning exploring the best-rated websites. Note what you experience as a visitor and create your top five factors for a Wow visit.

Team reflection
- When we improve it, which 'I' will make most difference to our customers?
- How human-friendly is our Internet system?
- Where do we need to use our imagination better to understand the customer's experience? And what will that mean in practice?

Team action
- Select one 'I' to be the top agenda item at your meetings for the next few weeks.
- Invent clear measures for tracking how well you are performing on each of the 'I's.
- Implement at least one gem of an idea you have gained imagining what to your customer will be *outstanding* rather than merely 'OK' service.

Recharging your batteries

Strategic actions
- Rate your organisation on its ability to dialogue with your customers. Make this a high-profile business aim.
- Ensure that the six fundamental 'I's are hard-wired into your Internet and e-commerce channels.
- Introduce systems that immediately register that the customer is known to you when he or she starts to place an order.

Training messages
- Customers want to be appreciated as individuals, not as a market!
- Customers are no longer passive – they want to be in control.
- Imagining the customer's experience – and responding creatively – is everyone's responsibility.

Logic flow
- Service hasn't got worse, it just hasn't improved as fast as customers expect and demand.
  ↓
- The Internet is becoming a primary channel for delivering customer service, but
  ↓
- The customer's needs for Individuality, Interactivity, Immediacy, Intimacy and Imagination need to be integrated with the new technology.

Challenging ideas
- Encourage as many customers as possible (especially the ones you don't see in the flesh) to exchange photographs of themselves with as many of your people as possible – casual at-home poses preferred.
- Bring in a group of 15-year-olds for a day to show your older managers how to surf the Net.
- Hold a story-telling competition, with great prizes, to see who can tell the best (most lifelike) tale of a day in the customer's life.

What is Legendary Service?

Individual reflection
- How far away is the goal of becoming a service legend for your organisation?
- What aspect should you focus on first to make an appreciable improvement to your customers' experience?
- What do you need to do actively to encourage customers to tell their story?

Individual action
- Circulate the checklist 'Characteristics of a legendary service provider' (page 58) to colleagues and selected customers.
- Analyse and act on at least one of the themes that emerge where you can make significant improvements.
- Use customers' stories to improve all your presentations, briefings and meetings.

Team reflection
- What well-known legends or myths come closest to describing your company story? Choose one positive and one negative.
- Do people believe that what they do shapes the destiny of the organisation?
- What are the most common tales our customers tell about us? Be honest!

Team action
- Agree which issue(s) to tackle from the checklist;
- Encourage your own people and customers to tell stories relevant to the issues.
- Present these stories – either in person or on video – at a decision-making meeting . . . and respond to them.

Recharging your batteries

Strategic actions
- Decide what stories you would most like your customers to be telling to develop the service promise of your brand. And the first steps to take to make this a reality.
- Make ethics a key element of marketing your product or service.
- Suspend all customer surveys and insist on using the story-telling form for a period.

Training messages
- Customers are screaming for 'wow', 'delight' and memorable experiences.
- The inner quality of relationships is transmitted to customers in each service encounter.
- Relationship is all.

Logic flow
- Customer satisfaction doesn't guarantee loyal customers.
  ↓
- To attract and retain customers everyone needs to be involved in the process of legend-building.
  ↓
- Creating a legend results in your customers doing your marketing for you.

Challenging ideas
- Appoint a corporate story-teller to build your legend;
- Ban the expression customer satisfaction, and
- Encourage everyone to take a 'second job' with personally selected projects that enrich the environment or community.

Change the Box

Individual reflection
- What box are you in? How would you describe it and how does this limit you in providing great service to your customers?
- From whom can you learn to see the box changed?
- What are the stereotyped perceptions of your industry? And which ones would you like to see changed?

Individual action
- Talk – and listen – to six different customers about their perception of your service 'box';
- Set up a discussion group (include customers) to decide what change(s) will make the most difference to your customers, and
- Select a company you admire for service that is *not* in your industry. Visit it with a colleague and translate at least two of their innovative ideas into your own business.

Team reflection
- What assumptions are we making about what the customer really wants? (S1 thinking).
- How can we challenge these assumptions with a small group of key customers? (S2 thinking).
- Where could we apply 'one-line' solutions to our service offering by challenging assumptions commonly held in our organisation about what's expected in our industry? (S3 thinking).

Team action
- Try a 'dawn raid' visit to competitors, especially new ones. Do it as a competition for who can 'steal' the most effective ideas for changing your box;
- Go and live with some of your customers for at least a week, and
- Bring a key customer into your box in a way that will touch the emotions of your front-line people.

Recharging your batteries

Strategic actions

- Design and implement a simple means of knowing what percentage of managers' time is spent on the *basic* and *expected* service.
- Survey employees' perception of themselves – are they proud of the way they are seen by customers?
- Discover how other organisations have strategically changed their box. Live with them long enough to find out the messy and exciting bits.

Training messages

- We need to focus resources on the latent and potential needs of our customers.
- We have to change customers' perception of *our industry*, not just our business.
- We have to decide how to change the box about (a) our people's self-perception and (h) the whole process by which our product or service is sold.
- We must realise that we are in a box – and *we* create it.

Logic flow

- We are limited by expectations of our industry or sector (the box).
  ↓
- We need to differentiate ourselves from this box by being different.
  ↓
- This is achieved by focusing time, attention and money on the full potential service we can deliver to the customer.

Challenging ideas

- Sacrifice a sacred cow: some part of the old box that people think is a permanent fixture. Make it a memorable ritual.
- Hire a key customer as a working consultant for a month to change perceptions about your box.
- Tell your customers you're moving in with them and won't budge until you understand their business – and *their* customers' business – as well as they do.

Learn From the Future

Individual reflection
- What kind of future would I like in this business for myself and my customers?
- Can I visualise it in a concrete form – for instance, by drawing it?
- What differences would this focus make to the way I think, act and feel in my daily work?

Individual action
- Create a story – with as much colour and detail as possible – for a desired future two or three years from now. Perhaps use Datalearn (page 104) as a starting point.
- Share it with colleagues – get them to add their views.
- Use the story at team meetings and briefings to inspire a stimulating dialogue about the future.

Team reflection
- Read and discuss the Datalearn story and its implications for your business.
- Are we a diverse enough group to think about the future imaginatively? If not, whom can we include to help us visualise the future better?
- Are there any signs that we are too limited in our thinking by current problems and what it could mean to us to learn from the future?

Team action
- Write your own team story of the future, ensuring you use the 'I's (from Chapter 1), ideas from Datalearn and your own wildest possible hopes.
- Test the story on a group of senior managers – integrate their views.
- Use conferences, meetings and training sessions to communicate the future story and its practical implications for today's behaviour.

Recharging your batteries

Strategic actions

- Create a story of the company's desired future at board level.
- Use ingredients of this story in corporate communications (magazines, conferences, Internet, etc.).
- Decide which aspects can be communicated as part of the growing legend outside the business.

Training messages

- Customer listening + benchmarking = maintaining the present.
  Creativity + Imagination = Securing the future.
- 'Learning from the future' means working backwards from the desired state, not forwards from today.
- Story-telling is the most powerful method of motivating and inspiring people.

Logic flow

- Perfecting the known tends to limit your horizon of possibilities.
  ↓
- Imperfectly imagining the future helps you to create that future.
  ↓
- It's necessary to write and communicate your *own* authentic story of the future.

Challenging ideas

- Hold a company party that's set three years in the future – dress, act and talk like you're really there. Invite some customers. What do you learn?
- Ask customers to write their story of how they would like you to be in the future – take it seriously!
- Put on a pantomime or play at senior management level that portrays both how things are now and how you would like them to be.

Develop Beginner's Mind

Individual reflection
- Recall the freshness of perception you had when you first came into the job. What did you immediately notice that needed improving?
- If you could begin this job again, how would you like it to be?
- If you were a customer of your business, what would you really (a) expect and (b) want?

Individual action
- Hang around more with customers, suppliers and parts of your organisation you rarely visit. Take a notebook and jot down both facts and perceptions as they occur.
- Listen to individual customers with no judgment or agenda.
- Run meetings with the sole aim of identifying customers' moments of truth. Action one insight this week.

Team reflection
- In what areas can we admit ignorance of our customers' real needs?
- How well do we *demonstrate* to customers that we understand the significance of their Moments of Truth?
- What different ways are there of describing what business we're in? And how will that make for practical improvements in what we deliver to our customers?

Team action
- Hold a meeting where customers set the agenda. Focus on one or two key Moments of Truth that can be improved. Monitor the difference both from customers' and your own people's perceptions.
- *Act* on one insight you've had from describing 'what business we're in' in a new way.
- Create project rooms, displays and chat-rooms, that are designed around the needs of specific clients – to give your customers a 'wow' when they come into your building.

Recharging your batteries

Strategic actions

- Find your organisation's DNA – what are its *real* values and beliefs?
- Ensure that everyone in the business has thought deeply about customers' Moments of Truth and acts to positively surprise the customer with this understanding;
- Hold an executive meeting with one agenda item: 'What business are we in?' Take a full day, and
- Communicate the message of each customer's uniqueness – a market of one – throughout the organisation.

Training messages

- We continually have to use our imagination to get into the customer's frame of experience.
- Customers need very few snapshots or perceptions of our business to make a judgment about us – manage those moments well and they will be much more loyal.
- We need continually to shock ourselves into beginner's mind to avoid the hardening of the categories that routine brings about.

Logic flow

- There's a tendency to 'go blind' and assume that we know what the customer really needs.
  ↓
- To combat this tendency we need constantly to revisit every aspect of our business with a fresh, childlike beginner's mind, assuming we 'know' nothing about the customer's experience.
  ↓
- This results in a closer understanding of the customer's actual experience.

Challenging ideas

- Ask your customers what they would most change about your service if they had a magic wand.
- Give key customers a magic wand – or whatever symbolises the power to change things instantly – and agree with them how it can be used.
- Ask some 12-year-olds to experience your service. Listen and act on their ideas for improvement.
- Make a video of a senior director's week on the front-line. Show it widely.

Think *Both/And*

Individual reflection
- Where in my life do I think *both/and* – for example, career *and* family, ambition *and* tranquillity, hard-headed *and* human?
- What could I do to focus more on the quality of individual relationships both with my colleagues *and* my customers?
- Do I love what I do?

Individual action
- Rate your processes and systems from the customer's point of view – share your perceptions with colleagues *and* customers.
- Design your version of the McCulloch card (page 161) for employees. Then think of a fresh way of communicating your messages other than on a card.
- Redesign your role so that you can move closer to truly loving what you do!

Team reflection
- Where are we efficient, but boring? Or where are we exciting, but inefficient?
- How can we measure the quality of customer *relationships* – empathy, psychic goodwill, etc.?
- Do we hire friendly, nice, sincere people?
- What can we do to encourage 'nasty' people/employees to become 'nicer'?

Team action
- Investigate processes and systems in the business from a customer design point of view.
- Identify the balance between operational and relational service.
- Ensure service-mindedness is the number one factor in recruiting new people.

Recharging your batteries

Strategic actions

- Include 'designers' in your customer team to look at all vital interfaces with the customer.
- Create a corporate scorecard that identifies and measures performance on relationship building – empathy, etc.
- Redesign all systems critical for the customers' happiness so they (a) appeal more to female customers and (b) are feminised to create a more emotional connection with all customers.

Training messages

- Relationship is all.
- Thinking *both/and* means realising that efficiency and effectiveness is not enough – customers also want to be made to feel valued as individuals.
- Customers leave you because the service relationship is poor more than for operational/technical/pricing reasons.

Logic flow

- The operational aspects of service performed well are not enough to ensure customer loyalty.
  ↓
- Relationship factors count for more in customers' minds.
  ↓
- Therefore, you win and keep customers by over-focusing on the more human, intangible factors.

Challenging ideas

- Introduce 'service beauty' awards for people and methodologies that are stunning in their simplicity and effectiveness.
- Use ballet dancers to train face-to-face customer representatives in movement and grace.
- Employ actors to give all your people voice and empathy coaching.

The Power of Attention

Individual reflection
- When did you really put your whole mind and heart to work on a task? How did it feel, and how did it turn out?
- If customers see through the quality of internal relationships you enjoy, what would they see that might make you sweat?
- How much *quality time* do you give to customers and customer issues?

Individual action
- Show sincere appreciation to someone who works for/with you. Make it specific, timely, direct and heartfelt.
- Make visible to your team how much of your diary time you spend with customers/focusing on customer issues – compare notes and agree to do more.
- Try and re-try *ad infinitum* improving some small aspect of service you've failed on in the past. Record the number of times you fail *until* you succeed.

Team reflection
- How would we rate the quality of attention in our team meetings?
- How does the quality of our internal relationships impact the customer negatively or positively?
- How can we really appreciate each other better?

Team action
- Make customer issues first on the agenda of every meeting, and the compulsory first point in any presentation.
- Build more enjoyment and 'getting to know each other' time into your schedule. Play together.
- Reward heroic actions on behalf of the customer immediately – don't wait for awards ceremonies, but make it a weekly or even daily practice.

Recharging your batteries

Strategic actions
- Spell out what a partnership orientation really means for your organisation in behavioural terms.
- Reinforce by example a climate of openness where people can talk honestly about their mistakes.
- Give over the first half of your company report to a description of your customers' experiences.

Training messages
- Put attention – intention, time, energy, resources – on improving internal relationships. They are transparent to the customer.
- Put your attention on appreciation and relationships *will* improve.
- You are your diary.

Logic flow
- You are transparent to your customers.
  ↓
- Therefore, they see to what extent you are putting your attention on them.
  ↓
- Improving the quality of partnership inside the organisation positively affects customers' perception of service quality.

Challenging ideas
- Hold a meeting where all have to brag about their biggest recent failures – and what they've learned from them.
- Institute a tribal behaviour award – perhaps a spear or bow and arrow – which is given to the function least responsive to partnering other functions.
- Declare a Touch Day during which you have to shake hands with everyone you meet, in the corridor or canteen, giving eye contact and a positive greeting.

What If? Why Not?

Individual reflection

- How often do I *yes, but* suggestions from my people and colleagues, and new ideas in general?
- . . . and when do I do it with my personal partner, or family?
- How can I stay more open – think *what if? why not?*– to unfamiliar ideas or those I expect to disagree with?

Individual action

- Implement one idea for improving service you feel strongly about – however small – that you expect to be *yes, butted.*
- Introduce a fine system – say £1 for every *yes, but* – in your office for a month.
- Take the seven provocations in the chapter – allow the ideas to flow and implement one at a time.

Team reflection

- Do we give ourselves enough agenda time to develop *what if?* scenarios? Do we stay in the blue long enough?
- Is the incidence of *yes, butting* high, medium, or low in our meetings?
- Why do we need to think *creatively* about our customer relationships?

Team action

- Hold a blue/red/green session with a different person, managing each phase to solve a specific customer's problems – work it through from ideas to action.
- Take a creative image of service – theatre, music, etc. – and apply insights back to your own business by thinking *what if? why not?*
- When experienced, introduce this process of thinking *what if?* to all customer-facing groups and implement several innovative ideas from the process this month.

Recharging your batteries

Strategic actions

- Decide which of the seven provocations – for example 'What if business was theatre?'– is most relevant to your business.
- Having chosen it, agree what new symbols and language will be needed to communicate your fresh thinking. If you use the theatre metaphor, what could you call your people – cast members? – and what effect would this have on the way they were trained and rewarded?

Training messages

- *Yes, butting* is the enemy of creative thinking.
- Blue thinking – time spent standing back from business as usual – always pays dividends. Make it important and urgent.
- All great achievements come from thinking *what if? why not?*

Logic flow

- Past experience (especially success) leads us to *yes, but* the new.
  ↓
- There are methods for breaking out of this *yes, butting* by using *what if? why not?* thinking.
  ↓
- Provocative questions help us to break out of our existing mindsets.

Challenging ideas

- Paint a room blue and call it the customer ideas room, used only for creative problem-solving. Invite customers.
- Fine yourself every time you *think* a *yes, but*.
- Take colleagues to a memorable event – circus, theatre, unusual ethnic ceremony – and afterwards discuss what connection it had to your business.
- Search for common spiritual values in order to give more soul to your service.

Useful Sources

For international conferences on customer service, contact Howard Kendall or Sheelagh Mundell at Customer Service Management, telephone +44 (0)1689 858808. They also publish the excellent *Customer Management Journal*. For creative partnership in change management call Ian Taylor or Karen Jackson at the Deva Partnership Ltd (of which I am also a partner) on +44 (0)191 386 8473, or visit their website at www. devapartner.com

For Empathy Audits contact Jamie Lywood at Harding & Yorke, telephone +44 (0)1235 462000. For Business in the Community contact Julia Cleverdon on +44 (0)171 224 1600. For the UK Society of Consumer Affairs Professionals (SOCAP), which also focuses on service excellence, contact Tony Mosely on +44 (0)1275 845511. For stress management through the Transcendental Meditation technique, contact Jonathan Hinde on +44 (0)171 402 3787.

Contact Richard King or Madeleine McGrath at the Tom Peters Company on +44 (0)1708 437380 for in-company support on Making Work Matter and the Pursuit of Wow.

Acknowledgements

My heartfelt thanks to everyone who has helped in the creation of *Batteries Included!* My research team, Dr Bob Dreher, Calvin Germain, Janet Hanson and Angie Kaye. Any mistakes in the text are entirely down to them! My thanks for inspiration and ideas go to Len Arvedson, Sven Atterhed, Phil Dourado, Tony Mosely, John Pearson, Michael Rant, Adrian Simpson and Jim Sterne. And to Rod Dadak of Lewis Silkin for his perceptive and patient advice in helping me to remove legally contentious material.

My very special thanks to my brilliant agent Caroline Davidson, and to Simon Wilson, Simon King and Clare Smith at Random House for their great support, which has made the book possible. Also to the Saltzmans, the Rodens and the Provos for loaning me their beautiful homes to start and finish *Batteries Included!* And to Richard Thompson, for creative inspiration.

And most of all to my assistant Janet Hanson, who has put a lot of herself into this book. I can never thank her enough for her insight, optimism and generous belief in this project which, but for her encouragement I would have given up on.

Contacting the Author

Nigel May Barlow would love to hear from you to discuss the ideas behind this book. He can be contacted at:

Service Legends Limited,
107 Plater Drive,
Oxford Waterside,
Oxford OX2 6QU.
Tel: +44 (0)1865 512301/512302
Fax: +44 (0)1865 512303
E-mail: nigelbarlow@servicelegends.com
Website: www.servicelegends.com

Service Legends provides keynote presentations, interactive conferences, team events and consultancy to help you create your own service legend. This applies to commercial entities, public bodies, and even cities or countries seeking to create a reputation for great service. Nigel also works with creative approaches to strategy, teamwork, organisational innovation and major projects. Contact Janet Hanson.

Browser's Guide

I expect you thought this would be a sales pitch about how your life will be incomplete unless you read this book. Not so – it's a way of saving you valuable browsing time in making your decision to read *Batteries Included!*

What you are interested in . . .	How *Batteries Included!* can help . . .
1. I've got a long plane journey ahead of me – will it make the trip pass more quickly?	1. Yes, judiciously interspersed with the John Grisham you're really longing to read.
2. The title sounds intriguing – but what does it mean?	2. Ever opened a Christmas present where batteries *weren't* included? Most service is similarly disappointing. There's a quick definition on page xii.
3. Will the book look impressive on my office shelf?	3. Not if you put it next to Booker prize-winning novels and illustrated encyclopedias, but alongside other business books it has a fair chance of intriguing your visitors.
4. Is there any new stuff I can use in my presentations and pass off as my own?	4. Lots! Try the checklist 'Characteristics of a legendary service provider' on page 57, or the provocative model on the Walking Dead, Spectators, Cynics and Players on page 191.
5. Come off it – isn't Legendary Service just a fancy name for very, very good, or 'excellent' service?	5. Nope! And isn't excellence rather a passé expression? You might actually have to read the book to find out the difference!
6. I've already got a stack of books on customer service – why should I read this one?	6. Because it's the first one applying creativity to service. But, on second thoughts, your bookshelf sounds rather sad. Perhaps you should move along to the poetry section instead.
7. I'm just shoplifting and happened on your book by mistake. Should I take a copy?	7. I can't condone it, but if you must steal any book this year, take this one.

Index